D1101313

TIME'S THIEVISH PROGRESS

Elizabeth and grand-daughters at Dynevor, 1968

TIME'S THIEVISH PROGRESS

AUTOBIOGRAPHY III

JOHN ROTHENSTEIN

CASSELL · LONDON

CASSELL & COMPANY LTD.
35 RED LION SQUARE, LONDON, W.C.1
Melbourne, Sydney, Toronto
Johannesburg, Auckland

First published 1970

I.S.B.N. 0 304 93578 6

Printed in Great Britain
by Ebenezer Baylis & Son, Ltd.,
The Trinity Press, Worcester, and London
F.470

FOR MIRANDA, SARAH,
SUSANNAH AND HUGO
WITH LOVE

FOREWORD

As was explained in the Foreword to the second volume of this autobiography, between that volume and the present one there is an overlap in chronology. The large amount of space taken up in the earlier volume by Tate Gallery affairs precluded the inclusion in it of various aspects of private life, and in particular some friendships with painters that I especially treasured, which were contemporary with the public affairs discussed. This omission is remedied in the present volume, but with the consequence that my accounts of artists reach back to the years of the Second World War.

John Rothenstein

Newington, Oxfordshire
  January 1970.

CONTENTS

ILLUSTRATIONS

ACKNOWLEDGEMENTS

The author wishes to record his indebtedness to all those who have granted permission for the use of copyright material, particularly to Tony Evans, Lucian Freud, the Hamlyn Publishing Group Limited (for permission to quote from *Painting as a Pastime* by Winston S. Churchill), Martin Holmes, Ian Joy, the late Mrs. Augustus John, Keystone Press, Mrs. Wyndham Lewis, Mrs. Dorothy Mahoney, Marlborough Fine Art, The Earl of Oxford and Asquith, the *South Wales Evening Post*, the Tate Gallery and United Press International.

He is indebted, too, for information to Henry Moore, Lord Clark and Michael Holroyd, and most particularly to his wife Elizabeth and Father Vincent Turner for their invaluable research, especially in connection with the concluding chapter and appendix. In this research much use has been made of a paper read before the St. Andrews University History Society in 1952-53, *The Office of Rector*, by Ian Ferrier, and of a list of the rectors of Newington, Oxfordshire, compiled about 1901 by the then incumbent, the Revd. J. S. Pendlebury, who also transcribed various parish documents no longer available.

Thou by thy dial's shady stealth mayst know
Time's thievish progress to eternity.

CHAPTER ONE

ARTISTS AND ECCENTRICS

IT WAS in the early 'forties that a friendly acquaintance with Matthew Smith, a painter whose work I increasingly admired, ripened into friendship. We had met briefly on several occasions, but the first on which we talked at any length was in November of 1940. Augustus John had become difficult about the reproductions that I proposed to include in the monograph I was writing about him for the Phaidon Press, and I had called at Tooths, his dealers, to select additional photographs from the compendious file that Dudley Tooth maintained of the works of artists whom he represented. Matthew Smith, who also showed at Tooths, was standing disconsolately before a recent canvas of his own. He asked me to look at it, but because it seemed to me to be one of his failures I said as little as circumstances allowed. His intuition that I shared his own critical estimate of it, instead of provoking him, as it might another, to a prickly defensiveness, set him musing frankly on his own temperamental shortcomings. 'I always work in a state of almost complete nervous prostration and exhaustion,' he said; 'I say *almost* complete, because until I've conquered it to some extent, regained some sort of self-possession, you know, I can't even begin. I worry so appallingly when I think about a picture that I'm intending to paint—I worry so, if you understand,' and his voice died away in a whisper. I could hardly believe that the man I was listening to, this pale melancholic man, peering helplessly through thick-lensed glasses, whose body was so inert that its movements left his suit uncreased, the man with the hollow, anxious voice, was the creator of the long series of opulent nudes and flower-pieces, so exultant in their ripeness, so startling in their audacious energy. The hollow voice sounded again: 'I used to draw a lot but lately I've almost given up drawing, in any case I never thought very much of my drawings. . . .' Again it died slowly away. Thinking afterwards of this encounter I was surprised to note how positively I had enjoyed the company of the melancholy figure whose voice was like a whisper echoing in a cellar.

B

I

From that time until towards the end of his life Matthew Smith and I used to meet in the evenings at fairly frequent intervals, sometimes with common friends, Edward le Bas and Charles Ginner for preference, and sometimes by long-standing arrangement by ourselves. But more characteristic evenings would be the result of last-minute improvisations. Long-standing arrangements, I fancy, oppressed him with a sense of confinement. What he preferred was to be telephoned quite late, up, say, to eight o'clock. Surprisingly often he would be unengaged and we would meet half an hour later, sometimes at the Café Royal, 'the resort of the lonely', he called it, occasionally at the Athenaeum Club, but more often in Chelsea where he lived at the time when I came to know him well. It was this dislike of prearrangement that caused this illustrious and affectionate man frequently to dine alone—before we met I noticed him dining alone at the Café Royal on a number of occasions. He was a hypochondriac, but a hypochondriac with a difference. I became accustomed to hearing him, barely audible over the telephone, explaining that he felt extremely unwell and wouldn't be able to drink anything, needed urgently to get to bed early, but he would be very happy, provided I understood all this, if we could have some dinner together. At first I was astonished at the way the evening would end, but soon came to accept it as characteristic that well after midnight and after a luxurious dinner with a good deal to drink, and after we had decided to return to our homes, he should order two double brandies and then suddenly remember, for example, that some actress had invited him to a party to which he would thereupon decide to go, expressing his regret that I did not feel 'up' to coming with him.

At the beginning of our friendship he occupied a studio with a leaking roof in Maida Vale and a room in a dilapidated and not very reputable boarding-house in Piccadilly; to both of these he had formed a gnawing aversion. The studio I never saw, but one day as we were leaving the room in Piccadilly there emerged from the murk of the corridor, into which she noiselessly disappeared like a huge bat, the Marchesa Casati wearing a three-tiered black cloak, leopard-skin gloves and her menacing black hat that framed a face in which I could discern no feature but the great dark eyes. 'Oh, hullo, hullo,' whispered Matthew Smith mildly into the unresponding gloom.

We talked on these evenings of many things, painting, our friends,

Yorkshire—he told me several wittily obscene Yorkshire stories—
but there was one topic to which he constantly reverted, his detestation of the places where he lived and worked. During those bomb-
ravaging times when most people lived in a more or less acute degree
of discomfort one's place of habitation was an obvious topic for
complaint, but I discovered after the war had ended that Matthew's
dissatisfaction with the places where he lived and worked became no
less pronounced. There was, in fact, something obsessional about
his dissatisfaction; it almost seemed that he deliberately sought after
unsatisfactory quarters in order to feed it. From the boarding-house
in Piccadilly he moved to a one-room flat, and one of unusually
narrow proportions, number 921 in Chelsea Cloisters, a block in
Sloane Avenue—a flat that might have been devised expressly to
exasperate. Another might have had no choice, but Matthew was a
rich man. Sometimes this tiny flat was almost impenetrable because
a lady whom he greatly loved and the possessor of many of his
pictures used to 'send back his presents' after they had quarrelled.
Dislike of the places where he currently lived contrasted with a
nostalgic preoccupation with the places where he had lived or might
have lived.

'There was a studio in Dieppe on which I had an option', he once
said to me with feeling, 'but I gave it up to somebody else, a friend,
who didn't eventually want it, and the owner wouldn't give me
another chance. I was terribly disappointed over that studio. I could
have worked there. I could see my future pictures stacked there in
rows. Stacked there in rows, you know.' He complained constantly
of the problems of having no home, but he made no sustained effort
to find one.

The man I am attempting to describe was melancholic, tired,
obsessed with problems of living accommodation; moreover,
although well-read, his intellect was neither wide-ranging nor profound, and he was not a wit. How was it, then, that I never spent an
evening with him without a sense of exhilaration, and of everything
being, if not exactly well with the world, at least much better than
it had seemed a few hours before? There was nothing unique about
my delight in the company of Matthew Smith: I never saw him
enter any company without its being evident how welcome he was
and I cannot recall his having any articulate enemies, in spite of his
Yorkshire candour.

The principal charm of his presence was due, I think, to the fact that almost any subject of conversation, and even in an odd way his silence, sufficed to reveal the qualities of the man: the courage of a nature constitutionally timid and without a vestige of aggressive impulse, and the benevolence that did not tempt him—except to avoid inflicting gratuitous pain—to refrain from expressing his own strong convictions about anything other than questions concerning himself. His benevolence enabled me to discuss our friends with him, even to their gravest shortcomings, without the sense of disloyalty that would make such discussion unthinkable in the presence of censoriousness or malice. Another quality that enhanced pleasure in his company was his extreme but unassertive independence. He accepted no honours or distinctions liable to compromise it and he was wary of needless entanglements, although he sometimes suffered acutely from entanglements that he deemed necessary. Most men, as they advance in the world, tend to forgather with the successful and the established, impelled by the sense of the appropriateness of such associations, and of their value to the maintenance of their own positions. Such considerations were entirely alien to Matthew Smith; indeed he positively avoided the successful and the important, and his friendships with the illustrious, such as Augustus John and Epstein, were usually of very long standing.

In his social relations he might have been a pleasure-loving student. When we went out together he enjoyed meeting the eccentric, the witty, the talented, above all, perhaps, beautiful women, whatever their position, but he was bored as spontaneously as a child by people whose 'importance' was their principal recommendation. Finally, so far as I know, he was without ambition: to paint well called for all his vital energies and to the rewards painting well might bring him he was almost indifferent. He once said to me, however, 'My painting is more French than English and I would enjoy a little recognition in France, but I have none. I once submitted five paintings to the Salon d'Automne, but only the smallest, and the worst, was accepted.' Many years later we went together to the private view of a big retrospective exhibition of the work of Augustus John at Burlington House, and pointing to the painter's name in big capitals above the entrance, he said 'I can't imagine myself having an exhibition here: can you?' But he had—after his death. 'Augustus', he continued, 'once sounded me out about joining the Academy. "But what would be the good?" I asked him, but Augustus didn't answer.'

Matthew showed at times a curious inability to speak frankly to the person concerned about any matter that caused him personal distress. He was no doubt shown a draft of Philip Hendy's appreciative and lucid essay that prefaced the volume of Penguin Modern Painters devoted to his work and published in 1944. He complained bitterly to me and on several occasions that his family's opposition to his becoming a painter had been ignored (although he had made, he said, a special point of it in talking to Philip Hendy), as well as the disastrous and lifelong effect of the consequent friction upon his nerves. He neglected, I fancy, to make these points with sufficient emphasis; had he done so the writer would surely have taken note of them. Years later a similar reticence allowed him to pass, indeed to commend with the utmost warmth, a text of mine about which he had harboured serious reservations but which he voiced too late.

Matthew's tendency to melancholy was increased by the death of his sons, who were both killed on active service with the R.A.F. One day towards the beginning of 1942 he invited me to lunch and showed me the draft of an unsent letter to the R.A.F. College at Cranwell, withdrawing a conditional offer to present a painting in their memory. When I had read it I said, as I believe he intended to give me an opportunity of saying, that I thought it would be more appropriate to present the painting to the Tate. Then he recalled our discussion of the proposed gift the previous August, when he had told me that he had mentioned the possible gift to Cranwell, which was to be conditional upon an art collection's being formed there, and the person to whom he had spoken had embarrassed him by informing the press, but that he himself preferred my suggestion that the picture should be given to the Tate. 'If you really think . . .' he said, his voice descending to a whisper . . . 'If you really think . . . I might present two, but . . .' and again the soft hesitant voice dwindled into silence. He asked after Lucy, our daughter, and I showed him some photographs of her, for which I afterwards reproached myself, feeling that the sight of them might further have sharpened his grief. As a consequence of this conversation he offered in 1943, jointly with his wife, a large 'Still Life', painted about 1936, which was gratefully accepted by the Tate Trustees. At the lunch at which our conversation took place he made a most characteristic reply to my observing that I had heard he had left London. With a hint of impatience at my want of comprehension he said, 'I've never really *left* any place.' There followed a dinner with his wife and me. For Gwen Smith and for her abilities as a painter (they had met at the Slade where she was a student of high promise) he had the utmost regard, but she and he differed so radically in almost every respect that I could only wonder not only that they married but that they should ever have become acquainted. But even had these two possessed something in common besides love for their sons and for painting, it would still have been difficult to imagine Matthew amenable to domestic life, at least to any domestic life that could not be suspended at frequent intervals. The tiny single-room 'flatlet' in Sloane Avenue was regarded by some of his acquaintances as incongruous to the point of absurdity for a man who was illustrious, rich and advanced in years. It was in fact well suited to a man who so valued his freedom—freedom without premeditation to sally out or remain indoors, to go abroad, to make friends with some improbable person and the like, which would have been stultified or at least circumscribed by the need to consult the wishes of a wife, by the risk of hurting her feelings or putting her to inconvenience, or by the demands of an elaborate household or by many possessions. His preference for making last-minute decisions about how he wished to pass his evenings would by itself have made him a difficult husband. But the dinner with him and his wife was a pleasant affair, and it was followed, once a year or so, by others, occasions which I enjoyed, for Matthew behaved with courtly consideration towards her, while she, as decisive and direct as he was tentative and on occasion oblique, was excellent company. I admired her retentive memory for what was worth remembering, about, for instance, such friends as Gwen John, and for the way in which she seemed to have detached entirely her life from Matthew's while preserving her affection for him. I never pass the little restaurant beside South Kensington Station without recalling those occasions with pleasure; also with a certain pride, for I was pretty well alone, I fancy, at least among his younger friends, in being invited to dine with him and his wife together.

Occasionally, however, Matthew lamented his homeless condition, its inconvenience, and especially did he lament the loss of his house at Aix, and, one day, the loss of a screen he had painted, from which, he said, the background of his 'Peaches' in the Tate was partly taken. The screen, moreover, he said, had served him as a sort of talisman.

Augustus John claimed the same almost total freedom of action as

Matthew Smith but the claim was asserted in accordance with the dictates of a very dissimilar temperament. At the very outset of his life he had in effect proclaimed his necessities and his tastes, and the way of life that their fulfilment involved, so that anyone united with him in matrimony or friendship or any other relationship could entertain no doubts about the attendant conditions. There was wisdom in such consistent forthrightness—a forthrightness impossible except on occasion for a man of Matthew's extreme sensibility; people are in general far less provoked by what they may regard as misconduct when it can be readily foreseen than when it is unexpected.

The fairly frequent although irregular meetings I had with Matthew and the ever closer friendship that resulted from them warmed and enhanced my life during the war and after. Besides this capacity to give warmth and comfort there was in his character a vein of eccentricity that delighted his friends, which often showed itself in Chekhovian dramas of non-action. For some time after the Tate had acquired one of his paintings entitled 'The Young Actress' he was troubled by the belief that it was marred by a remediable defect and he asked whether he might retouch it. At last permission was obtained from the Trustees, and one morning in January 1944 he arrived at the Gallery with a very small paintbox and I left him to make a minute rectification—'only a sixteenth of an inch, you know, only a sixteenth', he explained—on his very broadly, almost coarsely painted canvas. Two hours later I rejoined him and found that after anguished debate with himself he had decided that, after all, no rectification was needed. These two distressing hours, however, were not vainly spent: his doubts were resolved, and I have rarely known him more cheerful than he was at lunch that afternoon at the Café Royal. Like many people who sleep with difficulty he read much, and just then he was in the middle of one of his recurrent phases of dedication of his nights to Dickens. 'Too many readers of Dickens,' he said, 'read him with a wrong disposition: they treat his leading characters as they treat film stars; they follow them and their doings and neglect the rest. The way to read Dickens is to immerse oneself in his world, in all its aspects, as though one were walking through a strange and interesting town, taking note of just whatever happens to attract one's attention.'

Matthew was one of the very few people I have known (Clive Bell was another) who was acquainted with that still too little

recognized Canadian painter J. W. Morrice—his 'Lady in a Wicker
Chair' (in the Beaverbrook Gallery at Fredericton) would hang
without disadvantage beside a Whistler or an early Pasmore—whom
he frequented in his Paris days. Morrice used to work, he said,
without preliminary drawings but from tiny oil sketches; he painted
a series of nudes that so shocked his Canadian relatives that they had
them burnt.

Later that January, when we again met at the Café Royal, Matthew
was depressed by the eyestrain that prevented him from working,
and I went back with him to his gloomy room in Hamilton House,
Piccadilly, where he told me he had been spending whole days
listening on his tiny radio-set.

Depression had two almost invariable effects: it intensified his
dislike for wherever he happened to be living and working, and his
nostalgia for France and for Aix in particular, and he would
attribute his current depression to his having been compelled, by
the war, to leave.

On one particular evening he spoke of the supremacy of French
painting, of his confidence in its continuing supremacy, and of the
bracing effect for a painter of living in France. His belief in its
future derived from his reverence for the older painters, Matisse
especially, for I never heard him praise or even refer to the work of
any painter of a later generation. 'Who,' I asked him, 'are the successors of Matisse, Braque and Rouault?' He evaded my question, even
when I pressed for an answer. France was his second country (and
often, in elegiac retrospect at least, his first), but his interest in other
parts of the world was not easy to arouse. I could hardly imagine
him in any part of the New World. He described, I recollect,
lunching with Hemingway that summer, whom he found 'neither
forthcoming nor attractive'—a visitor from a world far beyond the
range of his natural sympathies.

One of Matthew's most conspicuous and endearing traits was his
ardent susceptibility to women who were beautiful or pretty, which,
with his charm, his open-handed hospitality and his celebrity, ensured him a considerable measure of response. This I never heard
him even remotely allude to—in spite of his preference for bohemian
company his own manners remained impeccably correct. But stories
about his somewhat Chekhovian failures he used to relate with an
obsessive melancholy that was far from excluding a sense of the
humour of his situations. There was one about a woman whom he

saw in a train in France and who attracted him desperately. She, he and another man occupied a compartment by themselves on a night journey and he lay awake envying the man with whom she exchanged an occasional brief word. Why, he asked himself in anguish, did one never encounter such women alone? Jealousy and desire denied him any sleep, and early in the morning the woman got out of the train, giving no more than a nod to the man he had supposed to be her husband. I forget the details of the succession of measures he took, elaborate but futile, to find her. There was another object of equally desperate attraction whom after an hour's manœuvring one night in a bar in France he managed to meet. A moment later she left for the railway station. 'I thought of following —following her, you see—but then I thought she was probably going to some small place on the Paris line and that she'd return. I stayed on for two further days at much inconvenience, looking out for her. But she never came back. What I ought to have done was to follow her. . . .'

Matthew was one of those with whom intimacy was not in the least impaired if one happened for a time to see little of him. It was not until some months after he had related these particular stories that we met again, ostensibly to discuss a modification in the wording on the label of the 'Still Life' he and his wife had given to the Tate in memory of their sons. Our previous conversation was resumed as though uninterrupted. He exclaimed, when I twitted him about the woman in the train, 'Oh, it was *awful*! I can just *see* that little foot, just down there, you know.' As so often his talk turned to France. 'I started to speak French too late ever to speak it well; I speak fluently but badly—fluently but badly', he repeated in his voice like a muffled echo. I said that I supposed the only way to learn it really well later in life was to live with a Frenchwoman. 'I did that,' he said; 'she was a delightful woman—a delightful woman. Many Frenchwomen are, but you must either avoid politics or agree with them.'

Although in general extremely tolerant Matthew was apt to be critical to the point of resentment of anything written about him that he considered in any way inaccurate or misleading. This evening he spoke bitterly, yet again, about Philip Hendy's laudatory monograph, which had appeared no less than six years before. 'He said that I *glazed*. I've never done that; never in my life.'

Just before we parted he described a visit to the studio of Ambrose

McEvoy, amused, I fancy, at the contrast it offered to his own: 'McEvoy was painting, beneath a dazzling arc-lamp, with as much concentration as though he were alone, in a studio full of gossiping visitors.'

At that moment Augustus John came into the Royal Court in Sloane Square, where we were dining, a favoured resort of both his and Matthew's. 'I'd like to avoid him,' Matthew said; 'we lunched and dined together not long ago, and we drank so much that I've felt unwell for days.' How ridiculous, we agreed, the current depreciation of Augustus. We dined together a week or two later when he gave me much pleasure by telling me of the admiration Augustus had expressed for my father's Memorial Exhibition at the Tate (this was held in 1950), saying that he had occasionally entertained a certain reserve about him as a painter which the exhibition had entirely dissipated, and he described certain paintings, including, in particular, 'The Coster Girls', from the Graves Gallery, Sheffield, in the utmost detail. My pleasure was not diminished by my knowledge that Augustus' attitude was and remained equivocal: in certain moods he could depreciate (though never in my presence) my father's art, and at others he could wholeheartedly praise it. Matthew himself was still worrying about the wording for the tablet on the 'Still Life' he was giving to the Tate. He reverted once again to the problem that so continually vexed him, of finding a studio that he did not positively dislike, and spoke of his distress at having just yielded an option on one studio and then realized it would have been the best he had had for years.

During the years after the war his sight grew perceptibly weaker, which had the effect of making him more acutely observant of the near as compensation for his inability to perceive the far. One evening in October he not only subjected a new tie I was wearing to a commendatory analysis, but he precisely described the weave of the suit I had worn when we had talked briefly at a Royal Garden Party months before. Not that his attention was directed more than momentarily at such trivialities.

At the beginning of May 1951 a dinner with Matthew was to have melancholy consequences. He complained gently of the hanging of the group of his paintings at the Tate (which were in an annexe adjoining the Sculpture Hall), saying that they needed stronger light. I contended that paintings extremely strong in colour such as his own looked better glowing out, as it were, of a moderate light, than challenged by a strong one. (I remembered how adversely the strong light of Venice affected his paintings in the Biennale one year.) He seemed half convinced. Before we parted I handed him, at his suggestion, the manuscript chapter on him for my *Modern English Painters*, for which he had given me unstinting help. That night, he confessed, he was low in spirits, owing to his struggle, renewed every morning and always unsuccessfully, against smoking cigarettes directly he woke—also on account of indecision about whose invitation to stay, of the number proffered him just then, he should accept.

Towards the end of the month I saw Matthew for the first time since I had given him my manuscript. He told me that he would take it as a favour to him if I would omit an unfriendly remark he had made to me about Epstein. This I had already excised, as it happened, from my own copy. He said that otherwise he very much liked the chapter, but that he had a few suggestions to make regarding matters of fact. A week later we met again, when he returned my manuscript, with a few minor corrections and suggestions, reaffirmed his satisfaction but added, 'I take no responsibility for your *praise*.'

On this occasion he was in a state of acute distress: his oculist had told him that both his eyes were afflicted by cataract, and he had been offered the choice between allowing their condition to deteriorate or undergoing two dangerous operations, each involving thirteen weeks' convalescence in darkness. Already he found difficulty in reading, although little as yet in painting. Before dinner we went to his studio in Thurloe Square, so that he could show me his painting by Ingres, or from the studio of the master (he was not certain which), and the paintings on which he was currently at work. There was no painter whom he mentioned more often than Ingres, developing, on this occasion, the theme that 'revolutionary' painters such as Matisse and Picasso had understood him much better than his professed followers and academic painters in general, especially his extraordinary *deliberateness* and his profound calculations regarding the division of space. Suddenly, as though her work had some special relevance to this theme, he said that he thought little of Frances Hodgkins, and that her reputation would quickly fade.

In chronicling some of my meetings with Matthew I am painfully aware that the charm of his society, highly personal though it was, has somehow eluded me, so that readers of a later generation may wonder at the eagerness with which his friends looked forward to evenings spent in the company of this invalidish man, much given to complaint about the state of his health and the shortcomings of his studios, in repeated phrases that emphasized the echo-like timbre of his faint voice.

One night I telephoned to invite him to dinner. In a scarcely audible voice he said that he was ill—too ill to go out, but that if I would have dinner with him in the restaurant on the ground floor of Chelsea Cloisters he would be delighted. As rain was falling heavily I welcomed an arrangement that would allow him to remain indoors. 'It's a beastly place,' he whispered; 'I hope you don't mind it.' Our waitress was neglectful and off-hand and Matthew studied the menu with distaste. Presently he said, 'I think we've had enough of this place', and he got up and walked into the street without an overcoat and hailing a taxi gave the name of some resort he favoured. He explained that he was too ill to have a drink; his spirits rose; we had a large dinner and much to drink, and he seemed happier than at any other time I could remember. On another occasion, after a sedate dinner with me at the Athenaeum, we wandered along the streets of Soho, he lamenting the drabness of English cafés and places of amusement, when we suddenly caught sight, framed in a tall window, sitting on a high stool, of Francis Bacon. We joined him and he presently swept us along from bar to bar and club to club, eventually from the Colony to the Gargoyle. The more Francis drank, the more physically helpless his condition, the more marked his imperious dignity. We were joined at the Gargoyle by the painter Robert Colquhoun, a wasted and a very drunk Don Quixote, and Robert McBride, his rotund, no soberer Sancho Panza, who accompanied noisy demands for whisky with abusive remarks about members of the party that had assembled in the meanwhile. Francis, although unable to rise from his chair at the head of the table, instantly quelled them with the grave authority of a judge.

It was a delight to be in the company of Matthew and Francis together. I never heard one praise—to his face—the painting of the other, but their tacit assumption of mutual regard and affection was manifest. Matthew used to say of the work of Francis that even at its least successful it never lacked absorbing interest, and Francis, who admires the work of few of his contemporaries, admires Matthew's with little qualification. When it was decided to hold a retrospective exhibition of Matthew's work at the Tate and I invited Francis— who, so far as I was aware, had never written a word for publication —to write a tribute for the catalogue, he readily accepted.

Dining with me one night early in 1952 Matthew talked of the humiliations he suffered in his early life: of meeting a schoolfriend walking in Darley Street, Bradford, with a well-dressed woman, when he himself was carrying a sack of wool, and of their mutual embarrassment; of how even at the Slade the habit persisted of doing menial tasks of the kind his father had laid upon him with 'character-forming' intention, and of the astonishment of Professor Fred Brown coming upon him in the performance of some such task.

During the early part of 1952 we often discussed his forthcoming retrospective exhibition at the Tate: on one occasion he said that it would be more appropriate if we showed John instead; on another that the prospect afforded him more apprehension than pleasure.

Essentially preoccupied as he was with personal endeavour and private life, his attitude towards public affairs was both sceptical and commonsensical. He laughed with unusual heartiness when I told him that Augustus had pressed me to bring him to an anti-Franco meeting, and, with reference to another friend's agitation for unilateral disarmament, he said, 'If we're to have armaments, and in the present state of the world we must, let's have the best possible.'

Every time I saw him his health had deteriorated and his vision in particular, but he bore his afflictions stoically.

Early in September I received a letter from Kathleen Follett, a common friend, which told me that Matthew had been deeply distressed by the chapter on him in my *Modern English Painters* (the first volume had recently been published) and that he had even talked of suicide.

I immediately told her on the telephone that Matthew had kept the chapter in manuscript for weeks, read every word of it and made a number of suggestions and corrections all of which were adopted. 'I don't for an instant doubt it,' she replied, 'and I admire the book, but,' she significantly added, '*you know what Matthew is.*' I wrote to him at once and he telephoned next day and asked me to dinner. I went first to Chelsea Cloisters, where we looked through some paintings and water-colours for possible inclusion in the forthcoming exhibition, and then to his studio in Thurloe Square to go through a very large accumulation of more recent work, with the same end in view—this without any allusion to the more immediate issue between us, uppermost in both our minds. The opportunity of comparing the new with the earlier led me to the conclusion that as Matthew became more melancholic his paintings became more exuberant. It only affected me as singular for an instant: as I had been long convinced that he was one of those artists whose work is the fulfilment of all that they themselves are not—as distinct from those, like Byron, for instance, whose work is a projection of what they are—it seemed to me inevitable that the exuberance of Matthew's work should be in inverse ratio to his own optimism. Few of the new works seemed to me consistently realized, though all had fine passages, but their shortcomings were no doubt mainly due to the deterioration of his eyesight.

It was not until we were half-way through dinner—at one of his favoured resorts, the Hanstown Club, off Sloane Square—that he thanked me for my letter, confirmed that my chapter had caused him distress, for which, however, he was no longer able to account, and he freely admitted having gone through my text minutely and that all his suggestions had been adopted: although he murmured something about having a vague impression that he might see the text with the revisions he had proposed. He made, under close questioning from me, no specific criticism whatever, either general or particular, other than a small point about his war service that he himself had overlooked. 'I thought', he said (and this brought to an end our discussion of the subject), 'you might have shown yourself a wiser man than I in relation to certain statements of mine you quoted. When I re-read the piece, early one morning, when I felt wretched anyhow, I could see no course but suicide. But it's all right now. Don't worry about it.' The subject was never again spoken of, nor had I ever cause to fear that our friendship was in the slightest degree impaired.

The affair left me bewildered. Maybe he had criticisms that his reticence prevented him from disclosing but which he mentioned to other friends. My conclusion is that he may have felt the whole chapter—the fullest account of him to be published hitherto—to constitute somehow a violation of his privacy.

We met even more often than usual the following summer to make plans for the exhibition at the Tate: Matthew was most helpful, ever ready with useful suggestions. He was anxious, he said, that certain works in Epstein's possession should be included, but he said that owing to his secretiveness he might be reluctant to lend. His finest example, however, 'Woman with a Fan', Epstein lent most readily. It was characteristic of Matthew's self-depreciatory attitude that he exclaimed, in the middle of a discussion of such matters, 'But this must be very boring for you.'

Dining with Matthew late in July 1953 it suddenly occurred to me that the person to augment Francis Bacon's tribute in the catalogue, which was to consist of no more than a couple of paragraphs, was Henry Green, an intimate friend and an ardent admirer of Matthew's, and a writer of unusual merit. At my persuasion Matthew telephoned to him at once, told him of my idea and Henry Green agreed to discuss it with us shortly. In the course of the evening I mentioned in passing our projected exhibition of the work of Graham Sutherland. Matthew suddenly looked sad: when I asked him what the matter was, it appeared that he had assumed—such was his diffidence—that we intended to hold the Sutherland exhibition in place of, instead of in addition to, his own!

He was elated by my idea of a catalogue introduction by Henry Green, but most anxious that his friend should not attribute it to him. Henry Green lunched with us next day and offered to write 2000 words (Matthew had suggested 400) and declined payment. 'What I shall write will be *poetry*, and people don't get paid for poetry, do they? Now let's say no more about it. You shall have it after next weekend.'

When the exhibition was hung, on 31 August, Matthew came with Epstein to see it. 'It's not so bad as I thought it was going to be—not so bad, you know', Matthew said in his toneless voice—from him extravagant praise. Epstein was most enthusiastic, and generously said that the choice could not be bettered. He spoke also of the essays in sculpture that Augustus had recently been making. 'It's the sculpture of a painter,' he declared; 'it's sensitive, but you could stick your finger through it. It's interesting, but it's not real sculpture.'

The behaviour of Matthew at the small party we gave for him in our minute flat in the basement of the Tate threw some light on his feelings about my account of him and his work: he lurked near the door and could barely be induced to enter, so desperate was his shyness. 'I'm in a terrible state of nerves,' he repeated. Matthew's wife told Elizabeth that she had muted her account of Gwen John when she had given me information about her for *Modern English Painters*, saying that in temperament she was a combination of her brother Augustus and St. John of the Cross. In the fullness of time Matthew overcame his nervousness, was cajoled into sitting down, and from that moment he exerted to the full his unobvious but potent charm. The lovely actress Valerie Hobson (later Mrs. John Profumo), deeply admired by and admiring of Matthew, asked me in a low voice to point out his wife, who, she said, she understood was in every way incompatible with him. When I did so she laughed, exclaiming, 'But they're alike as two sticks!'

It was at this same gathering that I first mentioned to Stanley Spencer my hope that an exhibition of his work would be held at the Tate. 'That will show 'em,' he exclaimed delightedly, with a simple assurance in comical contrast to Matthew's almost pathological diffidence.

The immense success of the exhibition did nothing to diminish his diffidence: he was pleased by the admiration of his friends, but they, he thought, and to infinitely greater degree the critics and the public, were unaware of the vast gulf between what he attempted and what he succeeded in achieving, so that they could not recognize failure even when it stared them in the face.

Although disposed to be critical of Epstein he warmed to him somewhat after his second marriage, to Kathleen Garman, whom he particularly liked and who fostered a more cordial relation between Epstein and his fellow-men. We met immediately after he had attended some sort of wedding celebration; never, he said, had he known Epstein so benevolent. Augustus, too, he had lately seen, also in high spirits, but just as he was rejoicing in the happiness of his two old friends his own mood was shadowed by the reflection that, after all, he disliked the studio to which he had recently moved even more than that he had left. But he had, I suspect, another and graver reason for distress: I had never seen his little room in Chelsea Cloisters so densely stacked with gifts, in the form of paintings, temporarily returned.

I do not think that he was ever reconciled to the new studio, but he was greatly pleased by the action of a friend to make it more habitable. Vera, then the wife of the art critic John Russell, had thoroughly scrubbed the floor, and when he asked why she did not leave that to the charwoman she replied, 'It's far too rough for a charwoman, but she should be able to manage it now.'

Matthew compulsively fed his strange nostalgia for habitations other than his own. 'I love to read advertisements for houses,' he said; 'I saw one today for a little cottage in Kent. It sounds ideal.' 'Are you going to look at it?' I asked. 'No,' he said, 'but I like to think of it—to think of it, you know.' That same evening—it was in

March 1957—he told me something that perfectly exemplified his extreme considerateness for his friends, which on occasion could become a cause of positive anguish. A married couple had given him a year's subscription to an art journal, and he had been a good deal troubled lest they, who were not well off, should feel under an obligation to renew it. After endless worry he accordingly took out a subscription for it for the following year—although he did not at all care for it—and casually let his friends know what he had done.

Matthew underwent the painful operations on his eyes and the prolonged and not less painful after-treatment, all of which he bore with exemplary courage. Their effect, he told me, was to enable him to see with an unaccustomed distinctness, which was in one sense disturbing, in that his broad handling of his paint, partly the product of myopia, although it had become habitual, was no longer quite spontaneous.

During 1958 many of his friends must have been oppressed, as I was, by a melancholy apprehension that he was gradually losing his hold on life. By 1959 he was fatally ill, and in hospital with cancer, though ignorant of his condition. 'Matthew', said a woman friend of his, 'must be crucified before he dies,' and she repaired his ignorance.

On 22 October St. James's Church, Piccadilly, was crowded with his friends and admirers for his memorial service. On the altar rested a vase of opulent red and yellow flowers: the incarnation of one of his own still-lifes.

After the service was over, Augustus, who sat just behind Elizabeth and me, wandered up and down the aisle, robustly kissing girls he fancied. In my mind's ear I heard Matthew describing the scene with dry relish in his muted voice: '. . . kissing the girls, you know.'

For months afterwards I would find myself in the act of telephoning to Matthew, and recall with a shock that somebody else was living in the 'flatlet' in Chelsea Cloisters and that I would never spend another evening in his company.

*

Augustus John spent more time, as the years passed, at Fryern Court, his house near Fordingbridge, and less in London (where for considerable periods he had no studio), and we met infrequently. Evenings in his company resembled those with Matthew in being improvised at the last moment, but even more informally. Augustus would telegraph or else would murmur in his deep voice over the telephone that he had just finished some studies for a wall painting, or found some old work that he had forgotten about, and if it would interest me to see them would I come to his studio around six. There he would show the works he had spoken of, always full of optimism about the prospect for carrying out his studies for wall paintings although, so far as I am aware, none was ever completed. In the meanwhile various people would arrive, including, usually, a girl or two. Augustus, vague-seeming and having drunk a good deal, was adroit nevertheless in ridding the studio of intruders at the appropriate time, it being understood that those of us who were present by invitation would spend the rest of the evening in his company. We would go to places in Chelsea for preference. After a longish visit to a bar he would apprehend that his guests might be inclined to eat. 'I want to stay here for a bit longer. There's a girl who's going to join us. Sturdy little thing. . . .' We would wait. Sometimes she would turn up and sometimes not. Augustus did not seem to mind, assured that before the evening was finished there would be others. At the Antelope Dylan Thomas, very drunk, briefly joined us once or twice. Upon those he spoke to he directed a cold, fanatical stare that put me in mind of Evelyn Waugh's, and he gave the impression of someone easily provoked to truculence. Augustus alluded to some poems he had recently completed, and Dylan Thomas, who had evidently seen them, declared with affectionate irony that Augustus was 'a most promising young poet'. I had never before heard Augustus mention having written poetry.

I must have been silent, distressed at some event or other. Dylan Thomas came up to the bar and giving me a searching, almost solicitous look, said 'You're a dull boy tonight. Why *be* a dull boy?' He was never, I imagine, a dull boy himself: his ordinary talk was as richly poetic as his writings, and spoken in his resonant but precisely modulated tones scarcely less effective. I would like to repeat a few of the best things I heard him say, but even the contemporary public would hardly tolerate some of the dicta of Dylan Thomas, although those who heard or overheard them made no demur, so beautifully, with such high spirits and assurance were they uttered, by this corpulent, innocent-faced boy with the untidy curls.

An occasion for several meetings with Augustus was his loved and revered sister Gwen. It was he, I believe, who proposed that a memorial exhibition of her work should be held at the Matthiesen, the Bond Street gallery now defunct.

Matthiesen and Maison [he wrote from Fryern on 12 August 1946] have been trying to persuade me to open Gwen's Exhibition. I hesitate to undertake this, 1st the accident of consanguinity seems to rule me out and 2nd I am subject to stage-fright on such occasions. I wonder if you would be so good as to perform this function or if that is impossible, whether you can propose any other suitable person to do it. I know your admiration for Gwen and your position of course enables you to speak with authority. For these reasons I hope you yourself will agree to this request. All the works are to be seen at Matthiesens. They are anxious to have this point settled at once so as to get the catalogue ready. I have just written a fore-word to this which I would like you to see.

On 11 September he wrote expressing his dissatisfaction with the exhibition:

I am glad to hear you will be able to open Gwen's exhibition. I have just received the catalogue which perplexes me. Many of the best pictures do not appear to be hung: the reproductions are ill-chosen and the self-portrait from the Tate I took some trouble about does not appear. I hope if you have time to go to the Gallery before the opening you will ask Mr. Maison to show you what he hasn't thought fit to hang.
Many thanks for consenting to do the opening.

It was a privilege to open this assembly of the work of one of the painters I admired most of her generation.

Let me thank you again [he wrote on 22 September, again from Fryern], for opening Gwen's Exhibition. Unfortunately we arrived rather late and thus missed the beginning of your speech: what I was in time to hear made me regret being late all the more. I was quite sure the Exhibition would move you deeply.

Augustus and his family gave me, to mark the occasion, a small but beautiful example of Gwen's work.

Augustus was greatly preoccupied by the problem of ensuring the perpetuation of his sister's memory. He was anxious that a book should be written about her, and at different times he suggested that Elizabeth and I should be entrusted with the writing of it, but he withdrew under a recurrent impulse to write it himself. The fore-word he contributed to the Matthiesen catalogue is among his best writing, but it was evident that he was not capable, at that period of his life, of writing a book involving research (his *Chiaroscuro* is made up of remembered, and often imperfectly remembered, fragments); of this he was at a certain level aware, but he never altogether abandoned the intention. No one, however, could have been kinder than he in helping me with the chapter on Gwen in *Modern English Painters*: he entrusted me with all the documents, including many letters, the very documents, in fact, on which he would chiefly have relied had he attempted to write her life himself; in addition he withdrew the right to consult them from someone he thought, on reflection, would not make good use of them, and who posted them back from abroad unregistered so that they were untraced for three weeks. Shortly after my book was published I received from him the following letter from Fryern accompanied by notes on my treatment of his sister and himself. These are worthy of publication as expressing a view of her character somewhat at variance with that hitherto accepted and on account of their intrinsic interest:

May 14, 1952

Dear John,

I received your new book and have been reading it with *great* interest. I think you have made a very good job of the subject *and a very difficult job it must have been*. I turned at once to your Essay on Gwen which I found very good, though a few oversights and some misunderstandings have occurred, which I will note down.

The early Whistlerian portrait is at present at Percy St. I would certainly have lent it had it been requested. I hope to come up and see the show very soon when I will gladly take a meal with you as you proposed. I had thought to come up before but got anchored down to some work as usual, and am now due for a short visit to S.W. Wales with a friend. I hope you got a copy of Chiaroscuro: though between me and the firm of Jonathan Cape many a slip has happened and may yet. If by somebody's negligence no such book has reached you I will see that the omission is rectified. I am at work on the second part which should largely complete the first with something over.

I regret only the near absence of one figure in your book, that of Dick Innes.[1] In a feverish and interrupted life he had time to

---

[1] As the subjects are arranged in the order of their birth Innes figures in the second volume, which was not published until 1956.

prove himself a true poet-painter. As different as chalk from cheese (neither of which substances are to be imitated) he was as far apart from his contemporaries, even when he admired them. I was surprised and pleased to see a letter to you from Dodo [Dorelia John] reproduced: her only appearance in print so far and not a bad one. I did not know she could write!

Many thanks for the book,

Yours ever,

AUGUSTUS

FIRST NOTES ON 'GWEN JOHN' FROM A CURSORY READING

Paragraph 1. With our common contempt for sentimentality, Gwen and I were not opposites but much the same really, but we took a different attitude. I am rarely 'exuberant'. She was always so; latterly in a tragic way. She wasn't chaste or subdued, but amorous and proud. She didn't steal through life, but preserved a haughty independence which some people mistook for humility. Her passions for both men and women were outrageous and irrational. She was never 'unnoticed' by those who had access to her.

2. In Maurice Cremnitz's bed-room, where I slept one night, hung a drawing by her of my host. 'Il n'y a personne,' he said, 'qui dessine comme cela.'

3. She concerned herself with very few people, ignoring all others or treating them with a ritual politeness only. She could hardly tolerate the occasional vulgarity of the Curé of Meudon nor the stupidity of most of the nuns. Jesus Christ alone seemed a worthy comrade, though even He seemed often absent-minded, negligent or dilatory and so far culpable. As to the friend who saw so much of her latterly, it is quite possible she wouldn't remember him.

4. Edwin John can hardly be called her favourite nephew, since she scarcely knew the others—except for Elfin, whom she didn't approve of. Her shack, in Rue Babie, wasn't on a piece of waste ground, but on an enclosed terrain and once cultivated. Gwen, in her notes, was not always reticent about herself, and some of them, as I told Edwin, must be destroyed. In any case they were not written for publication.

5. Lexden Terrace was the *last* house to be occupied by my family, when Gwen might have been about 16 or 17. She had no

help from McEvoy, whom she out-distanced immeasurably from the start.

We lived for a while on the corner of a statuary's shop in the Marylebone Rd. (on a turning out of Fitzroy Sq.).

The letter you quote on page 63 was written years later, like all the contents of Edwin's collection.

P. 167. There was no 'pity' in the portrait referred to. Gwen was *pityless* except in the case of cats.

The 'Artist's Room' was her room at Meudon, in The Rue Terre Neuve. The portrait 'Girl called Fennella', page 168, is of an English girl who had assumed the name of Fenella Lovell, a well-known gypsy name, for this girl pretended to be a gypsy and had learnt a considerable lot of the Romani language in which she used to write to me, mixing her dialects recklessly. When she offered me her virginity, I, like Queen Victoria, was not amused. She looked too unhealthy, even when naked . . .

P. 170. I don't understand what you mean by 'she was relentless with herself in her determination to transform her life'. She only wanted to *fulfil*, not transform, it, but her lovers were unsatisfactory. Rodin getting too old, Maritain too much of a Pasha, his niece too stupid, Rilke . . . ? I don't know about him.

Her notes *do* reveal a mind of exceptional quality. She might have been mad at moments, but she was never banal. She had an abnormal sensibility and in spite of her loathing for dishonesty was often blinded by emotion and easily taken in. The difficulty about coming to England with the cats was the imposition of quarantine. Ill manners she could never forgive.

Edwin says he found dozens of studies of Gwen by Rodin in the cellars of the Musée.

I haven't time to analyse your treatment of myself, but I must say at once, my collision with a rock at Tenby made no difference to my mentality. My skull is abnormally thick it appears: or maybe my scalp. I was born at *Belgrave House, The Esplanade*, Tenby. The 'Old Lady's'[1] head is very well modelled: the hands unfinished yet expressive. *She herself* couldn't move them easily. Never painted a 'peasant' in my life. My latest 'improvisation' has already taken three to four years to reach its present unfinished but hopeful stage. [Wyndham] Lewis is an ass to say that nature is for me a 'tremendous carnival' or 'saturnalia'. What

---

[1] 'Old Lady', by John. Bought by the Tate in 1941.

cheap journalistic tripe! No wonder that man has been struck blind. His own pictures, however, have prepared us for this mild calamity. Let us hope that it won't prevent him continuing his art criticism at least. As for Gypsies, I have not yet encountered a sounder 'Gypsy' than myself. My mother's name was Petulengro, remember, and we descend from Tubal-Cain via Paracelsus. Dodo and I did *not* get married following the death of Ida. My mountains were never Innes-conceived. Another silly legend. They were conceived by neither of us but seen by both, though more effectively by him, for I lacked his superstition and drew better. His limitations actually helped him: and yet if we both loved the same wandering girl, it was I who embraced her and obtained her response. He painted like a sophisticated and moon-struck bargee and I envied him this faculty, but of course was incapable of imitating it. He might get up before dawn, but it was I who went last to bed. I had to mind my Ps and Qs, for he was pernickety like all consumptives and I would have hated a quarrel or to have hurt him in any way. I conclude these straggling remarks which are for your ears only. They may throw an extra gleam of light on Gwen, Innes and even myself.

A. J.

It is relevant to mention that he had already read, just a year before, my drafts on both Gwen and himself as the following letter indicates. The corrections he made were in fact adopted.

May 29, 1951

Dear John,

I was very sorry not to be able to come up yesterday. I was quite inarticulate with my throat and the usual depression. I think I'll come up next week and will let you know so that we may have that dinner with which you tempt me. I have looked through the extracts you sent and made some useful corrections which I hope you will endorse. I was due to-day at a conference with aims at sanity and Peace (at the instigation of Victor Gollancz) but I felt my slogan 'To Hell with National Frontiers!' would have missed fire in the circumstances. I was probably wise to withhold it. I think I have the photographs you require.

I don't remember what 'candid comments' I made on Tenby. When last there I thought it an entrancing place and would not like to 'froisser' the Town Council—yet. I have been sufficiently

critical in my memoirs, which by-the-bye are due in the Autumn;
but, as usual, I am just now at loggerheads with my publishers . . .

In Gwen's documentary remains there are one or two passages
which should be suppressed. I would like to see the extracts you
have chosen—next week. Perhaps you should mention an evening
which suits you.

Yours ever

AUGUSTUS

After first approving of the illustrations for my Phaidon book on
him, he became critical of what he asserted to be the inadequate
representation of his most recent work, which, in fact, I admired less
than the earlier, on account of the softness of his contours and of a
growing tendency to force the lineaments of his sitters into con-
formity with a few favoured, often Grecoesque schemata. The
suspicion that his own estimate of it did not in fact differ substantially
from my own was confirmed one evening when I was at the house of
Hugo Pitman, one of his closest friends and a discriminating collector of his work. I must, Hugo insisted, stick to my guns about the
illustrations. A few days before he said he had come home to find
Augustus contemplating his big upright early 'Dorelia' standing in
front of a fence. Augustus was in tears: 'Dorelia was a lovely girl—
and I can't paint like that now—just can't do it.' Moved to sympathy
by what Hugo Pitman had told me, I went round to keep an appointment with Augustus at Tite Street, to find a brusque-ish letter
asking whether I could call instead next day. I did so, and found his
amiability restored and he finally approved the illustrations. It was
evident that the contemplation of the photographs stirred melancholy thoughts, for his hands trembled violently as he held the file,
and he knocked over and broke an ashtray.

That summer he seemed to be subject to frequent fits of melancholy. One night at dinner Matthew Smith told me that he felt sad
about Augustus, one of his oldest and closest friends, but who seemed
to have lost his old friendliness and candour, and although they
continued from habit to take meals together they found that they
had little to say.

I have never known a man more impervious to the effects of dissipation than Augustus: when he was nearly eighty he could out-
drink most of his companions and engage in amorous—if that is the
word—relations that would have debilitated constitutions generally

held robust. But by the late 'fifties the preternaturally ardent fire that had animated his majestic frame began to burn low. The last letter I had from him, dated 9 June 1959, written in response to the gift of a book, read in part: 'I was astonished to find myself included in the galère, being accustomed to consider myself, if not exactly dead, at least belonging to the *Baroque* age—or earlier. . . .' The following summer, when he called at the Tate and asked me to take him round the Picasso exhibition, he was quite deaf and very weak and it was plain that he was beginning to die; he died two years later.

*

Very different had been my last sight of H. G. Wells. He was bustling and alert, very much in the midst of life. I was lunching at the Café Royal and Wells, on his way out, sat down at my table for a few minutes. He seemed to be in excellent health; I can see in my mind's eye the large eyes, luminous with intelligence and a diffused benevolence that gave dignity and light to his commonplace features —a benevolence that was far from incompatible with a ready proneness to exasperation. It was in fact to exasperation that he immediately gave vent. 'I've just come back from America, as I dare say you've heard,' he said (like everyone else I had indeed heard, as certain opinions he had expressed there were under bitter attack as disloyal). 'On my way back I was held up for days in Bermuda, because the Germans had thrown the postal service into confusion by sending there four tons of postcards, each one inscribed, "Oh, you are brave", and of course the officials were afraid to take the responsibility for simply throwing the beastly things away. So I was held up.' Wells' step was jaunty, his clothes were dapper; in fact the voracity of his interest in wide and varied fields of knowledge, in life, public and private, had preserved him well: he was still very much the 'H.G.' I had known as a boy in Church Row, Hampstead. I was aware, all the same, of an exasperated melancholy that was new: it was caused perhaps by the persistent failure of mankind to heed his advice or to fulfil his prophecies. I had never met a man so deeply preoccupied with the future as he: the word was ever on his lips, and never had the 'future' looked a bloodier mess. But for Wells, as for another sage, 'cheerfulness kept breaking in'. In later years he had become less radical in his outlook. Not long before this last meeting Elizabeth and I had found ourselves sitting not far from Wells on the opening night in 1940 of the film version of *The Grapes of Wrath*.

Beside Baroness Budberg, his tall good-natured companion, Wells looked angry and little. In fact he was waiting for a pretext to vent his anger. As the four of us walked out together I inadvertently gave it to him by praising some feature of the film. 'I disagree,' he said, his voice rising, 'it's an anti-social, anti-democratic film. The forces of law are ridiculous throughout. A *beastly* film.'

A painter of the younger generation I was happy to meet again, in 1942, was Ceri Richards, to whom I was introduced, at the private view of the first London exhibition of his work, by Henry Moore, who had on several occasions told me of his admiration for him, once describing him as the finest draughtsman of his generation. Ceri (whom I had known slightly as a student at the Royal College of Art) was one of those Welshmen who seem to justify the claims of Welsh nationalists that Wales is a nation entirely distinct from England. Welsh was his native language, into which, he told me, he used inwardly to translate my father's criticisms of his work at the College, the better to understand their meaning. Like Henry, Ceri was short and strongly built, but while Henry was the personification of energy, a benevolent toughness and directness of purpose, Ceri was withdrawn and gentle, his large grey eyes fixed upon things far-off. Although I had lost touch with the painter I was familiar with the work, which was of slow growth and much indebted to Picasso, Miró, Arp and Ernst, but his debt was expressed without either subservience or disguise. I believed that a rare imaginative talent was emerging and shortly after our meeting I brought an oil painting from the exhibition, 'Blossoms', before the Tate Trustees, who readily acquired this first example of Ceri's work to enter the collection. The 'blossoms' could also be read as exploding bombs, for the picture was painted in 1940 when the air attacks on London began in earnest.

It is to the credit of the prevailing perceptiveness that Ceri won steady recognition, until by the following decade he had come to be recognized as among the foremost British artists of the time. His is an extremely complex art, impossible to place in any category, at once the product of a highly personal imagination and of an intimate knowledge of the work of contemporaries; of an extreme consciousness of the importance of formal relationships together with an intense preoccupation with his subjects, drawn as often from music and poetry as from the visual world. Neither his language nor his themes have ever shown any sign of dwindling into convention. The rich and varied tapestry he is tirelessly weaving grows year by year more impressive. Ceri himself, unaffected by his celebrity, retains the serenity and friendliness that marked his character in the 'forties. He retains, too, the same sheer good sense, however diffidently voiced, which I had cause to value when he became a Trustee of the Tate in 1958.

*

An artist of the same generation as Ceri and a fellow student at the Royal College with whom I was also acquainted was Edward Burra. Invited by Kenneth Clark to contribute a monograph to the Penguin Modern Painters he was editing I took the opportunity of paying tribute to this painter whom I had long particularly admired.

In mid-September 1942 I visited Springfield, his parents' house in Rye, where Edward lived in an upper storey. The contrast between the hall, a highly conventional place where tweed overcoats and mackintoshes hung and golf clubs and fishing tackle leaned, and the entrance to Edward's apartment, ornamented by an enlarged photographic portrait of a leper, far gone in his fearful affliction, was bizarre in the extreme. Edward was fascinated by decay; 'decaying' was a word frequently on his lips, as a term, moreover, of approbation. In his painting-room were a considerable number of completed water-colours—his poor health involves an enfeeblement of his hands which prevents him from painting in oils—some of Mediterranean low-life (sailors and prostitutes in bars and the like), of Mexican and Spanish subjects, some of them very large, and all highly finished and suffused with a spirit at once sinister and witty. They showed, too, his extraordinary powers of observation and his powers, no less extraordinary, of translating simple objects, whether baskets, chair seats, sailors' caps, wallpaper or bottles, into terms as formally fascinating as they are expressive.

Edward Burra himself was a silent pale long-faced man of thirty-seven who put me in mind of an electric battery almost run down, so near did his small reserve of energy seem to exhaustion. In spite of his poor health, this impression of exhaustion is misleading. His energy is carefully husbanded: he leads a quiet, regular life in jealously guarded seclusion, disturbed, I fancy, by few personal relations; he is as indifferent as an artist can be to the opinion of the public—a public which he allows infrequent opportunities of forming any opinion. Almost the sole interruptions of his secluded quiet were his visits abroad. There was a story, current among his friends, that he went out one evening, telling his mother that he was going into the garden to walk around. When night came he had not returned. It was weeks later when he walked casually in from the garden. It appeared that he had spent the intervening weeks in New York, making drawings of Negro dives in Harlem. When I asked him whether the story was apocryphal he answered, 'Not entirely.'

Upon the walls of his painting-room were pinned numerous photographs of paintings by Signorelli, Tiepolo, Magnasco and the Spanish masters, of Greek sculptures and pictures clipped from newspapers, English, French, Spanish, Italian, of dramatic incidents and evocative poses. Cluttering the floor, a wireless, a gramophone, chairs piled high with books in several languages, South American 'glossy' magazines, Victorian scrap-books, and on top of all this many long white paper cylinders were scattered: his own enormous water-colours, rolled up. As we talked I examined these high towers of books. Among them were volumes by Dickens, and, more significantly, novels of horror, such as Walpole's *Castle of Otranto*, and works of the Elizabethan dramatists such as Tourneur and Marston; and others pertaining to the cosmopolitan world of Montparnasse by such writers as Blaise Cendrars, Francis Carco and Pierre Macorlan. Edward makes no disguise of the nourishment he draws from books, and likewise from the paintings of the old masters, the Spaniards in particular, and among contemporaries Picasso, George Grosz, Chirico, Covarrubias, Dali and Wyndham Lewis. The real artist, Sickert used to say, is an avid borrower. A more avid borrower than Edward I have never known, yet the more freely he borrows the more highly personal the results. During the later 'thirties his interest shifted away from the low life of Harlem or Marseilles and his work assumed a more sombre character. Just before the Spanish Civil War he happened to be in Madrid. 'One day when I was lunching with some Spanish friends', he told me, 'smoke kept drifting past the restaurant window. I asked where it came from. "Oh, it's nothing," someone replied; "only a church being burnt!" That made me feel sick. It was all terrifying: pent-up hatred everywhere, violence, strikes, as well as burning churches. Everyone knew that something appalling was just about to happen.' From that time onwards his work often sounded a tragic note. The fact of Spain's being the theatre of war enhanced for him its tragic aspect, for he had been for some years under its spell: El Greco,

Zurbaran, Goya and the dramatic, luxuriant Jesuit-patronized Baroque architecture and sculpture he had studied, he told me, with intense excitement. He had taught himself Spanish (by the Hugo method) and had visited Mexico as well as Spain. On a visit to his studio, I asked him to show me a certain water-colour: 'A big picture, of Conquistadors' was how I described it. He looked puzzled, and when we found it he said, 'Oh! *That* was the one you wanted, was it? But it's of *this* war.' (It was 'Soldiers at Rye', which I shortly afterwards persuaded *The Studio* magazine to purchase for the Tate.) During my day-long first visit I came so to accept the reality of the world of Edward Burra, this place, with the presiding portrait of the leper, where the Baroque church with the dead Christ was as much at home as the young man meditating some unlawful pleasure in a dubious café, that I experienced something of a shock on walking downstairs to find myself in the world of normality once more. Were the cheap clothes of exuberant cut and fibrous texture of Edward's imagination less 'real' than the decent tweed overcoats in the hall?

On my way out Edward's mother described the attitude of the inhabitants of Rye towards Henry James. They regarded him, she said, with an awe bordering on veneration, but if he by chance addressed them, they suffered acutely from the length of his sentences.

*

A painter of a much older generation whom I formed the habit of seeing during the middle of the war was Charles Ginner, the last survivor of the Camden Town Group. His friends Harold Gilman and Spencer Gore, though familiar to me as close friends of my uncle Albert, I had not the privilege of knowing. I used to climb the narrow stairs that led up to Ginner's little painting-room at 66 Claverton Street, Pimlico, with the pleasurable anticipation not only of entering the presence of a friend but of one for whom the memory of these two others, whose work I greatly admired, was so very much alive. They had been dead for more than twenty years, and Pimlico is miles away from Camden Town, yet something of the way of life which the three of them lived in intimacy before the First World War was perpetuated in the little rooms in Claverton Street: the way the landlady's choice in wallpapers was accepted, the way the landlady herself loomed large. Similar, too, were the vistas offered by the streets outside, long, straight, symmetrical and grey. Along these, on certain auspicious evenings, I would be guided by Ginner to some 'eating-house' with shabby comfortable red-plush seats. Sickert used to say that English artists lived like gentlemen, but Ginner lived with a simplicity that put one in mind of the continental artist of tradition: two small (meticulously tidy) rooms furnished with the utmost simplicity and adorned by half a dozen small oil studies and drawings, the gifts of painter friends, a small library of well-read classics, half English and half French, an annual 'painting holiday'— these represented about the extent of Ginner's needs.

Like Matthew Smith, Ginner was one of those fortunate beings who charm without exertion, by their mere presence. One was aware, even when he was silent, of his modesty, generosity, candour and benevolence. But he was not habitually silent: he remembered his friends with admiration and affection and he stated his straightforward and sensible ideas with clarity. I recall his expressing resentment on only a single occasion, when he contrasted the effusive admiration expressed by J. B. Manson, my predecessor, for the work of the various members of the Camden Town Group—at the time when he was its secretary—especially for that of its leading members, Gilman, Gore and Ginner himself, with his neglect to represent it at the Tate. During the eight years when Manson had charge of its affairs nothing by Gilman or himself was acquired, even though their work was available for scarcely more than nominal sums, Ginner said, and only a single work by Gore.

One day he gave me a copy of his essay *Neo-Realism*, which first appeared in *The New Age* and was reprinted as the foreword to a catalogue of an exhibition he held with Gilman in 1914. This catalogue is something of a rarity and I was familiar with the ideas the essay propounded only through quotations drawn mainly from the long review of it contributed by Sickert to *The New Age*. Ginner had written little or nothing for publication since, I gathered, and admiring his loyalty to his friends and his rare good sense I urged him to write a brief account of the Camden Town Group, which appeared eventually in *The Studio*.

There was a reassuring unity about the life and work of this friend: he lived in the environment he most liked to represent; an environment fusty, lower-middle class, a Victorian survival. Characteristic, too, was his bachelor condition of a detachment that tempered even his affection for his friends. His painting is evidence of an ultimate lack of interest in human beings as subjects of pictorial art, suggested by his non-capacity to portray the figure. He preferred to treat them at a remove, in terms of their environment. But here he created an ineffable impression of their unseen presence: his walls are blackened by the smoke of their fires, his steps are worn by their tread, his flags are put out to signify their rejoicing or their mourning; there is little in his pictures that does not refer, however distantly or indirectly but always with an implicit affection and respect, to his fellow-men.

I never left Ginner (his high chuckle sounding in my ears) without enhanced affection and admiration for this kindly and honourable man, for his unassertive, but ardent, and so far as I could see, his ambitionless dedication to his art, his 'burning patience', as Sickert described it.

CHAPTER TWO

WYNDHAM LEWIS AND SOME OTHERS

A WISE man once declared that one ought to behave at each meeting with people one cares for as though it were the last.

One of the circumstances that made wartime London—and I have no doubt other parts of these Islands—an exhilarating place to live in, in spite of the endless harassments, deprivations and miseries of the war, was that so many people one knew or came across observed this injunction. They valued their families, their friends, as well as opportunities of reading the classics, looking at pictures and everything else that makes life precious, more intensely, more consciously than in time of peace, knowing that any day or night might deprive them of all of these forever. But after the war, even during the last phase of it, when the chance of that day or that night coming had diminished, the prevailing mood gradually approximated to the normal: people's relations became a little more casual and the serious tended to be postponed in favour of the trivial. But of course the amenities of peace, even though some were slow in making their appearance, afforded innumerable compensations. Of these one of the most delightful was the opportunity of meeting old friends and acquaintances lost sight of and making new ones; of living once again in a *city*, for during the war London assumed something of the character of a village.

One of those whose return I found particularly welcome was Wyndham Lewis. Owing to my visit to America early in the war, I was, I suppose, among the last of his English friends to see him and he seemed to regard me as a point of contact with London and he wrote me occasional letters—letters that he was evidently anxious to ensure the safe arrival of, for he sent them in duplicate. The first of these letters, from Toronto, reveals something of the feeling that inspired *Self-Condemned,* the book about Canada he published in 1955.

July 15, 1942

My dear Rothenstein, As you notice, I have landed up here.—
New York, as you probably foresaw it would, ended in disaster.
My dream of American dollars (which would help me to pay my
London debts) was beginning to fade already at the time we met.
—You, with your good practical sense, should have warned me!
But I suppose you thought I was old enough to divine such things
for myself.—You did not find the Tate in ruins I hope upon your
return; or did you get back before the Blitzes started? Anyway,
is that mausoleum intact? I hope the Blake drawings you had in
your office are safe: the Whistlers and Pre-Raphaelites, and several
moderns which I shall not name, though your father would be on
the list. How is he? I read that he had presided at some function
the other day in London, so I know he is safe. As a matter of fact,
I am glad that so far as I know nothing untoward has happened
to any friend of mine in England.

This bush-metropolis (where you find yourself in the presence
of a loathsome thing that is known as 'Methodism and Money')
has been my place of residence for upwards of 18 months. I have
never been able to make enough money to buy myself a ticket to
the coast, let alone to ship us back. I hope to get back, by hook
or crook, very soon. We have been miraculously fed and sheltered.
But no words of mine could paint the extreme grimness of life in
this country, and especially in this city. Please remember me to
anybody we know.—I have just written to your father. I should
welcome a note with a little news about anything that is happening—or that is likely to happen. Do you find scope for your
energies?

Yours,

WYNDHAM LEWIS

Nov. 17, 1942

My dear Rothenstein, A bad attack of influenza lasting about a
month has confused things. I have here a rough draft of a letter
but I cannot remember whether it was mailed. So I may be
repeating myself if I thank you for your excellent letter and the
enclosures about Tate exhibitions. You certainly seem to have
been uncommonly active, and what you tell regarding the demand
for good pictures in England is highly encouraging. On the other
hand I was distressed to hear about your father's health. I very
much hope that spell of illness is now at an end.

D

My 'Barcelona'[1] picture is still here in America as I understand are all the other things from the World's Fair in New York. It is the property of the Leicester Gallery I believe.

Now regarding my return to England. Were anyone to make me a present of two tickets this evening at 6 o'clock, tomorrow at 10 o'clock I should be telephoning whatever office it is handles the request for Atlantic bookings. It takes about 6 weeks I understand for them to fit you in. The more you pay the better—and safer—accommodation you get naturally. I say if *someone made me a present*, for I have not enough money to transport myself across Lake Ontario, much less to England.—Such has been my state of mind and purse ever since the time we met in New York. But neither you nor anybody else will or can send me two such tickets. So it remains a wish only. My mind is constantly focused upon means of getting back however. I shall make it before long.

But I wish you could tell me how I shall keep alive once I am back! The reason I am here, after all, is because conditions in my trade in England became so awful that I had to see whether I couldn't make a little money in the country where traditionally there is supposed to be a good deal of capital. One of my last experiences let us recall was the sale of a large painting of a bearded celebrity to the National Collection for one hundred pounds.[2] That was no fault of yours; for if they *won't* supply you with the funds to buy pictures. . . ! But to come down to realities —how shall I find the means to buy food, pay my rent and so forth when I return? It worries me a lot. Will they make me director of art education: could I secure the editorship of *The Listener* or something like that? Could I get some post like that occupied by Arthur Bliss at the B.B.C.? Would the King appoint me Keeper of his ceramics? Or shall I just be there, trying to sell a picture to a non-existent rentier, or an article to a paper whose space has been cut by half?

It is a very serious problem. I do not ask to be allowed to *create*: of course not—it has been my experience that creative persons are obliged to waste ninety per cent of their life in futile tasks: and I certainly am tired of being rewarded, for such creative activities as one may manage to cheat fate and perform, one tenth

---

[1] 'The Surrender of Barcelona', bought by the Tate in 1947.
[2] 'Portrait of Ezra Pound', bought by the Tate Gallery in 1939.

what some wise-guy receives for doing nothing.—But there *may* be some kind of a second or third-rate job, which nobody else wants, that would keep the wolf away from the door.—I am approaching the age when society usually says to itself: 'We might as well recognise the existence of that unpleasant person. He'll be dead soon.' So there may be some sort of chance. What do you think?

To be serious—for of course the above is merely my way of trying to be funny. Since life for a free-lance painter-novelist-journalist would be impossible at such a time as this, is there any *post* you know of that I could occupy? Is there such a thing as an art-professor at Oxford or Cambridge? Is Schwab moving from the Slade directorship by any chance?—South Kensington. You smile: but (for a short while) why not?—Or is there some old, much-bombed Lighthouse that needs a Keeper! Have they been asking for someone, on nights of Blitz, to accouch the Zebras at the Zoo?

Ponder these problems—study the landscape carefully—sound anybody who has fat livings, or lean ones, in his giving, and let me know the result. I will get back somehow, before long. If an appointment awaited me at the other end, this translation might be facilitated.—Meanwhile all the best to you, and great solicitude about your father, to whom I hope you will be the bearer of my affectionate greetings.

Yours ever,
WYNDHAM LEWIS

I was haunted by the indignities and frustrations suffered by one of the most powerful intellects and at moments one of the finest painters I knew, and by the failure of my own efforts to alleviate them. I was saddened by our first meeting. When I called on 2 July 1946, at his old studio at 29 Kensington Gardens Studios, Notting Hill Gate, I found him engaged upon a series of portraits weak in drawing and pallid in colour, which seemed designed merely to flatter. He correctly interpreted my silence as expressive of disapproval, and launched into a justification of flattery, contending that an indigent portrait painter must aim first of all to please his sitters. His arguments were as flimsy as the portraits and as unworthy of his powerful intellect and incisive hand. I had the impression that his having left his own country in time of war (although of course he was very well over military age) had aroused in him a sense of guilt that might have been assuaged had his expatriation been attended by more than a bare modicum of success, which to judge by his letters and his conversation it had not. There was one painting which, although not among his best, belonged to a very different order from the portraits. This was 'A Canadian War Factory', made in Toronto in 1943 under the auspices of the War Artists' Committee, by whom it was presented to the Tate. It being a serious painting, Lewis, far from excusing its defects, became so conscious of them that he asked permission to retain it in order to put them right. This he never succeeded in doing to his own satisfaction, and I was not able to obtain possession of it until after his death, when it was handed over to the Gallery by his widow. Earlier he had regarded the picture as finished as the following letter shows:

Aug. 17, 1943

Dear Rothenstein, Well, the picture representing 'Canada's War Effort' is finished. The 'advance' even arrived at last—three days before I had finished what it was supposed to enable me to paint— and *six months late*. Energetic people have succeeded in wresting the remainder too.

The sum agreed was three hundred pounds (no expenses) about 13 hundred dollars. I have very little left—for naturally I had to borrow money: in order (1) to hang about while the commission was getting born, and (2) to live while I was working on my picture.

I still owe more than what I have left (what I have not paid back but kept temporarily for myself). As to having the necessary cash to buy a clipper ticket (via Lisbon) for 2 people, that, I fear, is as remote as ever it was. It is still as much as I can do to keep alive. But there is something else, namely: Where would be the use of that fare to me if I had it? I don't want a fare back without some guarantee that at the other end I shall not be plunged into economic miseries worse than before. I have told you all this before, once or twice: but as I know you would like to know how I am getting on, I will say it over again.—I will not ever return to my hand-to-mouth existence in London. I have a great horror of it. I have a natural dislike of being patronised by sleek gentlemen for whom the Fine Arts is a fine lucrative official assignment, and a road up to the social summits for the clever climber. I don't like that, in fact it makes me feel a little sick: also *always* receiving my hundred pounds (once, or twice, perhaps, a year) where others are far more highly rewarded for what is grotesquely bad—I am through with that *hundred pounds* business too. (Clark as you may know offered me this time, too, to start with, *my figure*, one hundred pounds, and it took me many a long month to drag myself out of that dimension and obtain a more suitable—a more possible —sum!)

There is something to be said I know for keeping the place a land fit for mediocrity to live in but I can't help hoping that *some* day my disturbing influence will once more be felt in the British Isles: but I just have to wait I suppose until Somebody says to Somebody else that *some* paltry job had better be offered to the importunate Mr. Lewis—just so that we can have him back don't you know where we can do him a bad turn now and then. —Britannia has received more at my hands than I have at Britannia's: I should not mind a spell of fifty-fifty. What chances do you see of such a ratio?

Meanwhile I exist here (for 'The Royal Apartments—Windsor' is a somewhat deceptive address: I have no Clark to 'keep' my Rowlandsons). Being here, immersed in transatlantic civilisation malgré moi, I attempt to turn my experience to some profit. We shall see.

Remember me to your father if you see him.

Yours,
WYNDHAM LEWIS

I saw him only occasionally but my impression was that although his intellect regained its vigour, as painter and draughtsman his work had become nerveless: this falling-off was no doubt precipitated by the progressive failure of his sight, for in May 1951, in a tragic article entitled 'The Sea-Mists of the Winter', published in *The Listener*, he announced his blindness. I wrote to him about this calamity and received this touching reply:

June 9th, 1951

Dear Rothenstein, I have been over to Ireland which is why I have been so long in answering your letter. I have received many letters about my approaching blindness but hardly any which I found affected me so much, in its simple sincerity.—Your words about Rude Assignment gave me great pleasure: you are au courant in the matter of its subjects, which makes your opinion doubly valuable.

Yours,

W.L.

With characteristic courage he continued to write. He contributed regularly to *The Listener*, dealing, among other features, with 'Contemporary Art at the Tate' (20 April 1950), and wrote the Introduction to the Tate retrospective exhibition of his work in July 1956.

In mid-July of 1951 we had a long talk at his studio in the course of which I hoped to elicit information for the chapter I was writing on him for the second volume of my *Modern English Painters*. Lewis was very pale and his features were puffy: he looked seriously ill. When I arrived he was in an aggressive mood: he said that he did not value belated politeness inspired by his blindness, and he complained that he had been treated badly, indeed persecuted, although he grudgingly excepted me on account of 'the half-dozen of my pictures at the Tate'; but then, his ill-temper mounting, he complained that we never invited him to evening receptions at the Gallery and was unimpressed when I explained that these functions were all but invariably organized by independent societies to raise funds for some art charity. At first he declined to give me any biographical information (even the date of his birth), saying that as he could no longer paint or draw, writing was his only source of livelihood, and his own 'vast store of biographical information' his principal asset, and that he intended to write another, and this time fuller and much more factual autobiography. Upon one topic, however, he was anxious to impart information, namely his quarrel with Roger Fry that led to his departure from the Omega Workshops. This account, substantially confirmed in conversation with me by Frederick Etchells (who accompanied Lewis on his departure), is given in *Modern English Painters*.[1]

The effort of memory seemed to exhaust him and on the only occasion known to me the operation of that powerful intellect became confused, when he said that Fry had told him that at the private view of the First Post-Impressionist Exhibition my father

[1] A detailed study has been made by Messrs. Quentin Bell and Stephen Chaplin of the circumstances of this quarrel: 'The Ideal Home Rumpus' (*Apollo*, October 1964). The authors, who bring to light much new information, admit that elements of mystery remain unsolved.

had voiced indignation that his own work was not included; whereas my father was in India at the time and knew nothing about it except what he gathered from allusions in letters from friends; he had moreover declined some time earlier Fry's invitation to join him in support of the post-impressionist movement. Forgetful of his negative response to my request for help, Lewis became suddenly genial and forthcoming, talking about his own art—I did not risk breaking the spell by asking questions about his reference to the 'uncontrolled skill, and therefore the vulgar skill' of certain of his early drawings, or his assertions that he showed no real mastery as a draughtsman until he seriously applied himself to more or less naturalistic drawing just after the First World War. He denied that he was ever a cubist, and recalled his prompt indictment of cubism as entirely dependent on the natural appearances that it ostensibly rejected. The mood of depression presently again overcame him and he complained bitterly of the support given to other artists and of his own neglect; he ironically blamed himself for his defiance of Fry over the Omega quarrel, saying that he should have submitted without a word, as all the persecution of him stemmed from his alienation of Fry, and that Kenneth Clark, 'on whom Fry's mantle is supposed to have fallen', pursued him relentlessly. When I told him that in the course of wide-ranging talks with Clark over a longish period about living painters I had never heard him speak adversely about him either as man or artist, he affected momentary deafness. Lewis lamented the shortcomings of his own work, due, mostly, to illness and economic stress. The affliction of the eyes, he explained, now prevented his seeing clearly at the centre of his field of vision. The 'economic stress' from which he seemed pretty constantly to suffer used to surprise his friends for he was extremely industrious both as painter and writer and he always lived very simply.

At the private view of an exhibition of his work held in the spring of 1949 I found him expounding to a small group, which included T. S. Eliot, the contrast between the cubists, 'whose art was firmly rooted in the nature they affected to exclude', with a 'genuine inventor of abstract forms' such as he himself had been before the First World War. As I walked in he momentarily directed his discourse at me, as I had incautiously described one of his 'Timon of Athens' drawings made in 1913 and recently acquired by the Tate as cubist. I left the exhibition in the company of Eliot, who spoke with admiration of Lewis, but observed that one of the reasons why certain people so disliked him was that he was a 'pro.' both as writer and painter.

I had had an ardent admiration for Lewis ever since I first came to know him, and his near-blindness and the poor state of his health, both of which perhaps aggravated his morbid obsession about the hostility of his fellow-men (the more influential the more hostile), determined me to propose to the Trustees that we should arrange a retrospective exhibition of his work at the Tate. They readily agreed.

When I went to see him on 10 April 1955 to discuss the exhibition I was shocked to find him aged and ill, and obsessed by a painful operation on his hands which he described in detail; his sight was almost gone. It was a sad experience to see the powerful, militant personage I so clearly remembered on earlier visits to this same studio in Notting Hill Gate so utterly reduced, his features white and without form, his energy ebbed away. Apprehending how changed I found him he spoke with envy of Augustus John's health, and in sudden irrelevant disparagement of Matthew Smith's painting as 'the taste of the stupid'.

We discussed the catalogue of the projected exhibition, and I asked him whether he thought that T. S. Eliot would write a brief foreword. 'Tom's always been timid, and afraid of what "people" will say,' Lewis answered, ' "people" these days for him being "bishops", but I'll sound him out. Not long ago,' he continued, 'Tom expressed to me his misgivings for having, in effect, given Herbert Read his start, encouraging him to contribute to *The Criterion*, and publishing some of his books, saying that there was no one whose ideas he considered more pernicious, and I agree with Tom.' The growing divergence between the outlooks of Eliot and Lewis on the one hand and of Read on the other made their want of sympathy inevitable. Read often showed belief in 'The Demon of Progress in the Arts' which they abhorred, while their convictions led them to evolve new concepts of traditional values. Towards the end of a lifetime of discerning and courageous championship of pioneering art and artists Read himself suffered a degree of disillusion, not indeed with the causes and people he had championed, but with subsequent developments, aspects of Pop art, for example. Whatever his errors of judgment—and what contemporary champion of the new has not been guilty of them?—Read was not only the most consistent and the most influential advocate of the new but of all critics the most closely and affectionately identified with the objects of his admiration, Paul Nash, Moore, Nicholson, Hepworth and numerous others.

In view of his state of health we assembled the exhibition with minimum recourse to Lewis himself, who did, however, write a brief foreword to the catalogue. At the private view, on 5 July 1956, Lewis, very feeble and nearly blind, was present, and to Elizabeth expressed his pleasure without reserve and spoke of the consideration with which he had been treated by the Tate; he was deeply touched, he added, by all that I had done on his behalf. His words moved me, not only because of my admiration for this formidable artist-prophet, but because it is singularly difficult to give help to people in distress—and so easy to give help to the successful to whom it counts for little.

The private view was a remarkable assembly of Lewis's old friends: T. S. Eliot, the Sitwells, Kate Lechmere (who paid for *Blast* and the Rebel Art Centre), Mrs. Nevinson, and many others: the last occasion, I fancy, when the survivors and associates of the movement in which Lewis played so splendid a part would be gathered together. When I quoted to Eliot his own opinion of Lewis as 'the most fascinating personality of our time', he replied vaguely, 'but that was so many years ago'—it was not, I think, that he was implying the least denigration of the later Lewis but that at that particular moment he himself was also occupied with thought of happenings of 'many years ago'.

Lewis was so exhausted by the ordeal that it was only with difficulty that Mrs. Lewis, Elizabeth and I could get him into a taxi—exhausted, but touchingly happy.

A few days later he rang up, quite in his old style, to express his annoyance about a review of the exhibition by Myfanwy Piper in the *Sunday Times*. Shortly he was to have far more justifiable occasion for anger. In the Lewis exhibition we had included a section devoted to the work of his fellow-vorticists. This idea had not at all commended itself to Lewis himself, who observed that the work of other artists honoured by retrospective exhibitions had occupied the whole of the three galleries usually made available for their accommodation, and he felt it a little unfair that his should occupy two only if the third were devoted to that of his former associates. He allowed himself to be persuaded by me with a grace that did not disguise his disappointment. Had I agreed with him, we should have been spared some subsequent harassment from one of these associates.

After the private view I never saw Lewis again, but he telephoned to me from time to time, on one occasion expressing his enchantment with the recognition the exhibition had brought him and the renewal of relations with friends and associates long lost sight of.

In the 'fifties vorticism had not yet become a subject of research; it was in fact largely forgotten. Though mainly as a result of the outbreak of the First World War it was shortlived, it seemed to me to be a movement—an explosion would perhaps more appropriately describe it—with considerable achievements to its credit and far-ranging potentialities. As Lewis was its acknowledged leader, a retrospective exhibition of his work seemed a peculiarly fitting occasion to pay tribute to that of his unjustly neglected fellow vorticists.

William Roberts, however, interpreted this tribute as an attempt on the part of Lewis and myself to relegate his fellow vorticists to the status of mere disciples of Lewis. In a foreword to the catalogue Lewis did indeed claim that vorticism was 'What I, personally, did and said at a certain period,' but this provocative claim apart there was nothing either in the catalogue or the exhibition that could reasonably be regarded as disparaging of the other vorticists. No suggestion reached the Tate from any other artist that he felt himself disparaged, though it is possible on account of his refusal to lend his 'Rock Drill' that Epstein entertained similar suspicions.

Roberts ignored our invitation to suggest how he might most appropriately be represented in the vorticist section. His conviction that the exhibition was designed 'to minimize the standing' of Lewis' former associates roused Roberts' bitter resentment—a resentment that was intensified by his belief that I was a person whom he 'felt to be hostile' to him and that this 'hostility' was expressed in the chapter devoted to him in Volume II of my *Modern English Painters*, published shortly before the Wyndham Lewis and Vorticism exhibition. This suspicion was baseless: I had (nor have) no shadow of antipathy for Roberts the man and admiration for a single-minded artist by whom I have never seen a work unworthy of him. When I went to the Tate I found only one of his pictures and that unshown; during the ensuing years eight further examples were acquired and shown together, and arrangements were made with the Arts Council for a retrospective exhibition, though this was not held until shortly after my retirement.

Roberts' resentment expressed itself in a succession of privately printed pamphlets: *The Resurrection of Vorticism and Apotheosis of Wyndham Lewis at the Tate Gallery, Cometism and Vorticism, a Tate Gallery Catalogue Revised* (all three appearing in 1955) and in the following year *A Reply to my Biographer, Sir John Rothenstein.* The second has an entertaining frontispiece by the artist entitled 'Conversation Piece', purporting to show Wyndham Lewis, Michael Ayrton and me plotting to make the 'other vorticists' 'look like a lot of sprats a whale has caught'.

When the first of the pamphlets appeared Lewis telephoned to me deeply incensed, and asked whether I thought he should reply. I advised him to ignore it, for although his voice was combative, I thought that the strain of controversy might be harmful to the health, already precarious, of this blind, seventy-four-year-old man. Whether because he was already too near death or on account of my advice, Lewis made no reply.

*

An enlivening feature of London life was the visits of artists from abroad.

In mid-November 1950 Picasso arrived on his way to a Peace Congress in Sheffield. The Arts Council gave a large party for him before dinner on the fourteenth but because of the Government's explicit want of sympathy with the Peace Congress Picasso declined to attend an official function. Late that night he arrived, however, evidently in the highest spirits, at an enormous gathering, largely of artists, in the palatial but dilapidated studio, since demolished, of Feliks Topolski in Warwick Avenue, Maida Vale. Picasso showed himself particularly amiable to the assembled artists; Moore, Epstein, Pasmore, Sutherland and Roland Penrose were among those present. As he moved round the large and densely crowded room, greeting the few whom he knew and having presented to him those he did not, Picasso made everyone else seem by comparison lifeless and above all unresponsive: he was the most illustrious person present and the guest of honour, yet it was his face that lighted up at each new encounter, rather than those of the eagerly expectant guests who felt it so great a privilege to meet him. Lithe-figured, bronzed, he stepped quickly like a boxer light on his feet; his dark eyes, seeming to reflect no light, put me in mind of the untired eyes of a wild animal that gave nothing away yet missed nothing. (How impossible to imagine him wearing spectacles!)

Reminding me genially of the tin of coffee—a scarce commodity at the time—I had brought him after the Liberation, he said he was eager to visit the Tate. 'I hear you've magnificent things but what I most want to see are my own things. The "Femme Assise", which you bought last year,' he added, to my immense pleasure, 'is probably the best of all my cubist paintings.' I wondered how Roland Penrose, who was standing nearby, and who at that time owned his splendid 'Femme à la Mandoline', received this judgement.

There circulated at the party a story that I hope was true. Victor Pasmore, deputed to meet Picasso at Victoria, was reported to have said, to explain his presence: 'Moi, je suis peintre', and Picasso to have replied, 'Moi aussi.'

It was arranged that Picasso should come to the Gallery with Roland Penrose at eleven o'clock next morning. Feliks Topolski, with his range of friendship and acquaintance as various as it is wide, his quick wit and his acute social sense combined with a total absence of conventionality, was the ideal host.

Early next morning a message arrived from Picasso to say that as the British Government had taken further steps to impede the holding of the Peace Congress he was leaving England almost at once and he felt that he ought not at this particular moment to visit a national institution, but he wished me to know how bitterly disappointed he was and that there was nothing in England he wanted to see more than his paintings at the Tate.

Towards the end of the exhibition of the works of Cézanne, Rouault and Braque with which the Tate reopened in April-May 1946 Braque spent a morning at the Gallery. He was a gentle man, one of those fortunate beings whose success provokes little jealousy: I do not recall ever having heard an ill word spoken of him; he was as serene as Picasso is restless; unlike Picasso, he had no super-abundance of vitality and reserved all that he had for the pursuit of his art. What a delightful presence: his dark, friendly eyes, the darker by contrast with his snowy hair, his slow movements, his courtesy and his reassuring common sense.

As someone to whom it has often fallen to accompany exhibitions of British art abroad and to lecture on the work of British artists, I have had many occasions to resent the contempt, thinly disguised, sometimes not disguised at all, of certain French critics and officials for modern art other than Parisian, but I know no more perceptive or less prejudiced, more warmly appreciative judges of painting than French painters. In spite of the fact that *la belle peinture* features so little in the painting of today, indeed by most younger painters the whole concept is militantly rejected, I notice that French painters, whatever their own tendency or generation, are apt to be responsive to it when they see it, whether in the work of their predecessors or contemporaries.

The most memorable experience in showing French painters round the Tate is the impact of Turner (even if they have already seen his work). It is incredible to them that so little has been made of 'this formidable genius'; that he should be so little known abroad, that so relatively little has been written about him. This has been the response not only of Braque, Léger and Chagall, but no less of younger Parisian artists such as Giacometti and César. They are apt to look, too, with close attention, although with nothing like the same admiration, at the pre-raphaelites, instead of ignoring or even deriding them like some of their British fellow artists. Showing Braque round the British paintings (there was as yet little sculpture in position) I felt myself to be in a wonderfully rational world.

Braque did not stay more than a few days in London and remained shyly detached. Not so Léger, who came over for a big exhibition of his work held at the Tate in February-March 1950. He arrived at the Gallery on 14 February, and expressed delight in the arrangement of his own paintings, but concern that nothing by his friend and protégée the American sculptor Mary Callery was on view! When I reminded him that this was a retrospective of his own work and no question of the inclusion of that of anyone else had even been contemplated, he dismissed this objection as the merest pedantry.

Léger had more zest for London than Braque. Like Braque he was politely bored with official entertainment, but he took naturally to the indigenous life. After behaving as an extremely correct guest of honour at the few informal parties I took him to, he would eventually say, 'I've stood on my feet too long. Couldn't we go off to a pub?' And as we walked in search of one which took his fancy he would be full of lively comment on what he saw. 'Now just look at London taxis', he would say. 'Why do you suppose they're *higher* than any others in the world? Simply because they're built for men wearing *chapeaux d'haute forme*.' 'But they don't wear them much these days', I objected. 'Ah, but this is a country of *tradition*, so that doesn't matter, does it?' Or else he would say that he felt like a game of poker. I do not play cards myself but it was not difficult to find someone who did, and off they would go together.

There was a big lunch given in Léger's honour at the French Embassy. As I arrived the Ambassador said that he did not himself care for Léger's work and began to explain why, when I had to warn him that Léger was just outside the door. Henry Moore was present and as we left Léger shook him by the shoulders, exclaiming to me 'Type sympathique, eh?' No foreign visitor to the English-speaking world could have been less hampered by ignorance— almost total, I fancy, so far as speaking was concerned—of the language. He went confidently about seeing and obtaining just what he wanted. In the United States, he told me, he and a woman friend, posing as an engaged couple, used to amuse themselves by allowing house agents to drive them to inspect innumerable luxurious premises.

Kokoschka, though he moved to Switzerland after the war, maintained his ties with London. Before long he took his rightful place among the major European painters, but it seems to me that his adopted country treated him meanly; nor in this indictment do I except the Tate, which has never bought an example of his work. In 1962, however, there was a very large retrospective exhibition at the Tate which received enthusiastic acclaim and drew enormous crowds and which I hope made some amends for our failure to accord due recognition to a painter acclaimed in almost every country but that which he had chosen to make his own. Shortly after its opening, however, I brought his latest painting, a view of the Thames from Millbank—almost from the site of the Tate—before our Trustees, but they considered it with respect rather than enthusiasm; funds were low and it was not bought.

*

There was one person, the most authoritative figure in the art world of London, whom after the war I came to see less frequently. This was Kenneth Clark. After dinner at his house in Portland Place in June 1945 Jane told me that he saw no possibility of continuing as Director of the National Gallery; he had virtually no staff, the obligation to attend committees almost daily—and an ever more imperative desire to devote himself to writing. The news did not surprise me, for the previous March, in the course of a telephone conversation, he had said that he was determined, come what might, to leave the National Gallery within two years. At the end of November that same year I went to see him in his room there for the last time as its Director. Like innumerable others I regretted his decision to retire, but he was impelled by cogent reasons besides his desire to write and his weariness with committees; he told Elizabeth that he found the prevalent ill-will in the art world increasingly difficult to bear. In any case, as he said on the occasion of my last visit, it would have been unfair to his successor to deny him the opportunity of establishing himself at the outset of a new era.

During the seven years when we had been colleagues the relations between the National Gallery and the Tate had never, so far as I can recall, been flawed by the smallest disharmony, and retirement scarcely diminished his benevolent interest in the Tate, to which he made occasional gifts, and from time to time he left, after his visits, encouraging notes about rearrangements, acquisitions and the like. But whether one happened to see him or not one could not fail to be aware of his influence. K's extraordinary power of giving always exhilarating and elegant, and often profound, expression to his wide-ranging learning, as well as his all-round ability, his wealth and his social connections made him at an early age something of an 'elder statesman', above the clash of party and controversy—controversy indeed he abhors and I cannot recall anyone of comparable prominence so successful in its avoidance. It would do him no injustice, I think, to say that he is an ambitious man in most of the ordinary senses, but he is also ambitious in one elevated and extraordinary sense. Just as many kinds of artists and writers, moved poignantly by the transitory nature of the beauty and the drama of the world, desire to capture and give permanent form to some facet of them, so K with the world's art: he desires, by comprehension and by exposition, by patronage, by friendship with artists, somehow to identify himself with all that he conceives to be noblest in the paintings and sculpture, and the music and literature within the wide range of his experience. This desire reached its culmination in the series of television programmes, entitled *Civilisation*, shown in 1969, which gave full scope to his multifarious talents as performer, organizer and encyclopaedic scholar.

Through the most judicious management of his exceptional and various talents and other advantages he has made his life the story of exceptional and many-sided success.

One of K's qualities that always gave me particular pleasure is his imperviousness to fashionable taste. I have heard him maintain silence when some fashionable artist whom he despises was excessively praised, because he shrinks from avoidable controversy, but he is able to look with zest at painting and sculpture by the most obscure and neglected figures. He has a habit of regarding the art of today with the great panorama of the art of the past for background, and there are times when the comparison fills him with doubts. I remember a long discussion at the meeting of the Tate Trustees on 17 January 1945 provoked by discussion of a bare shaft of wood under consideration as a purchase. K declared that abstraction was a heresy and expressed doubts whether the Tate should admit it at all; and Henry Moore said that if sculpture was nothing more than abstract form it would be a poor affair. (It was eventually decided, however, that I should prepare a list for later consideration of unrepresented abstract artists of merit.) K's deepest interest, of course, is in the great figures of the Italian Renaissance but he has also been a generous patron of some of his own contemporaries, in particular of Henry Moore.

His understanding of all the visual arts, as well as of literature and music, has been wide and searching since his undergraduate days, but it seemed to me that his human sympathies were apt to be confined within the ample circle of his friends. But of recent years his outlook has undergone a marked change: scholarship for scholarship's sake—did he not once compare it to knitting?—has held a diminishing attraction, while his urge to share his knowledge and experience with a very wide public has correspondingly increased. This change owes much, perhaps, to the influence of Ruskin, to whose writings he has devoted sustained and intensive study and whose social preoccupations have affected his outlook. Unlike Ruskin, however, he has never ceased to be primarily a visual man to become a politico-economic one, but he has come to believe that by making more widely known those elements which in his view constitute 'civilisation' he can make a contribution to it.

Although I cannot recall our discussing religion, I believe that his feeling for it has deepened. Just before the showing of the programme on 'Grandeur and Obedience' in *Civilisation*, he wrote to me saying, 'I wonder what Elizabeth will make of the one about the Catholic revival. I have no doubt that it will enrage Protestants, but it may be almost equally distasteful to genuine Catholics.' Elizabeth and I thought that he treated a complex theme with extraordinary insight and lucidity.

CHAPTER THREE

STANLEY SPENCER

ONE very old friend there was whose absences from London rarely interrupted our intercourse for long. Even during the war, the last two years of which he spent mostly in Port Glasgow, Stanley Spencer never disappeared entirely from view. One day, I remember, I met him in high spirits and immensely voluble, on his way to visit Hilda in the Westminster Hospital, and shortly afterwards both of them together at an exhibition. She seemed normal enough, and with a touching absence of self-consciousness alluded to the infrequency of our meetings since my visits in the 'twenties to Vale Studios when Stanley was at work on 'The Resurrection, Cookham', which she recalled in detail. Even after their divorce Stanley remained obsessively devoted to Hilda, and in an emotional sense he never ceased to think of her as his wife. He painted pictures of his second wife nude but for her black lace underclothes, and he came to feel that in doing so he had been unfaithful to Hilda. To atone for his infidelity and set matters to rights he painted a nude of Hilda, confined at this time in a mental home, which she was occasionally permitted to leave in the company of her relations. This nude, austere and sad, remote from his black-laced close-ups of his second wife, has a gravity and an economy unlike any other of Stanley's nudes known to me. I persuaded Catherine Walston to buy it, and I was happy that it should belong to a friend.

A few weeks earlier I had met Stanley at the Café Royal. On account of his matrimonial involvements he rarely had more than his return fare to Cookham in his pocket; this was well understood by his friends, who saw to it that he was put to no expense. On this occasion I ordered some drinks and was about to pay for them when Stanley raised his hand in a prohibitory gesture: 'No!' he said, 'I've never paid for a drink before, but I intend to now'—and he did. 'Your father, criticizing a drawing by my brother,' he continued, 'said "Gilbert, remember, there are still standards". That is what

50

I'm remembering now.' He looked pathetically tired; he was worn out, he confessed, by the 'perpetual ineffectiveness' of his efforts to get Hilda out of the mental hospital for good, but the doctors would not release her. The Government, he was convinced, intended to keep all mentally unfit people under control, and this increased his anxiety for her welfare. He asked after Elizabeth and I told him that she was wiring our house in Garsington. 'She's always so delightful to watch whatever she does,' he said. 'When I was with you in Fellows Road I used to enjoy sitting beside her by the hour whenever she was working.' And recalling that time he asked, 'Do you remember that sinister drawing I did of you as "The Napoleon of Millbank"? I never took it away with me because it was so sinister, and for you it will be too sinister to hang.' Stanley, ever short of cash, was unusually generous with his work. There must be many people in Cookham today who called on Stanley as children, and had their portraits drawn and presented to them.

Meanwhile the circumstances of his life—his work apart, where cheerfulness was always breaking in—had become more tangled and distressing than ever. It would not surprise me were there to grow up around him a legend comparable to that about Van Gogh. (Malcolm MacDonald, immersed in politics, told me he would like to become his Boswell.) There is certainly ample material for such a legend, but it is my conviction that had he been happily and securely married he would never have become, never have been in the slightest danger of becoming, the homeless wanderer that he sometimes was. I have known no more impassioned painter and draughtsman; no one whose temperament more inclined him to an exclusive dedication to his work. Had he enjoyed the shelter of a home, he would have been too engrossed in his work to dream of wandering, but having no such home he was at the mercy of bitter circumstance.

Stanley I would meet more often by chance than design, but always, on my part, with pleasure. 'Do you know what good art is?' he asked me one day. 'It's just saying "ta" to God.' Partly because I thought them exceptionally fine and partly because they were begun immediately after he had left our house but was still our Hampstead neighbour, I followed with great interest the sporadic progress of his series 'The Forty Days in the Wilderness'. 'I would like to complete them,' he said, 'and I'd like to have them fixed inside a dome, where the white figures would look like mackerel in the sea, or rather, like a mackerel sky.' At one time I

considered proposing 'Christ with the Scorpion' as a Tate purchase but he was anxious that the series should be kept together,
so I agreed to relinquish my option. We bought 'The Bridge'
instead, which annoyed Stanley, who complained that 'of course the
artist has no voice in what he's represented by'. Many artists are
irritated, understandably, I think, at the way in which critics,
dealers, art gallery directors and others in one way or another
benefit from their work. This was to an exceptional degree the case
with Stanley: generous in giving his work to friends, he was jealous
of anyone who wrote about, bought or in almost any way actively
concerned himself with it.

*

After the war I saw more of him. There had been times when I had
found him desperately unhappy, unhappier even than when he had
stayed with us in 1938. Dudley Tooth, his dealer, told me that he
had come into the gallery very depressed. 'Expect no more of me,'
he had said; 'I died fifteen years ago. I've had no happiness since.
No one so miserable as I have been can paint. I'm bringing you just
one more thing that the public will like, but it's no good. As a
painter I'm finished', and he spoke to me in a similar strain. The
belief that he was finished must have faded quickly, for nobody had
less self-pity or more self-confidence, although he always maintained
that his early works were beyond comparison his best. The mood of
self-denigration was long forgotten by 1947 when he agreed to take
part in a broadcast with me to celebrate the Tate's half-centenary,
but he withdrew in indignation as soon as he discovered that the
work of other artists besides his own was to be discussed.

Stanley's self-confidence was in full spate when I spent an afternoon with him in his miniature red-brick house in Cookham Rise, on
13 April 1949. Never in fact did I remember him in higher spirits,
or in more conspicuous evidence that element that I can only
describe by that tedious and worn-out word 'genius': his ideas and
reminiscences which, if the first lacked logic and the second precision, were astonishingly original and evocative.

For a time Stanley's talk would hold his hearers entranced, but
eventually, as the torrent showed no faintest promise of abatement,
much less cessation, they became first resistant, then downright
bored. Stanley had many human failings—much advertised in a
biography and the reviews it evoked a few years ago—but one god-

like characteristic: except for his first wife, by whom he was obsessed as much after her death as during her life, and his second, by whom he was relatively briefly but superficially obsessed, he was almost entirely self-sufficient. In his 'conversation' no participation by the other parties was required; indeed it was apt even to be resented, but sometimes, if firmly persisted in, it could be received with unexpected appreciation and long remembered. No one who did not hear it will ever be able to form any notion of the rare quality of his talk; his writings, even the best of them, in spite of an occasional, a very occasional, flash of insight or beauty, are dull by comparison, and often just dull and devoid of any of the quality of his talk (I offer this opinion without having read the 3,000,000 words or so of manuscripts he left). He attached high importance to his writings, not merely so much, I think, because he over-estimated his talent as a writer, but because he attached high importance to himself and therefore to his writings as emanations of himself. (When in 1938 there had been some discussion between us about my wish to write a book about him he said, in a letter to Dudley Tooth, 'I am against a neat book. I would rather it be a confused heap than risk anything being left out. People would be prepared to wade through a thousand badly written pages by me than one page by anybody else.')

Reminiscence played a large part in his talk, of events long past for preference. The memory from which it so profusely flowed was as strange as all his other characteristics. If he had been asked to paint, say, a brick wall he had known as a child and not seen since, his representation of it would probably have been exact. His memory was in fact most retentive where it was most visual. And there were few details of any of his pictures, down to the merest scrap of pencilling, that he not only perfectly remembered, but also their precise significance and the impulse behind them. For many artists the act of creation is an act of parturition, but for Stanley all his pictures, even the earliest, most of all perhaps the earliest, existed in the present: he lived with them (wherever they happened to be) all his life. For him, in fact, there was scarcely any distinction between past and present: both existed in an undifferentiated flux. On the other hand his memory had extraordinary lapses. For instance, on one occasion when the conversation turned upon David Jones, he told Elizabeth and me that he had never even met him. Yet in fact he had been a fellow-guest of his at Campion Hall for more than a month (when the possibility of Stanley's painting the Lady Chapel was under consideration) and during that time had manifestly enjoyed his company and his conversation. Reminded of this, he persisted in his denial.

A fascinating account of his life in Port Glasgow (to return to the afternoon of my visit) in which he vividly evoked the startlingly nefarious doings of a gang of evil-looking young men, led by one 'Pope Ptolemy', came suddenly to an end, and all his zest and the breathtaking copiousness gave way to shrill complaint. People were avoiding him, he claimed, on account of his sexual paintings. (The neglect of him was due not to censoriousness but to the fact that most people were interested at this time either in the neo-romanticism of Piper, Sutherland and others, or in the 'Euston Road' neo-realism of Coldstream and Pasmore, and Stanley's work fell far outside either of these favoured categories.) He was financially embarrassed: he needed, he said, at least £2,400 a year to support Hilda and her two young daughters and his second wife and he had made no more than £400 in the previous year. Elizabeth and I had retained, he astonishingly asserted, 'all the work he had done' during his stay with us. (His breakdown, in fact, had been so complete that he was incapable of doing any work at all; he had begun to paint Elizabeth and to draw me but abandoned both attempts as total failures after one brief sitting.) Then, just as suddenly, his ill-nature and plaintiveness spent themselves and he cheerfully admitted that he had left nothing at our house (these two tentative failures apart) and showed me what he was about. 'The Resurrection, Port Glasgow', loosely rolled, was propped up against the wall of his tiny painting-room; he unrolled sections of it and tacked them up to enable me to see the completed parts on the right-hand side, amounting to about two-thirds. It was a source of wonder to me how he was able to paint this enormous picture—it measures some seven feet by twenty-three—in this cramped little room, piece by piece, able to see only the piece he was working on, and the whole only when it had been taken away and stretched at his dealers. There were some portrait drawings of astonishing penetration and energy, several of the best of the grim, fanatical and yet somehow touching face of Hilda; there were others of workers in the shipyards at Port Glasgow. As usual showing his work enhanced his good humour; that he was really happy I knew when he suggested that we should look through some of his sketch-books. These, the vast reservoirs of his ideas, were his most cherished possessions. Whether he ever parted with one of them I doubt; if he did it would have been with the utmost reluctance. There was an amusing incongruity between these cheap folio sketch-books, with such decorative features on their covers as Scotch terriers in silhouette, and the prodigal outpouring of grandiose projects they contained. As we looked through one after another of these yellowed sketch-books and he bitterly lamented lack of support for carrying out a single such project, an idea occurred to me how he might be given the opportunity he so ardently wished for. There was, I remembered, a fund, left by the mural painter E. A. Abbey, for the express purpose of giving commissions to painters to decorate walls in public buildings; I also remembered that one of the committee of Royal Academicians who controlled it had recently complained to me of the absence of calls upon it. Here, it seemed to me, was an ideal occasion for its use: the painter of the most splendid wall-paintings made in England during the century—I was thinking, of course, of those in the Oratory at Burghclere—was eager, for little more than the cost of his materials, to carry out a public decoration. I told Stanley—to his delight—that I would suggest to our Trustees that they should invoke the assistance of the Abbey Fund to enable him to paint a staircase or a corridor at the Tate. The project was welcomed by the Trustees; the Committee of the Abbey Fund, however, refused its help. They considered, perhaps, that Stanley was an unworthy artist, or that the Tate was an unworthy place.

It was not until the end of the following January, 1950, that I again had more than a casual meeting with Stanley, when he lunched with me at the Tate and spent the afternoon there. He was in his most benign humour, and he brought me as a gift a drawing of a girl's head that I had particularly admired on my last visit to Cookham. We examined his 'Resurrection, Cookham', which had shown, more particularly in the light greens, signs of disintegration. 'The trouble', Stanley said, 'is that the paint has got steam in it, as there was a gas-cooker in the Vale of Health studio where it was painted', and we recalled my first visit there when the great canvas was an expanse of white priming in which the glimpse of the river in the top left-hand corner and one or two other features showed as meticulously finished little islands of paint. But it was on a visit about two and a half years later that I noticed the effects of steam from a continuously steaming kettle, the baleful cause, he now decided, of the instability of certain areas of the paint, and he agreed to the surface being waxed.

Stanley expressed his pleasure at a recent visit Elizabeth had paid to him in Cookham (where she found him creeping about the little painting-room with his shoes off, over a part of 'The Resurrection, Port Glasgow', which covered the whole floor, and dabbing at the surface with one of his small brushes, like a little bird pecking in a barnyard); she understood his work, he said, better than anyone else, and he recalled that she had even understood it when she first came from America and had seen scarcely any of it. He praised her book on him (published some five years earlier) but wished it had been 'more intimate, with more of herself in it and less of Plato and Aristotle'. Then he related the circumstances of his rejoining the Royal Academy, from which he had resigned in 1935 on account of the rejection of his 'St. Francis and the Birds'. Meeting James Fitton and Henry Rushbury at an exhibition of French Landscape in 1949, he had discussed the reason for his resignation. Neither he nor his brother, he explained, had ever submitted pictures for consideration by juries, or exhibited except by invitation, and when he had objected to the rejection of 'St. Francis and the Birds' his fellow-Academicians had refused to listen to him, and the former Secretary, Walter Lamb, had simply told him that 'it was best in his own interest not to show the picture', and he now assured these two Academicians that had he 'been listened to' he would not have resigned. They then took him to see Gerald Kelly, the newly elected President, who invited him to rejoin. Stanley preferred, he said, to send some pictures for exhibition, and 'see how they got on', but Kelly insisted on his agreeing to rejoin at once. This incident perfectly illustrates the irrational workings of Stanley's mind, for 'to send some pictures for exhibition' (as an outsider), as he must have known, would have invited the very procedure he had objected to, namely their submission to a jury.

As so often he spoke of his partial loss of religious belief and of its deleterious effects on his painting, and he asked me, 'What would a Catholic priest say if I went to him and said, "I've got the wind up about Hell"—as I *have*? And living', he continued, 'is just like painting, one has no real compass. Hilda considered organized religion as a kind of blasphemy, as God, she used to say, "meant every man to act in accord with his own nature".'

As he left the Tate he recalled the failure of his attempt in 1938 to make a portrait drawing of me and said that he wanted to make another in place of the one with 'that tough "Napoleon of Millbank" look' that he didn't like. With this in mind he came to the Tate on the last day of January 1950. 'It was an awful drawing, that last one,' he said, giving me a bird-like look as though seeing me for the first time, 'but as a matter of fact I see much greater kindness in your face than I remember and that kindness makes me happy—and your nose is *beautiful*; I want to get it *exactly*.' It was not, however, upon my nose that he focused his attention. When after half an hour we briefly adjourned I noticed that the large white sheet of paper was still virgin except for one minutely detailed *eye*. From this right eye he worked outwards until the head was nearly finished. As he drew he leaned forward and I felt that the intensity of his scrutiny almost pierced my skin, and as he drew he talked: 'Do you know some fool said to me the other day that human beings have no significance because they are such tiny specks in the universe? "Isn't it *awful*," I replied, "to think that I'm only about the size of Beethoven?" ' When he had drawn for about two hours he laid down his pencil and we walked round the Gallery together, and I was reminded of how closely his love of painting and drawing (he appeared scarcely to respond to sculpture at all) resembled his love of people. Of course he was intensely aware of the differences between Giotto or Rembrandt and painters of minor attainment, yet his response to all of them was oddly similar: he examined any and every picture with the same warmth and the same eagerness to do justice to its good qualities, and the same indifference to its weaknesses. The seriousness with which he could appreciate inferior works, especially if they were elevated by the smallest manifestation of earnest feeling, put me in mind of Van Gogh.

I was greatly touched by his coming a second time from Cookham four days later to complete the drawing, and he worked with only a few moments' interruption from half-past ten until just before two.

In the nearly twenty-six or seven years since we became friends I had never known him in so radiantly happy a state of mind. 'Love,' he began, directly I had settled into my chair (being drawn by Stanley, one just sat down: no question of trying various poses and lights), 'love is the generating force of my art. There are, of course, all sorts of odd kinds of love, emotional, sexual, and a sort of generalized benignity towards all things. They all of them contribute to my art.' He talked unusually well that morning but as my circulation slowed down and my temperature fell my mind became too numb to remember anything of what he said except these opening sentences. As he spoke at length about sexual love, as he often did, I consider it to the point, in this context, to correct the impression that Maurice Collis's biography and other writings convey, that Stanley's sexual experience was extensive. It is in the nature of things that the sexual aspect of most people's lives—however much the subject of speculation—remains unknown, or at most imprecisely known, even to their intimates. With this reservation I would say that compared with that of the average man the sexual experience of Stanley Spencer was quite unusually meagre, and that this very meagreness was the cause of certain aberrations he was subject to.

As the drawing approached completion Stanley alternately scrutinized my face more intently and bent so closely over his paper that his long straight-cut fringe almost touched it; and as an accompaniment to his efforts of eye and hand he began to murmur odd phrases of description. 'More interesting to draw than I supposed at first . . . intellectual, yet alert to see what needs doing . . . nothing bloodless, like many people who think . . . not a person to browbeat . . .' and so on. Most of the artists known to me feel affection for people while they portray them, at least for those they portray of their own volition (there are, of course, blood-curdling exceptions); I remember Anna Bazell, the daughter of Ambrose McEvoy, telling me that he could not bear to hear the slightest criticism of the subject of any portrait on which he was currently engaged. This can be true even of the most ruthless caricaturists. Low complained to me on more than one occasion when he had been accused of being impelled by rancour. 'I spent my formative years in Australia,' he said, 'which is a combative, plain-spoken country, but as an artist I'm no more disposed to dislike people than I am as a man—and that is very little indeed.' For all Stanley Spencer's goodwill towards his subjects, his drawings of them are sometimes distorted in an unflattering sense owing to his habit of crouching down immediately beneath them with the result that their jaws are given an exaggerated prominence.

When the drawing was finished he tore it from the block and looked attentively at it, as though it had been done by someone else. 'Not bad', he said, and his child-like smile showed that he was satisfied.

Suddenly the smile faded: words poured out descriptive of his misery with his second wife: his marriage had never been consum-

mated; she had threatened him with legal proceedings for his
alleged description of herself and a friend as lesbians, whereas,
he assured me, he had never so described them; Patricia had
'stolen' certain of his pictures, including 'The Sword of the Lord
and of Gideon' (which the Tate had acquired some eight years
before) so that when his dealers had hedged before his enquiries,
he had asked them 'in whose favour, then, did you draw the cheques
in payment for these pictures?'

The candour with which he confessed to the misery of his second
marriage was in one respect a new departure. When he had stayed
with us in 1938 his misery was obvious, and although many of the
facts that escaped him in his voluminous talk suggested that she was
responsible for his state of mind, he never once complained
explicitly of Patricia.

In Collis' biography (*Stanley Spencer*, 1962) it is alleged that
during his visit to us in 1938 Stanley made complaints against
Patricia to Elizabeth 'delivered with a force which his powerful
emotions made irresistibly convincing. By the end of his stay, which
lasted six weeks, he had made out Patricia to be an even worse bully
than Hilda, a very fiend of a woman.'

Collis was not, of course, under any obligation to consult any
friends of Stanley's in the writing of his book. However, had he
talked with those in whose houses conversations that he alleges took
place he would have been saved from many serious errors of fact and
more of judgement. In our case, although we invited him to discuss
whatever he wished, he did not avail himself of the offer. Instead he
chose to suggest that Stanley, while in our house, won Elizabeth's
confidence as (so it is alleged) he won that of other women who—so
the suggestion goes—were gullible and leisured and flattered by the
confidences of a man who was in his way a celebrity, and having won
it spun them mendacious stories about his life and hard times,
giving full rein to an abundant self-pity. But as any friend who actually knew Stanley could have told his biographer, this version is,
quite plainly, nonsense. Stanley was perhaps the least self-pitiful man
I have ever met and, as I have already made clear, he never at any
moment in our house complained of Patricia or attacked or criticized
her. He could not speak of her with affection, but he referred to her
with admiration. For his misfortunes he blamed himself. I would
like, therefore, to make it explicitly a matter of record that in the
course of scores of long conversations Stanley never spoke to either

of us a word to Hilda's detriment, nor until his visit to the Tate in 1950—twelve years after his marriage had effectively ended—a word of criticism of Patricia. Had he known that she had married him for money he would then have spoken of her more harshly still. When they were engaged in 1935–6—as related by Collis—he was living on advances from Tooth and was in arrears with the £2 10s. a week he allowed Hilda, but Patricia accepted more than £1,500 worth of clothes and jewellery from him. Such conduct would have made almost any other man suspicious, but what he did not know was that Patricia made no secret of her motive. One night in 1938 we were dining with Harriet Cohen, the celebrated pianist, and the talk very naturally turned to our semi-permanent guest. Duncan Macdonald, a director of the Reid and Lefevre Gallery, said, 'Spencer is a man I feel very sorry for. Friends of mine who live near Cookham tell me he has never shared the house of his second wife. I'm not surprised to hear it. Some years ago Miss Preece brought some of her work to the gallery for me to see. She asked us to give her an exhibition, saying she was in financial difficulties and that she intended to use the proceeds to settle in France. I told her that we were unable to help her. "Then," she said angrily, "I suppose I have got to marry that dirty little Stanley Spencer."' Macdonald was a prudent and kindly man, yet he did not hesitate to speak frankly about the matter at a large dinner party.

In several respects and some of them crucial ones, Collis' account of the marriage of Stanley and Patricia Preece is false. 'After all,' he wrote, as an explanation of the events immediately following their marriage, 'they had been lovers for two years.' The exact nature of intimate relations between people is difficult to ascertain but there are very substantial reasons for not accepting this statement, among them Stanley's own melancholy references to the non-consummation of his second marriage made to me many years later—a disclosure from which he could have derived no conceivable advantage. I would not have thought it necessary to refer to this essentially private matter had Collis not drawn inferences from it that I believe to be entirely false, namely that Stanley gratuitously celebrated his marriage to his second wife by committing adultery with his first. The night of the marriage Stanley and Patricia spent each in their own house, and she went to St. Ives next morning with a woman friend, leaving a note tied to the front door, saying that they had left. There were difficulties with Hilda over arrears of alimony to be discussed and Collis states correctly that Patricia 'thought the best time for Hilda to come to Cookham would be immediately after the wedding'. Hilda came to Cookham and spent the night with Stanley. His suggestion is that what took place was in accordance with Stanley's 'plan'. But whose plan in fact was it? For some time Patricia had been posing for Stanley in black lace underwear and the like, at the same time insisting that she was (to use his expression) a 'swell', in such a way as to unnerve him. 'A little more kindness', he said to me, 'and things would have been different.' There is no evidence that she was ever in love with him, and much to the contrary. Her suggestion that Hilda should 'come to Cookham immediately after the wedding' and stay alone with an over-stimulated and sex-starved man who she knew was devoted to her, bears a contrary interpretation to that placed upon it by Collis, namely, that the 'plan' was Patricia's, and its object the creation of an extremely plausible objection to marital relations with Stanley for which—to say the least—she had no inclination.

We spent a day with him in Cookham on Whit Sunday 1950 and as usual he walked us round the village and showed us Fernlea, pointing out (not for the first time) the upstairs front room where he was born. Next door is a tiny cottage where his mother was born. Here, he told us, when Patricia turned him out of Lindworth, his handsome house since 1932 which he made over to her on their marriage, she had found him a room in this very cottage, without knowing the associations it had for him. Its tiny window gave onto the passage from Fernlea to the garden shed in which he had received his entire education. He pointed out Patricia's cottage and showed us the barn where he had painted 'The Nativity', his diploma picture at the Slade, and a little further along the street on the same side the cottage where lived Dot, who figures in his 'Two Girls and a Beehive'. Dot, he told us, he used to court, but he was frightened, he said, of calling on her as the doorbell was extraordinarily loud and her father was a butcher, who used to come out and confront him aggressively. When he returned to Cookham after the war, financially ruined by Patricia, he had for a time to live in a shed, walking to the railway station to make use of the lavatory.

In spite of his bouts of shrill querulousness, of nasty peasant suspicion, there was something elevated about Stanley's mind that always turned his attention after a while away from his grievances and towards some loftier subject. That day he spoke—not for the first time—of his fear of Hell, and of his dislike of abstract art, on account of the arrogance and the falsity of its practitioners' claim to a monopoly of formal relations, as though *all* art were not concerned with formal relations, and all formal relations were not abstract.

His talk then turned to his introduction of sex into his pictures. 'People are shocked by it, but I must include *myself* in my pictures, *all* of myself, and that must include my sensuality,' he said; 'I daresay I put it in the wrong places, in the wrong order, but it is fundamentally good that I should include it.'

Once again the memory of past afflictions surged up to trouble him and he described his summons for his failure to comply with the maintenance order Hilda had been compelled to take out against him, and his subsequent actions in court, including his refusal to discuss 'matters of a most intimate nature' in a public place; he spoke of his fear and horror at his predicament. (These events belonged to the period of his visit to us twelve years earlier, but he did not speak of them so candidly at the time.)

For some reason he had brought with him one of his sketch-books; this he showed us, but while he delighted to discourse indefinitely about his paintings, he was apt to be hesitant about showing his drawings, chiefly, I think, because he feared he might be asked to part with them, but also because many of them, being inspired by love of some person or other, had for him an essentially private character.

This particular sketch-book was filled with studies for the projected series of 'chapels' he had much in mind to commemorate Hilda and certain of his friends; because he talked much about Elsie, the little maid who had looked after them at Burghclere, it may have contained designs for her 'chapel'. Of her and, as always, of Hilda he spoke with the utmost affection, drawing a severe distinction between these two, who believed in themselves and were concerned with their own affairs, and the mistress who was interested only in him. 'There's nothing more exhausting than someone whose only interest is yourself,' he said irritably. '*I'm* so interested in myself that I keep every letter I get, every document relating to me—even bills and receipts. Just lately I've developed a great dislike of being *disturbed*: I want more and more to be left alone.' As we left he said, 'You know, John, I'm not a great artist, but I'm very busy grubbing about on my little rubbish heap. At least I've *got* one.' All these were just odd remarks snatched out of the torrent of his talk: I wish I could convey its quality, the huge variety of its expressions, drawn indiscriminately from the language of his native village, the popular press, Thames-side suburbia and the Bible—a medley compounded of the racy, the rustic, the downright cheap and the august.

Next day I described over dinner with Barnett Freedman these various visits. 'Stanley Spencer', he said, 'is only a Sunday painter —but he's the greatest of them, even better than old Douanier Rousseau.' From someone so critical and caustic this was a tribute indeed.

Stanley delighted in receiving invitations, which in general he was under some sort of inner compulsion to accept, but occasionally he initiated visits on his own account. On Sunday 24 August 1952 when we were at home at Beauforest he telephoned to propose coming to see us the following day. I looked forward with mixed feelings to his visit, for the pleasure I felt was tempered with reluctance to be disturbed, for it so happened, by an odd coincidence, that I had just reached a critical point in the chapter on Stanley himself in my *Modern English Painters*. He was at his most cheerful and benevolent when he arrived, carrying a big, dilapidated parcel under his arm. The least self-conscious of men, he came promptly to what I suspect was the main purpose of his visit. Undoing his parcel he said, 'I'm working on a big picture of Christ preaching at Cookham Regatta, and I've done a lot of drawings for it, but now I'm a bit stuck because I've never been able to see them all together.' The parcel contained over fifty drawings, which he then arranged on the floor of our drawing-room, and Elizabeth and I sat down beside him while he explained in the prolific detail customary with him the significance of every incident. In one important respect these somewhat sketchy studies differed from the finished painting: the figure of Christ was remoter, smaller and scarcely identifiable. When Elizabeth remarked upon the insignificance of the Preacher Stanley cackled heartily, 'Poor old Christ, I've got to find a better place for Him!' This observation of hers revived in him a wish he intermittently expressed that Elizabeth should write another book about him. The Phaidon book she had published about seven years before appeared to delight him when it first appeared, but he had been turned against it, he said, by members of his family who considered that it depicted him as too much the village boy, which accorded ill with his brother Gilbert's frequent hints, to which he later gave written expression, of the possibility of the family's descent from 'the aristocracy or the landed gentry',[1] and with his dismissal of their father's statement that his grandmother was a washerwoman as 'not to be taken seriously'.[2]

Early the following June we paid him a return visit. Before going to his miniature cottage in Cookham Rise we called upon the critic R. H. Wilenski. At the end of the lane leading to his house we saw him with Stanley—and Stanley was laughing. 'You won't believe me', he said, 'what's just happened to me. On my way over from Cliveden View I got lost. *Stanley Spencer lost in Cookham!* 'It was as though Gilbert White had got lost in Selborne.

Stanley was in high spirits that afternoon and exhilarated by the possibility of carrying out one or two of the vast projects on which his imagination was constantly engaged. The authorities had shown some interest in his making a big painting for Llandaff Cathedral, and on the strength of this interest he had ordered canvases measuring ten feet by thirty. He had named £2,500 as his price, but he was concerned lest this sum frighten the authorities out of giving a commission he was passionately eager to undertake. (The price or some other circumstance did eventually extinguish their interest.)

Suddenly all his good nature evaporated, and he spoke with bitterness of the Royal Academy. 'I scarcely ever', he said, 'attend their meetings, on account of the sickening things said against people. I've never seen anything like the ghoul-like gloating over the misfortune of those whom the Academicians dislike; over the dismissal, for instance, of Eric Newton from the post of art critic to the *Sunday Times*.'

During the following year I saw little of him, but Denis Mathews, who went with him on an expedition to China, described his arrival at London Airport clutching the two brown-paper parcels that constituted all his baggage, and pointing along the Great West Road saying, 'That's the way I go to Cookham.'

Stanley responded with enthusiasm to the proposal that a retrospective exhibition of his work should be held at the Tate, and with Elizabeth and Lucy I went in mid-August 1955 to see him. We had been with him for barely a few minutes when he burst out, looking anxiously up into our faces for signs of disagreement, '*Do* let's go down to the village. Would you rather look at the churchyard? Or walk beside the river?' Had we just arrived at the outskirts of

[1] *Stanley Spencer* by Gilbert Spencer (Gollancz, 1961), p. 12.
[2] *Ibid.*, p. 14.

The author in the 'sixties, plaster, by Oscar Nemon

Sir Matthew Smith, 1944, oil,
by Augustus John

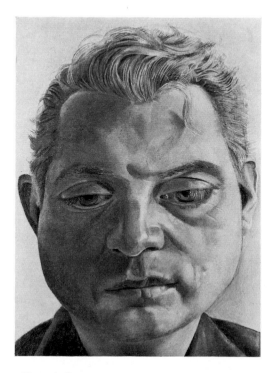

Francis Bacon, 1952, oil, by Lucian Freud

Lhasa or Samarkand his proposal that we should set out in explora-
tion could hardly have been made with a more passionate urgency.
We chose the churchyard, and Stanley showed us the family
graves, and then, taking us inside the church, he showed us the
family pew, the fourth from the back, facing the organ, and a fine
poem on a wall-tablet, in which there occurred the word 'turtle' in
the sense in which, he said, Shakespeare used it.

When we returned to his little cottage he showed us a painting of
himself with Patricia, both naked and portrayed on a scale and with a
realistic detail that startled. 'What a pity', Stanley mused, 'that you
can't have *that* for the exhibition. You can't, of course, but all the
same you *ought* to: it's *needed*.'

The necessity for turning out what he called trifles, small landscapes, flower-pieces and the like, in order to meet pressing obliga-
tions, combined with the lack of opportunity to engage upon more
ambitious themes has always depressed him. Low spirits even impelled him to complain of Tooth, his dealer, for having 'got him into
his debt' by advancing money to him in order to enable him to complete 'The Resurrection, Port Glasgow'! But the immediate source of
the bitterness he voiced was the alleged evasion by the canons of
Llandaff of their undertaking to commission him to make a big Day
of Judgement for their Cathedral, which, he claimed, had been
described in *The Times*. Their method of evasion, he said, was to
pretend to believe that what they had commissioned was not a
painting but a mosaic. It is only fair to the canons to mention that
Elizabeth later recalled Stanley telling us that he had warned the
canons a bit truculently that they would probably dislike what he
intended to paint. This afternoon, even though he had abandoned
any hope of a commission to paint the subject, he was obsessed by
it, and he described his projected treatment of it in the utmost
detail, except for one corner, which, he explained, 'I'm still waiting
for.' At one point his description seemed to me confused. 'I'm
sorry,' he said; 'you're right; I'd gone on to another big religious
subject that I have in mind. But I've got', he said in a serious tone,
'to be careful with this Day of Judgement business: I've my own
fate to consider.' (Stanley's conversation afforded frequent testimony
to his fear of Hell, a fear that was strange considering how little he
distinguished between bad acts and good or between the 'Good' and
the 'Bad' in the resurrecting people in his pictures.) He was convinced, too, that the canons had shown an excessive deference to

F

Epstein (who had modelled a 'Christ' for Llandaff), which made what he regarded as their slighting treatment of himself rankle the more.

I managed to stimulate the cheerfulness that with Stanley was always ready to break in by discussing the projected exhibition. When I suggested that he should write a foreword to the catalogue he was delighted, and the canons of Llandaff were momentarily forgotten. 'I've never had a chance', he said, 'to have my say about my own work; people would rather read something about it badly written by me than well written by anybody else.'

Some time that day Stanley talked to Elizabeth about his visit to China. On their way through Russia, A. J. Ayer, the philosopher, had been rattled by some minor misadventure and wanted to return to England. 'You can't, Ayer,' Stanley said; 'we're like death-watch beetles; we're facing in one direction, and all we can do is to go on till we come out the other side.' To Lucy he said that he told the Chinese that he was always at home in their country, as it seemed to him that Cookham was only just out of sight on the other side of the hill.

At the end of September and early October while the Spencer exhibition was being hung Stanley himself was constantly at the Tate, happy and helpful, not at all fussy about the arrangement of his pictures: 'I only want', he said, 'to be *surprised.*' In this he was unique in my experience: other artists have expressed pleasure in the appearance of their exhibitions when complete, but I knew no other to behave with equanimity, much less total satisfaction, while the arrangement was in progress. But as so often with Stanley his happiness was suddenly banished by the memory of some years-old grievance. Some thirty-four years earlier he had stayed for four months with Muirhead Bone, a consistently loyal supporter, but the visit turned out unhappily: his hopes of a commission and of a fee for giving painting lessons to Bone's son Stephen were disappointed, and Stanley felt himself, once settled in, unwanted and patronized. Angrily he described how Bone would insist on his going for walks which would take him past the post-office and then, as though by an afterthought, produce the letters for posting. 'Ye'll be after', Stanley used to mimic Bone's pleasant Scottish accent, 'possting Lady Bonn's laiters.' He also recalled with mounting fury his belief that Francis Dodd, Bone's brother-in-law, had put it about that Stanley had been asked to leave the house for opening his host's letters, an allegation which—if it in fact had been made—might have been based upon Stanley's having read a postcard from Sturge Moore as it lay on the breakfast table inviting the Bones to visit him and enjoining them 'to bring Stanley'. They left the house without mentioning the invitation and he complained to Sturge Moore, who in turn seems to have reproached the Bones. Stanley considered suing Dodd for libel. Collis, who alludes to the incident in his biography of Spencer, says that 'needless to say, nothing more was ever heard of this ridiculous affair' and that it was 'unlikely' that any coldness persisted between Stanley and the Bone family. Stanley did not sue Dodd, but the incident caused lasting resentment on his part, as his friends were frequently reminded.

Stanley's irrepressible spirits at the private view of his exhibition on 2 November 1955 were due, I fancy, not so much to the large crowd of attendant admirers as to the positively intoxicating presence of so great a number of his own pictures. This state of mind conduced to a candour about his family, usually repressed by his brother Gilbert. At a big tea at which Elizabeth and I entertained members of the Spencer family Stanley thus spoke about his father: 'a tiny little man with a big St. Peter-like white beard, but a beard more and more stained by tobacco. My mother objected to his smoking and prevented him from buying cigarettes, but the old man wasn't above picking up cigarette butts in the street.'

Stanley was elated by the success of the exhibition and friendly about a broadcast on his painting which I gave, but what delighted him most was the opportunity of writing the introduction to the catalogue. When I asked him to undertake it I had not fully understood how exasperated he was by the fact that so many others had published their opinions about his work and he, its creator, who cherished with loving minuteness the memory of every line, every brushstroke, to say nothing of every idea, every remotest impulse expressed, had been denied the opportunity of publishing anything but a few 'notes' and a letter. 'At last', his introduction began, 'I can say my say about my pictures.'

Stanley paid constant visits to the exhibition; on 17 December, the day before it closed, I saw him listening to a young lecturer speaking about his work, unaware of the presence of the artist listening intently and meekly, although ready perhaps at the proper time to voice opinions of his own.

At the end of October 1957 he came to Beauforest for a large lunch party we gave. As soon as we were settled at the table Stanley

thus began a long dissertation on the virtues of Hilda 'my first wife—
we're divorced and I did wrong to agree to a divorce—she often has
to go into an asylum, but even when she is in the asylum people go
there *to ask* her help and advice. That shows what a wonderful
person she is; [he named the mistress alluded to before] goes to the
asylum to *row* with her and she doesn't half row. But it does Hilda a
lot of good. You see nothing's better for deranged people than that
other people should take them seriously, and—going specially to
row with her and to have things out with her in detail shows Hilda
how seriously she takes her.'

'But I'm disappointed', he went on, 'not to have got that Llandaff
commission. When I went down there, the canons proposed to pay
me £2,000 for a very big painting. This was before they wriggled out
of it altogether. I said I hoped the Nonconformist chapels would
commission me to do paintings for *them*, and I think this may have
put the canons off a bit. But perhaps the canons were right to
wriggle out. After 1922 or thereabouts I began to lose my sureness—
the sureness that came from a sort of holy joy. The loss didn't begin
to show glaringly until the early 'thirties because up to then I'd
been carrying out ideas I'd settled in almost every detail ten years
before, and I'd been working from drawings done at that time. I was
losing my *vision*, being able to *see* my way clearly—*then* it was
unthinkable that I should find snags. Before the 1914 War I was in a
state of complete sureness about my work. As I finished one painting
I had no drawing or notion for the next. I wooed the empty air. But
the paintings I've done since the early 'thirties have been "selected"
from among hundreds of old drawings,' and he went on to describe
movingly but at immense length the effects of his loss of vision and
the grief and frustration it caused him. 'Just compare', he concluded,
'the *Glasgow* "Resurrection", which is just *contrived*, with the
Cookham "Resurrection", which is *seen*, seen whole from the
beginning.' All this he described even better and far more succinctly
in the introduction to the catalogue of the Tate exhibition. This is
one of the most lucid and revealing statements by a painter of this
age, and to me it is a matter for wonder that Stanley, the most
loquacious of men, whose talk and most of whose writings were
brought to a conclusion by external circumstances rather than because he had said his say, could have said so much, so well and so
very briefly. The omission of all references to this piece of writing
is perhaps the most curious feature of Collis' biography, more

especially in the light of its contention that Stanley's later work was finer than the earlier.

When I met him in March 1958 he was exhilarated by the Stanley Spencer Festival featuring a big exhibition of his work at Cookham. He was aware of his steadily growing reputation, and it was pleasing to him, but the highest honours that came to him from the world outside counted for less in themselves than as enhancements of his standing in his native village. No honour therefore meant so much to Stanley as the staging of the Cookham exhibition. The occasion of our meeting was a committee convened over lunch by the Lewis Partnership in connection with an exhibition they were sponsoring. 'He's gone on like this', the secretary told me, alluding to his continuous spate of ebullient talk, 'since ten o'clock this morning.'

The next time I saw him he was in almost equally high spirits, in circumstances that did the utmost credit to his courage. Lord Astor telephoned in January 1959 to Beauforest to tell us that Stanley was very ill and that he wanted to see Elizabeth and me. We immediately drove over to Cliveden and the three of us went together to the Canadian Hospital nearby.

Stanley was in an uproarious mood: he gave us, in all the detail with which, had he been well, he would have represented them with pencil and brush, a horrifying account of his illness, and the details, more horrifying still, of the operation which might enable him to live in spite of it. He spoke of his love for *The Book of Common Prayer*, and quoted from it at length; then his talk became bawdy—bawdier than I had ever heard it. As though to account for his uproarious spirits he remarked that he had made two portrait drawings that day. We left him astonished and humbled by his courage, for he must have known that his affliction would allow him to look forward only to a short span of life and that this would be lived in discomfort and indignity.

By the end of July he was well enough to propose coming to us for a weekend. Although he asked to go to bed directly Elizabeth had driven him from Cookham, it was evident that the colotomy operation he had undergone had deprived him of no whit of his vitality: he talked almost without cessation; when I brought him a drink I had difficulty in finding an opportunity to leave the room. Before he settled for the night he asked for a batch of Phaidon volumes and—of all books, for there was no painter with whom he had less in common than its subject—my *Life and Death of Conder*. Next morning he was extremely contentious about some opinion expressed in the book, and his contentiousness was exacerbated by my having forgotten it—I had not read it since its publication in 1938—and being therefore unable to argue the point.

The necessity for painting landscapes to ensure his survival, he said, had given him a positive antipathy for landscape, and he insisted throughout his visit upon sitting with his back to a window. If he were compelled to paint landscapes again, he said, he felt that he could be inspired by the Thame at Newington and asked if he might invite himself again at some future time.

On the Sunday John and Penelope Betjeman came over from Wantage to lunch and John evidently had much to say, but Stanley, at the top of his form, in volubility at least, denied him the opportunity of interposing a single word. He gave, in the fullest detail, an account of his operation, of his love affair, and his ideas, obscure and confused as ever, and as tinged with scepticism, about religion. When Penelope managed to ask him whether he believed in the Resurrection of the Body, he showed his annoyance at her interruption, treating the question as one of purely personal and peripheral concern.

John Betjeman was even more frustrated than fascinated by Stanley's monologue; so knowing his liking for boats I took him down the Thame in my canoe. Whether it was relief at being able, at last, to speak about the moonlight seascapes of Julius Olsen or some aspect of the architecture of Comper, or his response to the extraordinary beauty of both banks of the little river on that August afternoon, he said that the excursion had afforded him one of his rare moments of unshadowed happiness.

When the Betjemans had gone Stanley screamed at Elizabeth, his tiny frame shaking with fury: 'That bloody woman. Do you know what she asked me? *Whether I believed in the Resurrection of the Body!*' Whether his fury was provoked by her interruption of his talk, by her seeming to doubt his faith or to assume that he believed in fables, he did not explain. It was perhaps due to the intrusion of so concrete a concept into his muddled harangue, which he took as a reproach and an invitation to commit himself.

Next day, as Elizabeth drove him back to Cookham, he criticized abstract painters, saying that so many of them made pictures that did not grow out of their experience, and that with the true artist whatever he saw with his painterly eye became his unique possession; what need therefore to resort to invention? Suddenly he began to carp about me for my alleged 'dedication to abstract art' and he persisted in spite of Elizabeth's ridicule, but when she became annoyed he said placatingly, 'I'm glad John understood me so well when we discussed the matter last.' But he resumed his criticism of me on another pretext, asserting that a view expressed in my *Modern English Painters*[1] had done him more harm than anything ever written about him.

On 4 September of the same year—I record the date because it was the last occasion when I spoke with Stanley—he came over for the weekend, Elizabeth, as before, driving him from Cookham, having invited him in the hope that his presence would cheer Lucy, who was ill.

It was evident that the deterioration of his health was at last reflected in his spirits. On arrival he began querulously to recount how badly and persistently he had been bullied by fellow-students at the Slade. 'Wadsworth, with his Goering-like mouth, the leader, and Nevinson and John Fothergill the abettors. They once put me upside-down in a sack and they used to treat me in such a way that at times I was terrified of going to the School, and I once had hysteria there on account of it.'

'Communism', he said, recalling his visit to China, 'is coarsening and vulgarizing its wonderful, ancient civilization, and I was horrified that those who spoke about conditions in the world outside equated liberty with *social irresponsibility*.'

On his way upstairs he paused in front of the pen-and-ink 'Self Portrait' he had given me on the occasion of our first meeting, and at the sight of it his querulousness vanished. 'I was, I *am*, handsome, and I don't like people to think I'm not', he said. 'I cheered up the nurses in the Canadian Hospital by saying "When [he named his mistress] comes to call, tell her I'll be just where she wants me, *in bed*. It's narrow, so I may have to move over a bit."'

Next day he was in better spirits and made a drawing of Lucy,

---

[1] 'A few artists and a few critics have testified consistently to their belief that he is a major painter, but even these are mostly dead or belong to an older generation. The artists active today whose work seems to me most likely to withstand the erosion of time have expressed, in my hearing, their small regard for his work, and, with a few notable exceptions, others, too, whose judgement I most respect are sharers in this disregard. Most of them admit to some respect for his early works; it is the later that provoke their positive aversion.'

adding as he worked to the saga about his mistress. However much he was annoyed by her escapades, the unending saga was always a jolly one. 'Good luck to her', he said; 'God is on her side.' It was otherwise, and to an increasing degree, when he spoke of his second wife. When his Chinese hosts bade him goodbye, and they said, 'Your dear wife will be happy to see you', he replied, he said, 'My dear wife—she's never lived with *me*.' While Lucy sat with him he talked querulously about the Royal Academy. When he rejoined, he said, he had made it clear that he was not prepared to undertake any duties whatever. It was not long before Munnings 'found out about my male nudes, hunted them out, got photographs of them and showed them to the police'. It is characteristic of his querulousness that he should have made no mention of the handsome amends the Academy had made for the odious behaviour of Munnings.

On the Sunday he tried to make a drawing of Elizabeth, but he was already too weak. We drove him back to Cookham in the afternoon, and he gave us tea at the Copper Kettle, a favourite resort of his, and the scene of several important events in his life, his first meeting with his second wife among them.

On 19 October, driving through Cookham, we saw Stanley standing on the kerb of the main street. This was the last sight I had of him. Elizabeth, however, was to see him once again.

A day or two later I heard news of him which told me how fast his powers must be failing: Lord Astor told me that he thought it odd that Stanley, who always maintained that he wanted to devote himself to religious painting, was dilatory about finishing the 'Christ Preaching at Cookham Regatta' which he had commissioned, but that there was scarcely a schoolchild in Cookham whom he had not drawn.

On her way back from London on 6 November Elizabeth called to see him and to tell him that we would be very happy if he would paint us a small Resurrection. Stanley, however, was obviously gravely ill and incapable, Elizabeth thought, of painting any more. At first he was inclined to be quarrelsome, claiming that she had written that he had begun his professional life as a clerk in a builder's office, from which it was clear that his memory, too, was failing. But he was evidently touched by our proffered commission, and on this account and to atone for his flurry of quarrelsomeness he gave her a proof of his lithograph of 'The Supper at Emmaus'. As she left he urged that she and I should come to see him.

That afternoon, after Elizabeth had given me this account of her visit by telephone, I attended a meeting of the Fine Art Committee of the British Council convened to choose paintings for inclusion in an exhibition by British artists for Russia, the most representative to be sent from Britain anywhere since the war. I protested, vainly— even though I was responsible for taking it to Leningrad and hanging it in the Hermitage—against what seemed to me the absurdity of including only a single work by Stanley.

On 15 December, just over a month later, we heard over the radio that he was dead.

At the time of his death the love affair between Stanley and his native place was at its height: he had come to be known to all his fellow citizens as Stanley; before he was taken ill schoolchildren called at his cottage and asked him to draw their portraits; during his illness, he received numerous letters from schoolchildren and other neighbours. At his memorial service in Cookham Church I delivered the valediction to an audience of his friends and neighbours eager to hear the tribute of an outsider to the little man whom they had known all their lives, whom they had liked and laughed over and latterly come to love and revere in the fullest knowledge of all his shortcomings. This was the measure of their reverence and their love.

CHAPTER FOUR

STUDIOS AND PRIVATE FACES—I

EPSTEIN I knew far less well than I did Matthew Smith or Augustus John: partly because he was a less candid, indeed a secretive man; partly because my relations with him were for a time inhibited by some difference he had had with my father soon after his first arrival in England in 1902, when he came to our house with a letter from Bernard Shaw. My father, although he earned a less than modest income, made a small, regular allowance to this talented stranger, but the ensuing friendship was of brief duration, and it ended in circumstances which were never quite clearly explained but which precluded easy companionship between them.

My own acquaintance with him was slight until after the Second World War, when his reserve seemed gradually to diminish and a relaxed geniality to take its place. But suspicion of me was easy to arouse. When, for instance, in 1946 the Tate Trustees declined the proffered gift of his 'Lucifer' (now in Birmingham) he gave a press interview which showed that he attributed the adverse decision to me. He became a much easier companion under the influence of his second wife: Margaret, the first, shared and perhaps fanned his manifold suspicions and hostilities, but Kathleen, the second, allayed them. I called occasionally at 18 Hyde Park Gate during the lifetime of his first wife, sometimes with some visitor from abroad who wished to make his acquaintance, and Mrs. Epstein would sit at the long table in the main room on the ground floor, her expression at once blank and unfriendly, a sheet of paper before her and a pencil in her hand, noting the price and other particulars of any work under discussion but taking no part in it. Kathleen, on the contrary, was friendly and encouraged friendliness in her husband and disapproved frankly of his proneness to suspect and to dislike.

Epstein was one of those—and they are many—who often feel that they are in some way slighted, despised or worsted by those whom they meet, and who seek compensation in outbursts of hostility against them as soon as they have parted company. Frequenters of

the small closed circle of his family and intimates have more than
once described his outbursts against just-departed guests. I, however, was never anything like sufficiently familiar to witness any such
occurrence. Towards those present his manner was kindly, but
most people, I fancy, were conscious of his secretive reserve. This
characteristic was strikingly exemplified by his behaviour about
his own collection of early sculpture. His knowledge of such
sculpture was most exceptional and he would illustrate the points he
made in the course of his talk from the fine examples on view in the
house. Friends had told me that he possessed many others, but I
wonder if even his intimates suspected the existence of the superb
collection exhibited after his death. 'The greater part of this collection', Henry Green said to me, 'was kept locked up, likewise his stock
of whisky (small) and all his money in notes. During the spectacular
Mexican exhibition at the Tate in 1953, he arranged his own Mexican
sculptures around his breakfast table, stared at them lovingly, repeating at intervals, "better than anything *there*".' To Matthew Smith and
me he said, 'I have much better Negro sculpture than Picasso.' Like
Matthew's, his art was to some extent a compensation for what he
himself was not, for in the great company of his portrait busts I can
recall no secretive look; he brought out, on the contrary, the utmost
of generosity and openness his sitters possessed. Collecting, and the
multifarious questions of judgement and taste involved, particularly
interested Epstein. One day in the summer of 1952 he and Kathleen,
not yet married, had lunch with me at the Tate, and he talked about
Duveen, observing how extremely lacking in discernment he was,
and quoting him as saying, 'If I'd known Rembrandt was a great
painter when I was young I'd have made a fortune, but I didn't:
I thought he painted ugly things. And why', he asked me, 'do *you*
portray ugly things?' It was on this occasion that he said that he
doubted whether T. E. Hulme had in fact written the book about
him, Epstein, of which the manuscript was supposed to have
disappeared after his death.

Like most artists Epstein was very responsive to admiration, and I
could see that my own warm admiration for his 'Rock Drill' pleased
him, and at the private view of the retrospective exhibition at the
Tate held in the autumn of 1952 he cordially approved of my
attempting to secure its purchase by the Tate Trustees. (In the
event a cast was not acquired until the year after his death.) Of
later work in the exhibition he said that he thought the bust of his

daughter Esther was the best, and far preferable to the dramatic 'Haile Selassie', which was just then the object of particular admiration. Matthew Smith, who was present, endorsed Epstein's opinion.

The practice of an art being in essence lonely, artists are reassured by popular recognition—even those who have least belief in the validity of popular verdicts—which gives a momentary illusion of loneliness diminished. It so happened that I was a witness of a scene of acclamation that moved Epstein deeply. In mid-May 1953 his big 'Madonna and Child', commissioned by the Convent of the Holy Child, Cavendish Square, was dramatically unveiled by Mr. R. A. Butler, who appeared in a sort of improvised pulpit high above the pavement, and released a huge Holy Child flag which disclosed the figures—surely among Epstein's best—fixed to the bridge linking the two halves of the fine classical building. At the large gathering at tea afterwards with the Mother Provincial and the Reverend Mother, Epstein's face genuinely glowed with happiness at the general enthusiasm for the new statue, greeting me with a warmth that I had not experienced before, prompted, perhaps, by the allusion in Mr. Butler's speech to the modest part I had played in initiating the project. But even at such moments age-old resentments had a way of surging up. 'Do you know', he immediately said to me, 'that I've just refused membership of the Royal Society of British Sculptors because they refused me *their* support at the time of the trouble over the figures I carved for the British Medical Association.' The effect upon Epstein—a man innately combative and touchy, and long assailed with persistent venom such as no other British artist had ever had to endure—of acceptance as a national figure, regarded with respect and even with affection, was to inspire in him a measure of patriarchal benevolence. This was the mood, at least, in which during his last ten years I almost invariably encountered him: like Augustus he more than once offered to do Lucy's portrait, but to our regret in neither case was the portrait made. Not that his irascibility could not be aroused. He spoke bitterly about the mounting of his statue of Smuts: 'I model the figure,' he said; 'the South Africans can't even make a base.' But when I twitted him with having more commissions than the sculptor President of the Royal Academy his good humour returned: 'I've *far more*', he said.

Epstein threw light upon an important issue about which the

evidence is inadequate and opinion divided, namely, whether Rodin
was able to carve. John Tweed, Epstein said, who had worked with
Rodin and idolized him, assured him that he could not.

*

Henry Moore I often met, and his company many besides myself
find inspiriting and reassuring as that of a man who, although ready
to give his opinion with candour, seems always at peace with his
fellow-men and, more impressively, with himself. As a husband, a
father, a public personage, and simply as a human being, he must be
familiar with grief and anger, with self-mistrust and anxiety. Yet he
radiates a serene happiness—a happiness not remotely touched by
euphoria, for he has lost nothing of the precise appreciation, prevalent in his native Yorkshire, of the hard realities of life.

I remember the wry despair of a journalist who came to see me in
1952 about an article on Henry she was writing for *Time*. 'I'm
bewildered', she confessed, 'at his apparent inhuman perfection of
character: he seems equal to every situation, to be imbued with a
sense of social responsibility and immune from quarrels, to be
benevolent, patient and so on. It's difficult to write about somebody
without discernible faults.' 'And your researches', I asked, 'have
yielded no hint of any?' 'Well, when I was in Yorkshire collecting
material on his background, I heard a story, fairly well authenticated,
of his climbing roofs after girls in Wakefield—but that was *all*.
And that was when he was a *boy*. Since then *nothing*', she despair-
ingly went on, 'not befitting our model cultural representative
abroad.' I could not help her in this regard; all I could tell her was
that as a student at the Royal College of Art he was occasionally rough
and boisterous, but that for as long as I remembered it his character
in essentials had undergone little change.

It is difficult to know a man well unless you have worked with
him. I was involved in two projects with Henry which, although
abortive, gave me a fuller understanding of the reasons for his
exceptionally easy relations with those with whom he has dealings,
whether patrons, editors, assistants or critics.

I asked him in 1953 whether he would agree to my including him
among the occasional volumes of *British Artists* I had undertaken to
edit for the Phaidon Press some years before. He welcomed the idea
with enthusiasm, as did Kenneth Clark, who provisionally agreed to
write the text. Difficulties of a technical nature arose; K. was other-

wise heavily committed, and the volume—like several of the others planned—was never compiled. Henry's practical grasp, willingness to take trouble, and his good nature when the project came to nothing, yet further enhanced my respect.

It was in the autumn of the same year that another and far more important project in which we were jointly concerned also remained unrealized. I had recently been invited by Cardinal Griffin to join his newly established Art Advisory Committee for Westminster Cathedral, and I proposed to Monsignor Gordon Wheeler, the then Administrator, that Henry Moore should be commissioned to design mosaics for the baptistry. A few days later I took Henry to the Cathedral to ascertain whether, in the admittedly somewhat remote chance of his being offered the commission, he would be disposed to accept it. He paced out the baptistry, noted the way the light fell and was evidently fascinated by the possibilities it offered, telling me that Irina (his wife) had been greatly excited when I first mentioned the possibility not long before. He asked me to send him some reminders of the hieratic and monumental figures in certain of his Family Group drawings that I had mentioned in a general way as being particularly appropriate for the baptistry walls.

At a meeting of the Cathedral Committee held at the beginning of December, at which I formally proposed that Moore should be commissioned to design mosaics for the baptistry, Professor Tom Bodkin, who frequently alluded in his talk, and on occasion in his writings, to his conviction that the modern movement in the visual arts was nothing but a 'dealers' racket', boasted that he was determined to prevent charlatans such as Henry Moore from being considered for work in the Cathedral, and he also boasted that he had persuaded the Cardinal to appoint Professor Albert Richardson (who was just about to be elected President of the Royal Academy) and John Betjeman to the Committee—unlikely, as Anglicans, to express themselves strongly on controversial issues—in order, he said, to nullify my pernicious influence.

When my proposal came up for consideration and Bodkin abused Moore as a mere creation of dealers and of officialdom, I said that unless any proposal by a member was to be given serious consideration I could not continue to serve. My proposal was considered, but it was rejected, and once again Henry showed himself patient and unrancorous in the face of disappointment. Some fourteen years later I was authorized by Cardinal Heenan to write to Henry about the possibility of his designing mosaics for the still unfinished baptistry, but in the meanwhile his enthusiasm had cooled.

There happily came another occasion, a few years later, when we worked together to good purpose.

By the middle 'fifties it was evident that the Tate's collection of British painting and sculpture of the past half-century or so included examples of the work of all, or almost all, the more considerable artists, that the time had accordingly come to represent the most significant of them more fully and systematically, and that the Gallery should not deserve the reproach so often justly levelled at collections of modern art: 'when so and so was alive you neglected opportunities of acquiring his work and now you are compelled to atone for your neglect at enormous cost'.

It was decided that the first artist to be represented as completely as our resources allowed should be Henry Moore. He and I had a series of conversations about the subject in the spring of 1957; as a consequence his representation was increased substantially both in completeness and scale, and within a few years it included about forty examples, which were exhibited together. Henry made a list of suggestions for the representation of every important phase of his art then unrepresented and showed the utmost generosity and helpfulness in enabling the Trustees to fulfil their intentions, soliciting the permission of private owners for extra casts of bronzes to be made, himself supervising the casting, and arranging for the new bronzes to be obtained at only a fraction above cost. Thanks to his benevolent solicitude we were thus able radically to perfect and extend our Moore collection for what today would be the cost of two or three of his drawings.

Although serenely confident of his powers, Henry is far from being an egoist, and our conversations often turned to the work of other artists. Of Francis Bacon he spoke as beyond comparison the best of living dramatic or romantic figurative painters, although he had doubts about the degree to which it was possible to create enduring art out of such ephemera as press photographs, films and the like, and about whether drama created out of such materials might not eventually lose its compelling power.

Henry and Francis, in spite of their mutual liking and respect, sometimes treated each other with the aggressive caution of heavy-weight boxers. The three of us went together one night to a big reception at the Savoy, and Francis, attracted by some galaxy or

other which held no attraction for Henry, said, 'Let's go over there.'
'I think', said Henry, 'that for a few minutes I'll stay where I am,'
and Francis, whether in allusion to the sobriety of our friend's
life or the consistency of his attitude as an artist I do not know,
replied, 'Where you are is where you usually stay, isn't it, Henry?'
and he strode off into the crowd.

In the summer of 1958 Catherine Walston, Elizabeth and I paid
Henry a visit at Perry Green. When I referred to the extremely
tactile quality of one of his bronzes, he said, 'No wonder. When I was
a boy and my mother had arthritis she would say "Harry boy, just
give me some rubbing" and I would massage her shoulders and
back, and this gave me an acute tactile sense; in fact, although I
didn't know it, it was probably my beginning as a sculptor. I never
forgot those bosses and recessions.'

He showed us the 'King and Queen', recently cast and destined
for the Tate but reposing in his 'landscape'—as he terms the long-
vistaed, wood-fringed series of fields that he had adapted to the
display of a number of his larger works—until he should be satisfied
with its patina, beside the half-size model, in travertine, for his
UNESCO bronze, and he showed how several vistas from its site in
Paris would be seen between the limbs.

The talk of Henry Moore is marked, I think above everything else,
by sheer good sense, expressed with extreme directness, yet unless
conscience forbids qualified by kindliness. Having many intellectual
friends he just occasionally utters a cliché in current usage among
them, but it sounds as alien in his mouth as a quotation from a foreign
language.

At lunch one day the talented Portuguese Parisian painter Vieira de
Silva was contending at length that 'pure' form, that is to say form
devoid of any but aesthetic significance, was intrinsically superior to
form with extra-aesthetic significance. Henry voiced an emphatically
contrary view, denying that formal qualities were the first essential
for a great work of art, which was, he declared, an informing
humanity. 'Look', he said, 'at a late self-portrait by Rembrandt.
The head has no more *formal* qualities than a pudding—*but look at
it*!' From the expression of the talented lady you would have judged
that he had made an obscene remark.

When we hoped to acquire a Brancusi 'Study for Mlle. Pogany'
for the Tate (which Mr. Charles Clore generously presented) I
sought Henry's opinion and he called to see it. 'Of course it's a

Roy de Maistre, c. 1935

Cecil Collins, 1960

Edward Burra: in the background his painting
'The Three Fates', 1939

scandal', he said, 'that there's not a single Brancusi in the British public collection, but his heads are among his least good things— they're like heads to show a hat on. I can't quite make up my mind about this particular head; I like the chin and the neck, but I'm glad I don't have to decide. I suppose if I were still a Trustee I'd find my hand going up in favour. But I wish the Tate were going to get one of his finest things. Brancusi remained a *peasant*: his greatest asset was his strength; his greatest liability the susceptibility of a very simple man to the trivial fashions of a big city.'

On a visit to Perry Green in July 1960 I found him even happier than usual, enjoying, in particular, the affluence that came to him in the decade after the war. He showed me an ample new room he had built and additions to his holdings of land behind the house, in which he delighted to place his sculptures. But what afforded him still greater joy was the Cézanne landscape he had bought. 'When I was still a student at the Royal College I asked your father for a week's leave to go to Paris,' he said; 'it was warmly granted; in addition he gave me a letter to Pellerin, where I first received the full impact of Cézanne, and a letter to Maillol: meeting him would have been a terrific experience for a student, but I was too shy to use it.'

All Henry's sterling qualities were given full scope during his two seven-year terms of service as a Trustee of the Tate, above all his particular combination of the down-to-earth and the humane. There were, to be sure, a few artists who seemed to me to have merit, yet who were beyond the range of his sympathies—Ethel Walker, for instance, whom he considered as a mere decorator—but they were not many. The generosity of his attitude towards the work of younger sculptors in particular and to fellow artists in general was conspicuous, although he was ever vigilant for weakness of execution: he was the last person to take the will for the deed. I recall, in particular, another of his forthright statements about sculptors at board meetings. When we were planning to secure Rodin's 'Le Baiser', he said that it was far from being one of his finest works but he gave it his support as a creation of the greatest sculptor since Michelangelo.

One of the rare occasions on which I remember his being angry was in 1952 when the Whitechapel Art Gallery offered to sell to the Tate a half-length stone-carving by him, made in 1931, entitled 'Girl'. Being short of funds, as was invariably the case, we put the piece forward as a purchase—its cost was about £500—under the terms of the Chantrey Bequest. The Royal Academy members of

G

the Recommending Committee refused even to allow it to go forward for consideration by the President and Council. When I gave Henry this news I was astonished by his anger, but understood when he explained that only recently, and for the third time, he had been subjected to heavy pressure by Royal Academicians to allow his name to be put down for Associateship: 'They wanted my *name*, but they find my *work* unacceptable as ever. If there was one thing of mine they might have accepted it was that "Girl". This insincerity in their attitude makes acceptance of their offers unthinkable.' (We eventually acquired this carving out of our own funds.) Straightforward want of sympathy with his work does not trouble him at all.

As Henry and I walked round the Manzù exhibition at the Tate in 1960—which he regarded with great respect, except for the seated cardinals, saying 'You can't represent a proper figure without *shoulders*'—we recalled the attitude of my predecessor towards him. Manson had invited the loan of a Degas bronze to the Tate from Robert Sainsbury, who replied that he would agree provided that the loan of a Moore was also accepted. 'Nothing by Moore', Manson had declared, 'shall ever be shown there as long as I am Director.' (In order to secure the Degas a Moore was accepted on loan but never exhibited.) Henry could not have discussed the incident with more detachment had he himself not been concerned.

*

There was one painter, who has already figured briefly in these pages, whom I slowly came to know, namely, Francis Bacon. Because we had, in Roy de Maistre, an intimate friend in common, I had heard a good deal about him before we became friends. I admired his work when I first saw it at the Lefevre Gallery in 1946, but we did not meet until six years later, incongruously, at a fashionable dance, when he was very drunk. It was obvious from his dress— he was the only man present wearing a day suit—and no less from his conversation that he was anything but a regular frequenter of the fashionable world, but even if he had been his command of every social situation could not have been easier or more complete. It was evident that he attended such gatherings entirely on his own terms. He had a way, I was able to notice, even at this densely packed function, of making clear, with an imperious courtesy, that his life was lived, and his interests lay, in very different worlds from this.

At that time he was in his early forties—he looked taller than he was; his hair had the springy look of a boy's; his face was full and rounded, slightly narrowing towards the forehead; his stride was long and a little undulant, his voice caressing with just a perceptible undertone of menace.

For a time we made no effort to meet but by the following year, 1953, we had formed the habit of spending together an evening every few months. These evenings assumed two contrary patterns: when he dined with me I would call at his studio and look at what he was doing; we would eat a leisurely dinner either at a Soho restaurant or occasionally the Athenaeum Club, spending the rest of the evening at one or two Soho clubs with exclusively male membership. When I dined with him (as was more frequently the case), the order would be reversed and the evening would begin at one of these clubs, and meeting there painters and others we would drink until nine, ten, or even eleven, by which time I would be starving and my spirits would begin to flag, but he genial and elated. But my starvation and incipiently flagging spirits would be quickly cured by Francis' magnificent hospitality. If Max Beerbohm's division of human kind into hosts and guests is valid Francis is emphatically a host. Being a guest in fact frustrates his large impulse to offer hospitality and his sudden cravings for some very expensive food or wine which it would not occur to him to satisfy at the expense of a friend. Hospitality plays a very important part in Francis' life.

In the course of these evenings he would talk about painting (as about other subjects) in a way that riveted the attention. Precisely why what he says about painting so excites the imagination of his listeners—I have heard more than one person qualified to express an opinion declare that he talks about it better than any other painter of his generation—is difficult to define, but it is intimately connected with his own method, or rather his lack of method, as a painter. He has had no formal training, though Roy de Maistre, with whom he became friends in 1929, gave him occasional instruction, and he has few routine procedures and feels, with an intensity improbable for a painter who derives a measure of assurance from following well-tried methods, that the making of a painting is a hazardous adventure, far more likely to end in disaster, or in an even more exasperating 'near-miss', than in success. This sense of being constantly at hazard is reflected in his view of other painters, whose best work is accordingly the outcome of dangers overcome and always—and this is an essential element in his thinking and feeling—

with the help of sheer chance. I believe that he considers that no talent—least of all his own—can prevail without the aid of chance, a word frequently on his lips. The theatre of a painter's actions, when Francis speaks of it, is therefore a dangerous and exciting place, where, however favourable circumstances may seem, disaster always threatens. It is therefore inevitable that he should admire only a minority of the works of the artists he most admires. For Velazquez I would say that his reverence is unqualified and for the late Rembrandt also, although to a slightly lesser degree. Among living painters I have never heard him criticize Picasso, but for the rest his admirations are not for a painter's 'oeuvre' but for his rare successes achieved, so Francis believes, only when he has been favoured by chance. 'I hope the painter friends whom I respect', he said to me, 'will never know on how *few* of their pictures my respect depends.'

There are people of preternaturally strong sense of purpose who habitually act—with whatever intellectual qualifications—as though this sense of purpose were sufficient to ensure the attainment of their aims; there are also the Micawbers who put all their trust in chance. Francis acts—and his life is as original and audacious as his painting —with the conviction that he can attain his aims only when his strong sense of purpose is favoured by chance. He once told me that no day passed without his thinking of death: he is not less pre-occupied, I suspect, by chance, and it is this preoccupation that largely accounts for his fascination with gambling. For him it represents chance in its purest form. One autumn a well-wisher gave him £250 to enable him to spend the winter working in Monte Carlo: he lost the whole of it at the tables on the night of his arrival.

His preference for having his paintings glazed, although it owes something to his wish that they should be protected, and set some-what apart from their environment, is due to a greater degree, I think, to his liking for the play of chance, in the form of reflections. Of his dark blue paintings he said that the glazing enabled the spectator to see himself in the glass, and thus gave variety to their effect.

When one of his friends goes out with Francis fate is in the ascendant: anything may happen. Yet as a host no one could be more vigilant against the untoward. I recall, for instance, an incident at an evening party given at the Hanover Gallery in March 1957 to celebrate the opening of an exhibition of his paintings. The small rooms were densely crowded with artists, collectors, students, and the teddy-boys with exotic haircuts and leather jackets (many of them very drunk), who mysteriously arrive as a matter of course, and in considerable numbers, at any quasi-public function of which Francis is the occasion. Above the noise a cry of pain was suddenly though faintly to be heard. Before anybody else had even seen what caused it, Francis had appeared, instantly, from the far side of the turbulent room and was staunching a wound. Some object from the balcony had fallen upon a man below and laid open his scalp.

Because of his authority as a host people who might otherwise have been apprehensive at the presence of a number of drunk toughs moved among them without the slightest sign of disquiet.

It was not until 1962 that I came to know Francis well, when we met fairly often, at first largely in connection with the retrospective exhibition of his work at the Tate in May that year. The Trustees had agreed to my proposal that such an exhibition should be held— and it had the strong support of the staff, in particular of Ronald Alley—though with a conspicuous lack of enthusiasm.

Several common friends and acquaintances warned me that Francis would be an extremely troublesome collaborator; one of them—someone who knew him far better than I—even declared that if any of his early works were shown Francis would come to the Gallery and destroy them. These warnings did not surprise me, for there are aspects of everyone's character that remain hidden until one works with them. (How different, both for better and for worse, the performance of colleagues at their selection interviews and at their duties after appointment!) In any case I was aware of the lengths to which Francis could carry his waywardness. I recalled a characteristic instance. He had had many sittings for a commissioned portrait of one of his most devoted patrons, about which he mentioned to a friend that he had had a splendid day's work. The friend, remarking that the subject was abroad, expressed mild surprise. 'Abroad?' Francis said; 'of course I know he's abroad. But the portrait isn't of him any more. It's of a *chimpanzee*, and I've had a really splendid day with *him*.' 'Is there no chance', enquired the friend, 'that the subject will object?' 'I don't think there is,' Francis lightly replied; 'you see, I'd half told him about the impending change.'

In the event no one could have been more wholehearted than Francis in his co-operation over the exhibition. For a time I regarded each of our fruitful and agreeable consultations as the proverbial calm before the storm, but the storm never came. He was consistent in maintaining that he had done nothing of any value before 1944 when he painted the Tate's 'Three Figures at the base of a Crucifixion', and in opposing the inclusion of anything beyond a token representation of his earlier work. He was zealous in helping us to trace paintings lost sight of, and more surprisingly he imparted a considerable volume of information hitherto unpublished, speaking freely about his painting and his life in a series of conversations arranged to enable me to prepare my introduction to the catalogue. I appreciated his helpfulness in this respect, as he is apt to be guarded about giving biographical facts for publication—he had flatly refused, he told me, even to meet an unusually perceptive American scholar-collector who was writing a book about him. But Francis did even more than afford us his utmost help: he painted pictures especially for the exhibition. Towards the end of March I received an urgent invitation to his studio to look at a new painting which he hoped that I would like sufficiently to include. A huge triptych (it is eighteen feet wide) stood across the studio like a wall of lurid orange, red and black; two Nazi-like figures with two butcher's carcases on the left panel, a crushed bleeding body on a shabby bed—an allusion, pointed though remote, to the Crucifixion. (It was eventually titled 'Three Studies for a Crucifixion'.) For a long time I gazed at this extraordinary painting with fascination touched with horror. 'You know, of course,' Francis eventually announced, 'where all this comes from—it's inspired by *you*.' I must have made a gesture of incredulity. 'When you were here last week,' he replied, 'you spoke about artists as conveyors of religious truth. . . .' The assertion that this remarkable work owed anything to me was not seriously meant: it was no more than a humorous reminder of a recent conversation. Its sole source was the imagination of the painter, an imagination on this occasion working under the direct effects of alcohol. 'I was drunk', he said, 'pretty well all the time I was working on it.' His addiction to alcohol is prompted partly by the hope that it will intensify the workings of his imagination, but I think it relates also to his desire to invite the participation of chance in his work in the hope that it will both bring into play impulses unconsciously entertained and be productive of happy accidents in the actual application of the paint. But on no other occasion, he told me, had he completed a painting while drunk.

'Three Studies for a Crucifixion' and another painting, 'Red Pope on Dais', completed at high speed just before the exhibition opened, both showed him at his most inspired. It was evident that Francis, who generally works intensively (and occasionally not at all), was stimulated by the near prospect of the exhibition to extraordinary productivity.

He had moved not long before into a studio in a mews off Old Brompton Road, where these pictures were painted. Almost immediately the place reflected his character and habits, most conspicuously his lack of the acquisitive impulse (with most people superabundant). Beside his painting materials, the press photographs tacked on the studio walls, some of them, from their tattered and yellow look, long treasured, and the reproductions of paintings by the masters he most reveres, Velazquez chief among them, torn out of books, often expensive ones, that are then given or thrown away, Muybridge's volumes of photographs of men and animals in motion, Francis possesses the barest minimum: a table well stocked with spirits, a bedside table piled high with books, Aeschylus and other Greek dramatists (in translation), Pascal, Shakespeare, Montaigne, Baudelaire, Nietzsche, Dostoievsky, Van Gogh's letters, *The Golden Bough*, and a fine green Moroccan bedspread, but no rug or carpet anywhere. A splendid Buhl chest of drawers stood incongruously between two kitchen chairs. In the studio there had been brushed into a corner some miscellaneous objects, which I had supposed were rubbish. Following my glance he observed, 'I haven't had time to unpack properly yet.'

It was on the occasion of this visit that he showed an interest in his reputation as a painter that surprised me. Before this I had never known him otherwise than impatient of any discussion which might bear, however remotely, upon his painting as in any sense a 'career'. It was within my direct knowledge that he had declined honours and distinctions of several kinds; he had taken trouble to avoid publicity and always seemed indifferent even to the judgement of posterity. But this evening on the contrary he expressed the liveliest interest in the forthcoming exhibition and the utmost gratitude to me for what I might have done to bring it about (he was quite oblivious, of course, of the privilege the opportunity of arranging it conferred upon the Tate). In fact the whole project seemed to move him deeply, and he was manifestly anxious that it should be mounted as well as possible. We were later joined by our common friend, Alfred Hecht, the picture framer, whose shop in the King's Road, Chelsea, had become a sort of club which had many influential 'members' and where issues significant for the art world were discussed and even resolved.

A few weeks later I invited Lucian Freud to dine with me, partly in the hope of obtaining information about Francis for my introduction to the catalogue. Francis, divining my intention, and although most ready to provide information himself, wishing perhaps to exercise some supervision over the interrogation of an intimate friend, asked if he might join us. We dined at the Athenaeum. I had only a moment alone with Lucian in which he barely had time to say, 'Don't overlook the influence of Nietzsche on Francis,' before Francis himself arrived. As we were going in to dinner we encountered another visitor, Herbert Read, who hinted at his mild surprise at the presence of two such uncompromising 'bohemians' within these columned halls. I thought this so amusing that I told my guests of the impression they had made upon this sedate anarchist, adding that the Athenaeum had been founded for just such as them, and that they should allow me to put down their names forthwith. Francis clearly regarded the suggestion as too wild to call for comment, while Lucian, glancing at the sober figures of atomic scientists, judges and the like, gravely discoursing over their port, murmured, 'I couldn't face a place without *girls*.'

The occasion was unique among my evenings with Francis. Lucian and I were prepared for a late night, but Francis, suffering from asthma and worried at having come out on so cold a night without an overcoat, went early to bed.

Towards the end of April I finished the introduction, and because of Francis' habitual candour and the help he had so freely given in its preparation, to publish it without his approval was out of the question. It so happened that both of us were much occupied and the only time we were able to meet was on the 27th at breakfast at his studio. I arrived beset by misgivings: I knew, for instance, that he had given interviews—one at least of unusual interest—which he had unexpectedly at the last moment refused to allow to be published; not long earlier it had been agreed that I should write a book about him, yet a few days later he wrote to say that he could not bear to contemplate himself as the subject of a book. As we sat down to breakfast I was accordingly prepared for every sort of difficulty: even total prohibition to publish. He agreed to my proposal that I should read the introduction aloud and mark for subsequent discussion any paragraph which he might consider to be inaccurate or in any way misleading.

I read paragraph after paragraph, without the slightest interruption, and as I reached the end I concluded that he said nothing because he disapproved and would withhold permission to publish the greater part, if not the whole, of what I had written. I looked up to find him in tears, and I was deeply touched (as well as relieved) by the far too generous things he said. 'I *feel* like the painter you've described,' he said; 'it's an experience I've never had before, partly, I think, because you've treated my art in such a matter-of-fact way.' These words gave me great pleasure, although I did not agree with them: David Sylvester, for one, in my opinion, had written about him with acuter perception than I.

Francis had been up late gambling the previous night, he told me, and during his absence somebody—he suspected an acquaintance just out of prison—had broken into the studio through a skylight and stolen two paintings. We talked of Lucian Freud, whom he described as one of the most intelligent and entertaining people he knew, and gave a lively account of his life with a girl-friend: 'to bed, or rather to sleep, at three, then up again at seven, she posing as his model'.

A few days later I called at his studio before dinner and found him with Roy de Maistre, looking in silence at a painting in progress, a standing male nude casting a dark shadow on the floor. When Francis invited my opinion, I gave it, momentarily forgetful of the liability of a critical word to impel him to destroy the object of it. Roy's warning glance was too late: I had pointed to what seemed to me a weakening want of cohesion between the head-and-shoulders and the body, owing to an arbitrary horizontal line dividing the pink of the upper part of the figure too sharply from the yellow of the lower. The criticism, however, did not seem to disturb him, but my anxiety was not allayed until a few days later, when I saw the painting again, not only intact but with the defect (as I thought it) rectified.

Painters are inclined to welcome criticism of work in progress from visitors to their studios, not so much on account of any high opinion of their perception, but because artists become, by the act of creation, so deeply involved with their work that for the time being they are unable to see it with detachment, and they are accordingly apt to be interested by the way in which it affects a friendly out-sider. (When he was staying with us during the First World War Max Beerbohm asked my opinion of a caricature of somebody play-ing the double-bass, and when I pointed out that he had drawn the upper part of this instrument as larger than the lower, he actually insisted for a while that double-basses were like that, to such an extent had the identification of the artist with his work paralysed his critical faculty.)

Francis came to a party given by the Phaidon Press on 15 May to celebrate the publication of a book of mine, *British Art since 1900*, attended by many painters and sculptors, who glanced surrep-titiously, William Coldstream observed, at copies of it to see the reproductions of their own works 'as though it were about sex'. At this gathering I noticed in Francis the same determination that had struck me at our first meeting nine years before to encounter the Establishment, of whatever kind, on his own terms. When I introduced him to Lord Cottesloe, he said, 'I've such a hangover that I can hardly stand up', but having made his point he carried on the conversation with the utmost suavity.

On 23 May, when his Tate exhibition opened, I had the pleasure of his company almost all day. He even attended the press conference in the morning—the kind of occasion he usually avoids as though plague-infested—speaking most amiably to the critics; the private view in the afternoon and a party at night. At this last, a very formal occasion, he appeared in the clothes he had worn since morning: black and white check shirt and blue jeans, but instead of wearing his black leather coat he swung it about as a toreador his cloak. At a few paces distant he was followed by a few youths similarly dressed. He was very drunk, but his condition did not in the least diminish his dignity or the charm he so powerfully exerts. When he left he again thanked me for my part in the exhibition, embraced me, and kissed me on both cheeks, making me feel like a French officer receiving a decoration.

The exhibition was a resounding success, attracting more praise than any exhibition by a British painter within my memory, *The Times*, for instance, describing it as 'the most stunning exhibition'. I sent a copy of the catalogue to Picasso, who acknowledged it with an admiring message. The Gallery was presently crowded not only by the general public, artists, and students, but by 'teddy-boys' who came in unprecedented numbers. The exhibition itself would have

been less complete and the catalogue less exhaustive and scholarly
but for the highly informed enthusiasm of Ronald Alley.

I do not believe that I am liable to be suspected of prejudice
against artists, but I have found that they lack one quality even more
conspicuously than other people, namely gratitude. How many
times has one heard their patrons, in particular their early patrons
who bought their work when others ignored it, described as people
who exploited them?

The Tate retrospective exhibitions of the work of British painters
are widely regarded as enhancing or even creating reputations in a
national and sometimes an international context, and they are complex and expensive to organize. Nevertheless, only a small minority
of the artists concerned have ever shown any sign of awareness that
anything unusual has been done on their behalf. To this minority
Francis belonged. Had he never been offered a retrospective he would
not have noticed the omission; had it been cancelled he would not
have demurred, yet no one could have responded to it more warmly.

The overwhelming preoccupation of the vast majority of men and
women is with their fellow men and women, their relations with one
another, their environments, and abstract art, which is precluded by
its nature from making any communication upon these universally
absorbing themes, cannot dominate for ever, or even, it seems to
me, for very much longer. Abstract art is a logical manifestation
of the division of function which is industrial society's basic law;
it is therefore not, as many hold, esoteric; it is on the contrary, a
conspicuous example of specialization. It is not only in close
harmony with the procedures that distinguish most of the collective
activities of modern man, but—and perhaps for this very reason—
it attracts a high proportion of outstanding talent. When the abstract
movement has shown signs of exhaustion, students are reassured by
the adherence to it of such admired figures as Mark Tobey, S. W.
Hayter, Ben Nicholson, Victor Pasmore, Jackson Pollock, Barbara
Hepworth and David Smith. It hardly needs saying that there are
a number of figurative painters in England today whose work
attracts the admiration it merits, but it does them no injustice, I
think, to claim that, for the younger generation at least, Bacon's is
the only name to conjure with, the only reputation to make them
think that figurative painting may after all be more than a survival,
that it may even have a future. (Pop art is of course figurative, but
in a special sense which I shall discuss in a later chapter.) How

widespread the interest in Bacon was brought home to me when early in 1962 I was being entertained to tea in the Museum of Modern Art, New York, by Alfred Barr. Along the table sat the senior officials of that brilliantly directed institution and a few artists, in animated conversation. Somebody happened to ask me if I knew Francis Bacon. When I admitted that this was the case there was a sudden silence, broken only by eager questions about his personality, his ideas, the estimation of him by younger painters, and his latest work. The emerging pop painters owe nothing to the actual painting of Bacon, but his presence affords them a measure of assurance in the validity of 'the image', rather as, some years earlier, the presence of Henry Moore assured English sculptors—however dissimilar their work from his—that they could hold up their heads in any company. Nobody known to me is so aloof from organized society, so indifferent to its future as Francis. Yet however indifferent, he is aware of the part that his painting may play in a revival of figurative art. Although he passionately reveres certain of the old masters, he believes that for the time being traditional modes of expression are entirely played out, no longer effective vehicles for conveying either feelings or ideas, and that what is needed now is a kind of shorthand. ' "What modern man wants",' he said to me, quoting Valéry, ' "is the grin without the cat", the essential without the traditional elaboration, the all-over finish to which people of today have become so resistant.' He believes, like many another, that the proper study of mankind is man, but that if painters are to participate in that study they must look at man from unexpected angles, catch him off guard. He is fascinated by man—though it be man in the hell of his situation. Art unconcerned with men I have heard him impatiently dismiss. At dinner at our house in Chelsea that summer Roy de Maistre, Alfred Hecht, Bryan Robertson, Elizabeth and I were discussing abstraction. Bryan said that the tragedy of the painters of the New York school was that they were essentially social protesters who were patronized by the rich, to which Francis replied that they were not protesters, in that they had evolved an art through which protest was impossible, an art which suited them well since it seemed audacious yet could express nothing that could affront their rich patrons—a theme which he developed with vehement brilliance.

*

Roy de Maistre was one of Francis Bacon's oldest and closest friends. I came to know him slightly during the war when I visited his studio residence, 13 Eccleston Street, Victoria, and although I liked the man and respected his painting, I only gradually came to appreciate both at their true worth. Our friendly acquaintance ripened suddenly into friendship. At the height of the Tate Affair we met one afternoon by chance and he intimated in very few words, with the utmost delicacy, that he might perhaps be of help to me, and he invited me that same evening to his house. My evening visit was the first of many; over the years I saw more of him than of any of my London friends. During those dark days, by the information he had and by his combination of serenity with profound solicitude, he fostered in me a revival of spirits for which I can never be sufficiently grateful. Never, either at that time or later, have I been in his company without feeling the better for it. As a host—and like Francis Bacon he was essentially a host rather than a guest—he was a rare combination of the cosy and the exhilarating, of the correct to the point of courtliness with the original and the candid.

It would be difficult to find two people more different than Roy and Francis. Roy's life was organized and lived with meticulous precision, his environment exquisite, the relics of his past were preserved with tender care, whereas the life of Francis is anarchic, his environment one of spartan disorder, for he cares nothing for possessions of whatever kind, except for the photographs and other materials which he requires for the practice of his profession, and a handful of books. Roy was a strictly practising Catholic; Francis is constantly preoccupied with death, but for him there is no resurrection, nor does he discern any ultimate meaning in the sinister confusion of human life. Yet such can be the contradictions between temperament and belief that Roy was often oppressed by melancholy whereas Francis is exuberant and full of plans for the enhancement of life: 'I'm going to Athens,' he said to me one evening, 'where there are the two things I enjoy most, bars and the sea.' The theatre of Roy's actions was his home, his studio, the place where he preferred to see his friends, and which he was for ever embellishing. For Francis his studio is not a 'home', but the roof and walls needful for work and shelter, a place without emotional overtones. When a spell of work is upon him he paints hard and continuously, seeing nobody and scarcely going out, but for living as distinct from working he goes out to bars and clubs and restaurants in Soho, or the East

End for preference, or abroad to Mediterranean places such as Tangier or Monte Carlo. Their clothes might suggest—however erroneously—that they belonged to mutually exclusive social worlds: in these libertarian days, however, wearers of black leather jackets and blue jeans consort without discomfort with wearers of Edwardian clothes (in the most formal sense) such as Roy, even whose painting overalls were of distinguished colour and cut. Francis' studio, in a pleasantly sequestered South Kensington mews, is as unembellished, even as 'unlived in', as the day he entered into occupation, its wooden partitions still mostly unpainted, and if another studio of comparable convenience were offered him he would leave as indifferently as one leaves a room in a hotel. Roy's studio was a work of art, and, like Courbet's, a repertory of his whole life. The Roman Missal and the opera hat reposing on a small table inside the front door, miscellaneous chairs and pieces of porcelain, of fine design and inherited from remote French ancestors, a screen painting by Francis (one of his earliest surviving works), and an art nouveau settee also of his design; paintings of Roy's own from his early Australian years to work in progress, characteristic gifts from generations of his friends. All these miscellaneous objects, arranged with the art that conceals art, created an environment of tenebrous beauty, but a beauty not at all inconsistent with informality and comfort, this last attested by a simple iron coal-burning stove flanked by two ordinary armchairs, as was an element of fantasy by the palettes placed on a high shelf showing as black silhouettes against the sky. If Roy had been suddenly evicted from his Eccleston Street home and his possessions perished or scattered he would not long have survived what would have affected him as the amputation of his past. One feature of his past, namely his descent, was worthy of note: a direct ancestor was a son of Queen Victoria's father, the Duke of Kent, and a Frenchwoman, Madame de Saint-Laurent.

Such solicitude and ingenuity lavished upon an environment might have struck even the most sympathetic visitor as dilettantish were it not for the respect that the painter himself and his paintings hanging on wall and easel would have compelled even from the least sympathetic visitor: the man, a small upright figure, a miniature Roman emperor, dignified, discreetly dandified, courteous in an old-fashioned style, unyielding in his principles, exacting in his standards of behaviour, to his friends boundlessly benevolent. Modest to a degree though his resources were, he gladly extended his friendship to include men and women in need—often in desperate need—of the help he so unselfishly and secretly gave them. To the rest of the world he was indifferent—respectfully, admiringly, contemptuously—but still in essence indifferent. And the painting: austere and complex, yet radiant, not inviting but richly rewarding attention. How many of my happiest hours have been spent in front of the iron stove of Roy de Maistre!

From some time in 1966 the character of the evenings I spent with him—I was rarely in London for a week and almost never for a fortnight without spending an evening with him—began to alter. Roy was a diabetic, and I suspected that he suffered from other ailments as well. In that year I noticed that, for the first time, there were no new paintings on wall or easel, no work in progress; that in fact he had ceased to paint. He received his friends in a lounge suit instead of his painting overall. The following year, to my surprise, he showed me a new painting. 'It's no good,' he observed with intense melancholy, and he was right. His sight suffered progressive deterioration; eventually there were no books or newspapers to be seen on the little table beside the chair in which he habitually sat. Nothing in Roy's conduct of his life moved me to a greater admiration than his stoicism in the face of his inability to paint. What agonies of frustration and boredom he must have suffered, this impassioned painter, this intensely visual man, at having to sit, month after month, unable to paint; surrounded by his own paintings, constant testimony to what, but for some failure of the optic nerves, he could achieve. (A number of his best works remained in his studio, for, though he was usually in urgent need of money, he never parted with a painting without reluctance.) But he never complained; never referred to his deteriorating sight except, when necessary, with a terse word of explanation, and he never alluded to his inability to paint.

One evening in mid-September 1967 I was delighted to find him in livelier spirits than for months; he told me of the first objects to arouse in him a conscious aesthetic interest: the dolls in his nursery, which he used to dress in period clothes copied from history books. Of all the experiences of his life, he said, the completion of his colour charts and harmonies in pure colour gave him the highest sense of exaltation. (He began to work on them about 1918 in Australia and one of them—a disc-shape device for determining the relative degrees of harmony and contrast between different colours—was patented and published in Sydney.) On the 25th of the same month I went to say goodbye before leaving for New York to take up a visiting professorship at Fordham University, and found him in muted spirits. When I saw him next, on 19 December, I was distressed to find him ill and despondent. In my eagerness to see him I forgot to bring the small Christmas present I had for him; when I brought it the following day he seemed for a moment not to know who I was. Nine days later a common friend telephoned to me at Beauforest to tell me that he was gravely ill and in King's College Hospital, Denmark Hill. When I visited him it was clear to me that he was disappointed that the stroke he had suffered had not killed him: that he had no will to live. But on each visit I noticed a slight improvement, although I doubted whether he would ever be strong enough to care for himself. When I expressed my doubts to Francis Bacon he immediately offered to send him, accompanied by a friend to look after him, to some Mediterranean resort, for three weeks or whatever period was necessary for convalescence. One evening I found him in higher spirits. On my way out of the hospital, impelled by sudden inexplicable anxiety, I retraced my steps along the corridors, revisited his room for a moment. 'Goodbye, old boy,' he said, smiling and holding out his hands. It was goodbye.

He was sent home towards the end of February 1968. On 29 February the young friend who had been very kind to him during his illness telephoned news of him. He had cooked dinner for him, intending to serve it on a tray, but Roy insisted on getting up and eating it at his little dining-table. He was radiantly happy to be home. Immediately after dinner he suffered another stroke and was in a coma from which he would never recover. The following morning the same friend telephoned again to say that Roy had died in the night. So went the third of the four men whose friendship I have valued above all others—and a painter not valued at his true worth. He was a master of lucid, expressive composition, but also of colour achieved through scientific knowledge as well as sensibility. The brilliant light of a summer afternoon and winter twilight revealed different but equally moving ranges of his colour harmonies.

Today, when interest in the arts is more widespread than ever before and talent more promptly recognized, I am surprised by Roy's neglect. He was loved and admired by Samuel Courtauld, one of the foremost of the few major British collectors of the age, who owned a number of his paintings.

In Roy's studio when he died there remained many still-lifes— mostly of his own possessions, lamps, flowers, fruit, chairs, and the like—also some of his most characteristic works, those which expressed deeper reaches of his nature—a certain sombreness and harshness—rarely apparent in his conduct, at least towards his friends. 'In one's life one ought to be gentle and forebearing,' he said to me, 'but in one's art one should conduct oneself quite differently. It's often necessary, for instance, to give the spectator an ugly left uppercut.' Spectators don't care for uppercuts and as he was associated with no fashionable tendency and had no dealer— he was reluctant to sell his pictures—he was neglected by collectors both public and private. Four of his paintings were acquired while I was at the Tate but the Trustees made me aware that they regarded my advocacy of his work as a personal idiosyncrasy which they could afford to indulge, as three of these four were gifts, one of them from his friend R. A. Butler, a former Chancellor of the Exchequer, and heir to a large part of the Courtauld collection, which it would have been imprudent to decline.

H

CHAPTER FIVE

STUDIOS AND PRIVATE FACES—II

AN INCONVENIENT feature of the social structure of the present day is the virtual disappearance of places where friends and acquaintances meet by chance. Such resorts as the Café Royal, where people connected, however distantly, with any of the arts (as well as many other pursuits) might expect to see their friends or acquaintances, have changed their character, and they have not been replaced. Friends now accordingly meet by arrangement, made usually over the telephone. Some of my friends' numbers are 'ex directory', but one of the very few who values his privacy so highly that he has no telephone at all is Lucian Freud (grandson of Sigmund Freud). He has never been an intimate of mine and our lives run very different courses, but I have admired his work ever since I came to know it in the middle 'forties.

I also took a lively pleasure in the company of Lucian himself, but because of his refusal to have a telephone it is a pleasure I have enjoyed less often than I would have wished. I not only liked Lucian but admired certain features of his character: most of all his independence of conventional ways of life and of aesthetic fashions.

One afternoon, descending from a bus in a main road in Paddington (the district where he has always lived), I enquired about the street—it was Delamere Terrace—that he had given as his address. 'But it's all been pulled down', my informant said. Another passer-by gave the same answer, then with a searching look added, 'You're not looking for an artist, Mr. Frood, are you? There's one or two houses in the street that's left, he's there.' Outside the house stood an antique but handsome convertible, a Bentley, I think; inside the studio a welcoming bottle of champagne. Water and electricity however, seemed to have been cut off in view of the house's impending demolition. The studio was minute and derelict. Like Francis Bacon, a close friend, Lucian meets his fellow-men strictly on his own terms. Like Roy de Maistre—though it would not be easy to find two people more different in almost every respect—Lucian is often admired more as a person than an artist. In my opinion, in relation to his achievement he is one of the least regarded artists at work in Britain today. His portrait of Francis Bacon, which we bought for the Tate in 1952, is surely a combination of acute perception and skill very rarely found in 'the dying art', as a dealer advertised an exhibition of portraiture in his gallery. Marked by the same insight and crystalline lucidity are portraits of his friends and fellow-painters John Minton and John Craxton.

When I first came to know him he had not long freed himself from youthful imitation of a variety of European painters (of whom his knowledge was detailed and wide-ranging) and was evolving the extraordinary way of painting and drawing which won him the ardent recognition not of a wide public but of a circle of close friends, several of them, fortunately, able to buy his work and to give him support of various other kinds. The works on which he was engaged were surrealist in character but, representing everyday subjects— people, fishing-boats, animals, shellfish—they are without any surrealist devices. Although suffused with the fascinating dream-world strangeness of the best surrealist art, their subjects are entirely credible, belonging unambiguously to the phenomenal world. The fascinated, minute, unblinking stare with which he fixed his subjects makes it impossible for the spectator (or this spectator at least) ever to regard them casually. He is compelled to scrutinize them, down to the smallest detail—the errant lock on Francis Bacon's forehead or John Craxton's collar—with something of Freud's own intensity. But at the very time, around the middle 'fifties, when general recognition seemed imminent, he gradually abandoned his linear, minutely 'close-up' scrutiny of his subjects in favour of a broader and more painterly view. He was becoming, in fact, increasingly affected by the urge to *paint* rather than to continue to make coloured drawings. The learning of an entirely different form of art (for it was nothing less) has involved a solitary struggle and prolonged periods of professional near-obscurity, productive of failures as well as hard-won successes. There have been times when he has been mastered by paint but he has gradually shown himself its master.

There is one respect in which the social conduct of Francis Bacon and Lucian Freud differs from that of anyone else I know. The desirability of a classless society is questioned as rarely as its conditions are observed. I heard a disillusioned former member of a group of aristocratic but extreme radicals at Harvard state that the private prejudices and practices prevailing within it were snobbish and racist. Most people continue to consort with people of their own kind of upbringing, though accepting others, whatever their origins, who are successful. Francis and Lucian consort as naturally with barrow boys as with the privileged who often assiduously seek their company.

*

Other intimate friends whom I saw regularly and most often with Elizabeth were Albert and Catherine Houthuesen. I had known him well since he was a student at the Royal College of Art. Even then he showed imaginative and technical gifts of a high order, exemplified by his 'Supper at Emmaus', of which one of the two versions is among our most precious possessions.

In several respects Albert was very different from the great majority of his fellow students. He was the son of a Dutchman, Jean Charles Pierre Houthuesen (named after his French mother Charlotte Houllier, from Besançon, Burgundy), who only during the last ten years of his life, until his early and tragic death at the age of thirty-three, had realized his ambition to be a painter. Albert inherited, therefore, a special sense of the privilege of being an artist—a sense enhanced by his own difficulties in realizing a similar ambition. For Albert (born in Amsterdam in 1903) was brought to London when he was eight, worked for six years after leaving school at fourteen (and even before) as an errand-boy, a grocer's assistant, and at other similar jobs. He had a sense of the privilege of being even a student; in fact he took no good thing for granted. I remember him, at twenty, as old beyond his years, and at a time when other students had moments of frivolity—Henry Moore could behave gaily and even wildly at students' parties—Albert was always obsessed by a tragic sense of life, which did not, however, inhibit a highly developed sense of humour. This tragic sense of life was partly temperamental, but partly due to a family tragedy of which his friends remained unaware until many years later.

There was tension between Albert's father and mother originating from the circumstance that she, in a modest way an heiress—a member of the Wedemeyer family (Albert Wedemeyer, her grand-father, was conductor during the early years of the Crystal Palace and devoted to the work of Handel)—expected of her husband a more materially successful career. When shortly after their marriage he renounced an assured income from his maternal relatives' piano-manufacturing firm of Houllier in order to become a painter, the struggle to make a living for their growing family could only exacerbate this tension, which grew steadily more ominous. In particular she resented her husband's fostering the desire of Albert, their eldest son, to draw and paint. One day, soon after Albert's eighth birthday, his father was giving him a drawing lesson. 'For Heaven's sake,' his mother exclaimed, '*not another* artist in the family.' 'He understands it better than I do', his father replied. There was an angry altercation and Albert ran out of the room. On his way along the corridor he heard cries of agony. Hurrying back he saw his father staggering into the bedroom, clutching his head between his hands, shouting 'My head! My head!', and his demented mother, a shoe in her hand, following him. The last words he spoke as he lay on his bed, handing his purse to his wife, were, 'Take this; I shall never use it again.' And making a gesture to Albert meaning he should come to him to be embraced (which the child was too stunned to obey, being unable either to move or to speak) his father said, 'Look after your mother and brothers and sister.' Three weeks later he was dead.

All his life Albert has heard these terrifying cries; he told me that scarcely a day has passed when the terrible scene has not been re-enacted; and if a day comes when it is forgotten, it is re-enacted during the night. Yet he never spoke of it even to Catherine until at long last they were living in their own house in Camberwell, where they moved in 1952. The secret had been kept for more than forty-five years.

Shortly after his father's death, the family left Amsterdam and settled permanently in London, where the widow kept a boarding-house in Constantine Road, Hampstead. They became poorer and poorer. For the last two years before leaving school Albert stood each morning in a queue for stale bread and had the humiliation of regular visits to the pawnbroker. Finally the London County Council had to supply his boots.

The move to London deprived Albert of every link with the past, as was his mother's intention, since it left him entirely dependent upon her. He tried constantly to reject what he knew to be the true cause of his father's death, which his mother explained by insisting that in playing with Albert he had struck his head against a chandelier, thereby associating Albert directly with it.

I have related these sombre circumstances because they do much to explain the overtones of tragedy that mark much of Albert's work, especially his stormy seas and skies. One of his paintings cannot be other than an allegorical allusion to his own past. A sailing ship is sinking in an angry red sea beneath a red sky: its title 'The Wreck of the Early Hope'. It is, in my belief, a masterpiece. The element of allegory is both obvious—at least to one who knows the circumstance that inspired it—but also recondite. The artist pointed out to me that the boat is a Chinese junk, which though it looks as fragile as an autumn leaf also conveys a suggestion of eternity, thus expressing a degree of hope in mitigation of utter despair. A halo-like light surrounds the boat in silhouette, just as in his 'Last Will and Testament' the painter has lived to see dawn lighting his cluttered workroom. Another drawing which expresses a similar idea is 'Man praying': a painter is on his knee, on the floor lie his palette and brushes, and, as if in a vision, stands a table, and on it bread, salt and water.

It was at the Fleet Road London County Council School that Albert first received recognition as an artist. By way of compensation for his inability to speak English he drew a thrush on a blackboard. The headmaster and other teachers came to admire it. The drawing was left untouched for several days. But many years were to pass before public recognition came to him. Albert is a man of extreme reticence; the public at large remained ignorant of him, although, like Roy de Maistre, he had a small circle of friends to whom this dedicated figure was the object of admiration and deep affection. He might be without recognition still had it not been for Elizabeth's enterprise and perseverance, which resulted, in 1961, in his being given a retrospective exhibition. The time was propitious: his outlook on the world had not changed, his sense, above all, of the fragility and transitoriness of all that he holds most precious, under constant threat from time and chaos. (I remember his saying to me that often, before beginning a painting or a drawing, he is almost overcome by foreseeing their inevitable destruction—canvas or paper already disintegrated into dust.) But it often happens that with the passage of years a painter's brushstroke becomes freer and more fluent. Of course it remains as precisely controlled as it was before, but it can assume a spontaneous, audacious look. This was the case with Albert. It made it possible to see his paint, although applied with sombre exaltation, simply as paint and even to relate it, however remotely, to that of certain of the abstract expressionists. The resemblance was accidental and superficial—but it momentarily obscured the fact that the artist was as solitary a figure among his contemporaries as he had ever been, and it impelled many who had ignored or discounted his work to scrutinize it with close attention. Many recognized it as the expression of a rare spirit: dedicated, highly imaginative yet intimately conversant with the natural world.

This exhibition and the four that followed won him a wide circle of ardent admirers and enabled him, for the first time in his life, to earn his living as an artist.

One of the most remarkable things about Albert's art is its achievement in the face of misfortunes—poverty, persistent ill-health and the memory of the appalling event that he witnessed as a boy—that would have frustrated or destroyed another's.

There is one circumstance in his life that could hardly have been more fortunate, namely his marriage to Catherine Dean, a fellow student at the Royal College of Art, herself an artist of rare gifts. In the sitting-room of their house in Camberwell, facing the door, hangs an upright painting by Catherine of a cat asleep in a high-backed chair which would hold its own in any museum. (Another, in the Tate, 'Sheep's Head and Ferns', shows the same delicacy of perception with reticent firmness of construction.)

Every visit to this house has been memorable. Behind the pleasant but conventional, almost standard early Victorian front, is an interior that puts one in mind of a Vermeer. In spite of a lifetime of extreme poverty they have been able to assemble pieces of furniture, china and the like, all of which reflect the perceptiveness of their purchasers who, in earlier days, had shillings rather than pounds to spend.

The Houthuesens have a genius for friendship, and I know few people who concern themselves so consistently with the high peaks of achievement and experience.

*

Another artist whom I particularly admire but see too infrequently for my liking is Cecil Collins. We were first acquainted when he was a student at the Royal College of Art, but it was not until the 'forties that we became friends.

Unlike most artists Cecil had evolved a philosophy of life. When he spoke of it, his ideas were not taken seriously and were even the object of ridicule, in particular when they were explicitly formulated in an essay written in 1944 and published three years later: *The Vision of the Fool*. In the intervening years this philosophy has come to be widely shared and often militantly expressed by successive student generations. It is only one among many contributions to present-day student attitudes, but it is significant that *The Vision of the Fool* should have become a subject of discussion at the University of California. Its central theme may be simply stated: Cecil's Fool personifies spiritual, imaginative man who 'opts out' of today's utilitarian conformist society and rejects without compromise its materialistic values. 'Modern society'—to quote from this essay—'has succeeded very well in rendering poetic imagination, Art, and Religion, the three magical representatives of life, an heresy; and the living symbol of that heresy is the Fool. The Fool is the poetic imagination of life—inexplicable as life itself.' This owes something to Blake and more to Mark Tobey whom he met in 1938 and who fostered his interest in the thought and the art of the Far East.

Cecil's philosophy, consistent, poetically and lucidly expounded in words, has intrinsic interest but its essential value derives from its expression in pictorial terms.

In Cecil's art *subject* is of cardinal importance. There are of course many artists today who attach importance to their subjects, but the concept of an art which exists in its own right, subject only to its own aesthetic laws, abstraction in brief, exercises a pervasive influence.

The old dictum of Roger Fry's, 'a man's head is no more and no less important than a pumpkin', and the correlative judgement of Clive Bell's that 'to appreciate a work of art we need bring with us nothing from life, no knowledge of its ideas and affairs, no familiarity with its emotions'—such beliefs are still widely held or accepted by artists and critics. Even a man as independent and audacious as Francis Bacon, who treats of subjects of crucial human significance, used to dislike any titling of his pictures, saying 'I want my paint to speak louder than my subjects.' Cecil is one of the few creative artists who reject without any compromise the total exclusion of subject or its relegation to being a mere pretext for the exercise of the aesthetic faculty. 'If the subject is unimportant in a picture, we may well ask: unimportant to whom? The subject of the Crucifixion to Grünewald? To Fra Angelico? The subject unimportant to

Rembrandt, to Goya ?'[1] Cecil does not in this regard stand alone, but he is of a small company. Many years earlier, for example, Wyndham Lewis had written 'that [art] is about something is an axiom for me, *art-for-art's sake* I do not even trouble to confute'.

Even though Cecil regretfully accepts the fact that 'all we have left to us is to paint for the art trade'[2], he has consistently striven to show that 'beneath our commercial travellers' civilizations, there still flows the living river of human consciousness, within which is concentrated in continuity the life of the kingdoms of life, animals, plants, stars, the earth and the sea, the flowing generations of men and women, as they flower in their brief and tragic beauty', and that 'the artist is the vehicle of the continuity of that life, and its guardian, and his instrument is the myth, and the archetypal image'.[3]

This is an exalted aim, so exalted that no artist, not even a Blake, could consistently achieve it. Cecil at his finest moments does achieve it. Such, for instance, is 'The Sleeping Fool', a painting of extraordinary imaginative intensity—a painting which, ever since I first saw it a quarter of a century ago (and bought it for the Contemporary Art Society which gave it to the Tate), has been as vividly present to me as any on our own walls.

The Tate Trustees, sometimes responsive to my particular admirations, in the case of Collins, as in those of de Maistre and Houthuesen, were merely tolerant—and their tolerance had well-marked limits. They bought a second outstanding example, 'The Golden Wheel', and accepted a third as a gift from the Friends of the Tate, 'Hymn to Death'. A letter he wrote to us at the Tate about this last work testifies to the artist's intense and prolonged identification with his theme: 'The "Hymn to Death" was in my mind for a great many years and like most of my works it was a concentration of the essence of an accumulated experience. It is a vision of Death as a moment of "Transfiguration".'

Elizabeth, his wife, appears almost as an intermediary between everyday life and the mythological world where Cecil mostly dwells.

Cecil is diffident and retiring and at times even solemn in manner, which enhances his moods of gay extravagance. On a brief visit to us he said of Cambridge, where he has mostly lived since 1947, 'It's so

---

[1] Notes by the Artist, catalogue of the retrospective exhibition of his work at the Whitechapel Art Gallery, 1959.

[2] *Ibid.*

[3] *Ibid.*

hygienic; but Oxford is redolent of *evil*. I'd emigrate if we weren't so fond of our house.'

*

As Director of the Tate I was concerned primarily with painting and sculpture, but I was also much attracted by print-making. This was due in part to the sheer imaginative quality of many of the prints that were supplanting the widely collected but predominantly dreary prints that I remembered as a boy. I have often heard champions of academic art describe the pioneering art of this century as the 'product of a dealer's racket'. It did not, however, occur to them that the type of art most vulnerable to this stigma were the etchings, published in extremely expensive editions, of academic artists whose original drawings, owing to their shoddy quality, were virtually unsaleable.

But my interest in print-making was also stimulated by sociological considerations. It was year by year becoming more apparent that art produced only in very small quantities and obtainable only in very limited areas, around Bond Street or Fifty-seventh Street, for instance, was extremely poorly adapted to meet the requirements of a public in which enthusiasm for the visual arts was becoming more and more widespread. One of the art forms best adapted to satisfy this public is the print, in which outstanding quality may be combined with wide distribution. It was also a matter of concern that while entire editions of the work of the most highly regarded British print-makers were often bought on publication by foreign collectors, Britain remained—as it still remains—one of the very few European countries without a representative collection of modern prints. The United States has over thirty. Our melancholy situation—which could have been avoided at a modest annual expenditure, or even by legislation requiring selected print-makers to take an extra pull for a national collection as authors have an obligation to designated libraries—can be retrieved only at very considerable cost, and many desirable prints once easy to obtain are now beyond our reach.

My two chief points of contact with print-making have enabled me to see almost diametrically different aspects of it. The one is S. W. Hayter, my brother Michael the other.

I was not a regular visitor to Paris but over the past twenty years I have rarely been there without spending an evening at Bill Hayter's studio-flat.

Some engravers have employed their skill as a means of reproducing the work of others, as Raimondi did Raphael's or, like Turner, of reproducing their own. There have been yet others such as Rembrandt, Goya and Blake, and in our times Gauguin, Bonnard, Klee and Picasso, who have used it to realize their own imaginative experience. It is to this category that Hayter belongs. But he is far more than an engraver of rare and original gifts. He is an animating spirit, on the grand scale, of print-making and of many of its finest exponents. By reviving the workshop conception, 'of the artist, not as a lone wolf howling on the fringes of an indifferent society', as Herbert Read has written, 'but as a member of a group of artists working together', Hayter has done more than anyone else to transform engraving, 'the Cinderella of the arts', into a Princess who did not, however, vanish as midnight struck but continued to engage the attention of an ever-widening circle of artists, collectors and members of the public. The visitor to 36 rue Boissonade or to Atelier 17 becomes instantly aware of the personality who has so largely effected this transformation: a personality warm, highly and precisely articulate, eager to share his wide-ranging knowledge and his extraordinary technical mastery. (His own modest view of his attainments was summed up in a phrase I heard him use: 'the technical difficulties of engraving are in my view greatly exaggerated'.) Eager also to listen: I know nobody who listens with closer attention. It is not surprising that artists from every continent—including the most illustrious—have availed themselves of his knowledge. The art of Hayter's is that of engraving: 'the art of incising a groove into some resistant material'. The product is the work of the human hand.

My brother has taken an extremely active part in the evolution of print-making of an entirely different kind. How different from Hayter's is indicated by the title of one of Michael's writings: 'Look no Hands'.[1] Its themes are the print made, partly or wholly, without the intervention of the human hand, and the sharp distinction 'between past and present, between the agrarian culture that produced the woodcut and the world of technology that produced sophisticated photo-aids'. It warns against 'the love of hand-gesture in art for its own sake [that] may show an unattractive attachment to the past' and quotes another author who maintains that 'gestural print-making . . . as a medium that still has work to do . . . is over

[1] *Art and Artists*, March 1967.

with'. My brother does not entirely agree and believes that the print-maker should keep both options open: 'gestural treatment, on the one hand ... photo-aids on the other'. He himself, however, has become more and more deeply concerned with the second option; though he believes that the print made entirely with photo-aids 'will sometimes have a thinness, a coldness, a lack of presence', he increasingly responds to 'the strangeness, the richness, and fabulous diversification of the electronic age in which we live'.

This is not the place for an attempt to evaluate my brother's work, an undertaking in any case for which many others are better qualified than I. It may, however, be of interest to attempt to throw some light on a question that many of those who know him have asked, namely, how it came about that someone of precocious talent, brought up in an environment that seemed highly favourable to its development, should have taken so long to find his way. His was indeed a circuitous and at times a painful path.

This was due largely to our father. No-one among his contemporaries had shown such perceptive generosity towards his brother artists of succeeding generations, from Augustus John and Epstein to Henry Moore and Ceri Richards, but although he ardently admired Michael's talent he was unable to discern his most urgent need.

This need (which Michael himself was long unaware of) was that of many artists, in particular young artists in the modern world: a need for a degree of identification with pioneering art; however intense their admiration for their predecessors, their prime interest is directed to their most adventurous contemporaries. Our father was certainly able to respond wholeheartedly to the art of many of his juniors, but it is also the case that over the early years of the century he underwent a change of outlook which qualified, and at times impaired, his sympathy with the pioneering art of his own time. Whether this change was due to some shaking personal experience, to the bitter divisions of opinion resulting from the post-impressionist exhibitions of 1910 and 1912, or simply an effect of middle-age, or a combination of these, his family does not know. An exclamation in Volume II of his *Men and Memories* gives an indication of his attitude: 'A generation that sanctifies the austere devotion of a Cézanne and acclaims a Picasso is not easy to comprehend'. I am not here in the least concerned to criticize or to justify, but only to observe that it was an attitude with disastrous effects for a young man who would have been exhilarated and fulfilled by participation in a pioneering movement.

In 1920, when Michael was twelve, our family moved, on our father's appointment as Principal of the Royal College of Art, from Gloucestershire to London. Eager to foster his talent, our father devised for Michael a course of training which looked backwards towards the pre-raphaelites and to a William Morris concept of guild-craftsmanship. Why our father should have done this I do not know. Certain of the paintings he had recently made as an Official War Artist, of scenes of devastation on the western front, did not look out of place when shown with those of Wyndham Lewis and Paul Nash—both artists whose work he admired. For whatever reason it was devised, such training had grievous results. At the Central School of Art, which Michael attended half-time, he was, to use his own words, 'a half-baked prodigy too young to identify with the life there'. This combination of circumstances caused him to develop an almost neurotic inner life, and to become increasingly alienated from his surroundings. By the age of eighteen and for the next ten years he suffered near-breakdowns. During Oxford vacations and during the four subsequent years when I had a flat in our parents' house I was too obtuse or too much occupied with my own concerns to see more than that he was periodically in a neurotic state, but awareness of our parents' immense admiration and solicitude for him and the fact that he steadily produced drawings and water-colours of merit reassured me. I did not know, nor even remotely suspect, until he told me many years later, that his condition culminated in a suicide mania so intense that a journey or the crossing of a bridge, for instance, would bring about heart-attacks and that there were nights when he wanted to rope his legs together to stop himself jumping out of the window. With good psychiatric treatment and the encouragement of some commissions for the Pilgrim Trust's *Recording Britain* project his state improved. Like many British artists during the war, isolated from the art of other countries, he became especially susceptible to the influence of earlier British artists, which brought about the fruitful but short-lived neo-romantic movement, but he was also responsive to abstract art. Michael's move to Great Bardfield in Essex towards the end of the war marked the end of his years of uncertainty: a new beginning, a true beginning, rather. Michael was exhilarated by the surrounding landscape; in the village itself a small group of artists, Edward

Bawden, Kenneth Rowntree and John Aldridge among them, was already at work and they had even evolved something approaching a common style, which enabled them to treat the surrounding world convincingly but in terms of simplified form and colour and which made an immediate appeal to Michael.

It was Edward Bawden, the senior member of this small community, who by a chance remark put him on to print-making. 'There's nothing to it,' Bawden said; 'take a pen-knife and a bit of lino, and go ahead.' 'I tried it,' Michael said to me, 'and never looked back.' This new technique fascinated him; at the same time it cut him off from his family heritage and made it possible as never before to forget the years of illness and uncertainty. 'I suddenly felt an extraordinary vigour,' he wrote to me, 'and as I went on to develop ways of work that answered my needs, I also found there were new ways (to some extent), ways that hadn't been tried before, and this feeling of opening up and pioneering in the medium was very exciting. Then, for the first time, I *blessed* my horrible art training: the art training that had been so incomplete that I'd never even done any prints at school. And here was this whole enormous territory of print-making fresh, with no tracks from the bad past, glowing there under a new sort of sky!'

Study under Hayter in Atelier 17 was a further revelation. Here he began etching, but after a few months he encountered a serious, twofold difficulty: he wished to use colour, but London lacked the necessary printers and the process in any case was too indirect to suit him. So he turned back to linoleum printing which allows of the direct use of colour.

Soon after his return home he and his wife went on a Sunday picnic and sat down to eat their sandwiches outside a woodyard at Castle Hedingham. The wood—huge irregularly shaped planks of elm—was stacked in sheds to protect it from the weather. He looked up from chewing his sandwich and saw these huge planks, growth patterns in the likeness of a landscape on every one of them and wonderful movements like the shifts and eddies of a tide along a narrow foreshore. It was magic: there, *in* the material, landscapes and rhythmic movements were embedded—gifts, he felt, that he could hardly refuse. Climbing over the woodyard barrier he wandered around the place in a revelatory daze. A few days later he went back and bought a lorry-load of these planks.

This experience led to his using wood in his prints, for the sake not of texture but of energy and movement. It quickly had other consequences: the realization that he could print from anything with a flat main face that could be inked up and put in the press; that the ability to photograph an object that he couldn't print from and have a block made of it that he could print from gave him an endless range of objects, surfaces, fragments with which he could, so to speak, conspire in creating his images. (Nature rediscovered in different terms?) In his studio are stacks and heaps of 'found' objects, the spoil of intensive raids on garage scrapheaps, junkyards, the waste-ground of the city tip, iron wheels, fragments of television sets, mouldings of smashed-up furniture, as well, of course, as planks of elm, which he handles lovingly, as though they were precious objects. Michael's use of these miscellanea in this manner has come to be known as 'open block' printing and is specially associated with his Essex workshop.

The essence of his art, as I understand it, lies in the visual balance and tension between hand-drawn marks, the gestural element, and the 'received' photographic material and his found objects. The first, a direct expression of feeling or ideas, is intended to induce in the spectator a state of empathy; the second offers no lines the eye can follow to re-enact a pattern of recognizable feeling. Incapable of charging the imagination, it is intended to charge only the nerves.

CHAPTER SIX

ARTISTS ABROAD

VISITS abroad, brief though they mostly were, gave me opportunities of meeting several of the foreign painters and sculptors whom I particularly admired.

It was in July 1949 that I first went to see Giacometti in his studio at 46 rue Hippolyte Maindron, Montparnasse.

Giacometti, with his fine straight features animated by an extraordinary intensity of feeling, his black untidy hair and his slight figure charged with an electric energy, was an impressive presence. He seemed devoid of vanity. His success seemed only to increase his sense of the distance between his achievement and his intention, and generally to sharpen his self-critical disposition. At moments he showed a positive dislike for his work, to 'have it in for it', so to say. Discussing a passage in a clay figure, for instance, he would mark it with savage cross-strokes of his thumbnail.

The most beautiful sculptor's studio I had ever seen was Brancusi's, where I had been just before the war. Giacometti—like Francis Bacon—cared nothing at all about his surroundings, and his studio, minute and untidy, was the sort of place that one would expect a student, fresh from art school, to occupy while he looked for something better. On my first visit to this disorderly little place I recalled the work of art that Brancusi had created for his own environment—which he told me he hoped the city of Paris would preserve just as it was. The wooden shafts Brancusi had carved, scrubbed to a fine silver or else gleaming with dark polish, resembled cherished columns from some ruined temple. The brasses shone with a pristine, flawless radiance as he removed their perfectly fitting covers and invited my admiration with looks of childlike simplicity, mumbling nonsense in the meanwhile about the danger of catching leprosy from eating fish. 'I'd like you to have something of mine for the Tate,' he said, 'but I only sell when I'm absolutely forced to, just to enable me to carry on. As far as possible I want to keep my work here, so that it can be preserved together.'

Lucy, 1959, pencil, by Sir Stanley Spencer

The author with Lucy and Stanley Spencer at Beauforest shortly
before the painter's death in 1959

Richard at Dynevor, 1965

Nothing, I supposed, would have seemed to Giacometti so repugnant, indeed so fantastic, as the preservation in his little workroom of all the works he could afford not to sell. Far from cherishing his works as Brancusi did (he was disturbed by the suspicion of a stain on a shining surface of bird or fish) Giacometti, like Francis Bacon, was inclined to iconoclasm. When his work fell short of his intention, as was usual with him, it was in danger of destruction. On a later occasion he showed me two attenuated standing figures, and asked me which I preferred. To my praise of one of them he listened for a few moments with benevolent impatience. 'But what defects', he eagerly enquired, 'do you find in the other?' Confident in his awareness of my admiration for his work, I did not hesitate to detail what seemed to me to be the shortcomings of this particular example. The attitude of Giacometti as he watched and listened was that of an extremely partial spectator at a boxing-match: he applauded every critical blow I landed upon the unfortunate bronze. I was the agent of his vicarious iconoclasm so that from the time of this incident I was aware of an increased warmth of feeling on his part.

On this first visit, after he had shown me the bronzes and plasters that would have intolerably crowded the tiny studio had they not been such attenuated waifs, I asked him who had made some brush strokes on the wall, and when he answered, 'I, of course,' I asked whether I might see his paintings, for not one was visible. With a gesture of surprise that I should wish to see them, he got out several canvases and a number of pencil drawings. These I thought were marked by the same obsessive beauty as his sculpture, and was the more delighted by them as I had been unaware that he was a painter and draughtsman, and I reserved three examples. I was not, however, alone in my ignorance. Later that day I was the guest at an official lunch given by the Ministry of Fine Arts. To the question of one of my hosts about whom I thought the most interesting painter of the younger generation I answered 'Giacometti'. With a gesture conveying exaggerated tolerance for the almost invincible ignorance of foreigners he said, 'But you know, Giacometti is a *sculptor*, *not* a painter.' Of the three paintings I had reserved two were bought by the Tate for £60 each and the third was made available, by a message to Kenneth Clark, to the Contemporary Art Society, by which it was given to the Birmingham Art Gallery. (Paintings of such a kind would today cost £10,000 to £12,000 each.) These three paintings

I

were, he believed, among the first to be acquired by public collections. It was as a result of this visit that the bronze 'Man Pointing' was also bought for the Tate, for £250.

The letter he wrote me shortly afterwards, on 29 August 1949, shows the modesty of his attitude towards his own work, and the absence of intimations, so common from successful artists, of mysterious difficulties where selling their work is concerned.

> Pardonnez moi de ne vous remercier qu'aujourd'hui pour votre lettre qui m'a fait un très grand plaisir mais il m'était impossible de répondre plus vite, je n'étais pas très bien tous ces jours passés.
>
> La nouvelle de l'achat de la sculpture et des deux tableaux était une grande surprise pour moi, je ne m'attendai pas à tout cela et je ne sais pas très bien comment m'exprimer sur tout cela ni comment vous remercier. Je regrette seulement que mes choses ne soient pas un peu mieux qu'elles ne soient.
>
> Je ne comprends pas pourquoi les deux tableaux achetés reviennent à Paris, est nécessaire? Je suis d'accord avec les titres de ces tableaux, 'homme assis' et 'nature morte' mais pour celui-ci peut-être mieux 'Intérieur' mais c'est comme vous voulez. Je fais très volontiers une concession sur les prix—(naturellement et pour la sculpture surtout j'avais déjà fait un prix autre pour la Tate Gallery) *30 ou 40 livres ou 50 de moins* sur le tout est possible? ou est trop peu? Mais j'aime mieux si vous décidez vous même je suis d'accord d'avance avec vous.
>
> Dites moi si je peux faire fondre tout de suite la sculpture. Je pourrai la faire fondre pendant mes vacances. J'ai beaucoup travaillé tous ce temps ci et je suis impatient de partir bientôt en vacance un peu.

Thereafter on my visits to Paris I usually called at his studio. On one occasion we were going through some drawings when there was a tapping on the door. This Giacometti at first ignored. When he eventually said 'Come in' a pretty girl emerged. 'You see,' he said, as though some explanation were called for, 'we were married this morning.'

Of all the artists I have known Giacometti (with Francis Bacon) was the least satisfied with his work. Whenever we were together he complained of the difficulty he had in realizing his ideas, of the number of his failures.

As an example of his self-dissatisfaction and of the re-working
this involved, I recall the sequel to my selection, on 3 March 1959,
of an almost finished painting for the Tate Trustees to consider.
In response to a reminder that I had heard nothing of its progress,
I received the following letter dated 22 November:

> Je suis très touché par votre lettre et par l'intérêt que vous
> portez à ma peinture, cela me fait une très grand plaisir.
>
> Mais je dois vous dire que la peinture dont vous parlez je l'ai
> totalement faite et défaite trois fois depuis que vous l'avez vue et
> je l'ai recommencé dernièrement. J'espère arriver à un résultat
> dans pas trop longtemps et dès qu'elle sera un peu ce que je veux
> je vous le ferais savoir.
>
> J'espère arriver vite à m'approcher un peu à ce que je veux et
> je serais très heureux si le résultat vous intéresse encore.
>
> Je vous écrirai donc le plus tôt possible et en vous remerciant
> encore je vous prie d'agréer, cher Monsieur Rothenstein, mes
> très amicales salutations.
>
> Pardonnez, je vous prie, cette lettre très mal écrite, fatigué et
> très tard le soir.

At the time of this March visit he was also working on a plaster
of a girl, about seven feet high. 'The success or failure of my figures',
he said, 'is decided in the first few moments. The difficulty is to
begin right. I find it easy to model a figure once I get the head right.
But to get it right—that's difficult.' He spoke contemptuously of
abstract art. An American visitor, he said, had recently asked him
what he was working on, and when he said, 'a portrait of my wife',
his visitor had exclaimed 'ha, ha, ha' to express his incredulity
that a serious artist could really occupy himself with a 'subject'.
He spoke contemptuously, too, of the exaggerated importance
currently attributed to an artist's 'temperament'. 'For me', he said,
'everything becomes beautiful under scrutiny. What matters isn't
me and my "temperament", but how much I can convey of my *subject*
to the onlooker.'
An endearing characteristic of Giacometti's was the way in which
his propensity to savage criticism of himself was complemented by
one of readiness to admire the work of others. No visitor to the Tate
found more paintings and sculpture in which he discerned fine
qualities than Giacometti. In fact he was among the three or four
most responsive visitors that the Tate has welcomed in my time.

The most extreme contrast to Giacometti in this respect was offered by Ben Nicholson. Meeting him by chance in the Tate in the spring of 1963, I showed him a room recently rehung predominantly with abstract paintings of recent decades (including a group of his own). I then indicated, by way of contrast, an adjacent room, also recently rehung, but with figurative paintings of the same epoch by Bacon, Ceri Richards, Freud, Cecil Collins and Colquhoun. 'I can't', he said, irritably, 'even *look* at paintings like that,' and as though to emphasize his disapproval he added, 'I hoped, when I came in, that I shouldn't meet anyone I knew.' (In *Modern English Painters* I had devoted an appreciative chapter to him. But I had been constrained to argue that there were no metaphysics in his art and indeed that he was not so much an innovator as the most accomplished living practitioner of a new academism. This he had deeply and articulately resented.)

My encounters with Giacometti were too infrequent to allow of anything approaching friendship to grow between us, but I never saw him, his regular classical features so ready to darken with exasperation at the thought of his failure—real or supposed—to realize his intention in some current work, his abrupt gestures expressing his contempt for any notion of making his art a means of personal advancement, without a lifting of the heart.

Our last meeting took place at the time of the retrospective exhibition arranged at the Tate by the Arts Council in July and August 1965, when he came to London. On the evening of 15 July before the reception in his honour, arranged by the Friends of the Tate, Robert Adeane said to me on the telephone, 'Giacometti's here. I doubt if he'll agree to go to the reception at the Tate, but can you come to my house, as soon as you can? I know he wants to see you.' Giacometti was in the highest spirits, mainly, it seemed to me, on account of the St. Ermin's Hotel, Westminster, where he was staying, and he described at length the glories and fantasies and the great scale of its Edwardian architecture, which, he said, stimulated him to make a number of sketches out of the windows of his room. In the course of the afternoon, he said, he had visited Pierre Matisse, who was staying at one of the most famous and expensive London hotels, and Giacometti had contrasted the smallness and simplicity of the room he occupied with the magnificence of his own quarters at the St. Ermin's. Such was his good humour that, though detesting crowds and official functions, he agreed to come to the Friends' reception, remaining there, however, for barely twenty minutes. He also attended—and with evident pleasure—the dinner given in his honour at the Tate the next evening; he even made a speech in characteristic self-depreciatory terms. His pleasure the occasion offered to talk with Henry Moore, Francis Bacon and other artists was evident. Elizabeth and I had heard that he was ill, but neither of us knew that we would never again feel his firm impulsive handshake. Giacometti died of cancer shortly after his London visit.

*

I had occasionally heard people speak slightingly of Chagall, representing him as a hypocritical man, concealing an extreme materialism behind a smoke-screen of high ideals. When he and his wife came to lunch with me at the Tate in early January 1953 I formed a very different impression, which was confirmed as I came to know him better.

Chagall spoke of his friend Velona Pilcher, lately dead, a founder of the little Watergate Theatre, off the Strand, designed to be an experimental centre for all the arts. I expressed regret that the murals which he had painted especially for it (and which I had unveiled there some two years before) had been recalled for exhibition in France, where they remained. 'Very well,' said Chagall, 'I'll give the two oil studies for them to the Tate in memory of Velona.' Thus 'The Dance' and 'The Circus' entered the collection. I was touched by his ready generosity. These two studies were welcome for themselves and as the preliminary studies for the only public decoration he has made for a building in Britain and his first mural for a theatre since those he had made for the State Jewish Theatre, Moscow, in 1919–20.

Like the painters in the French tradition whom I have been privileged to take round the Tate Chagall was more attentive and more appreciative than his British confrères. He looked with particular interest at Turner, Constable, the pre-raphaelites, and he gave me pleasure by admiring my father's 'Doll's House' and asking to be shown other examples of his work.

'There's scarcely a trace of talent', he said, 'among the younger French painters, but what remains in Paris is an extraordinary sense of quality.' When I spoke of the adaptability of Russian-born painters which had enabled him and others to succeed in Paris he replied that they were indebted to French perceptiveness. 'If I, or any of us, had gone somewhere other than Paris, I doubt whether our talents would have been recognized—the French have such a sense of quality that they can discern even a suspicion of it.'

The following year in mid-July he again came to lunch at the Tate. Something set him talking about his likes and dislikes among his contemporaries, and he expressed himself simply and with vehemence: 'I loved Gris and Matisse; Picasso I wish I'd never known. Rouault disliked me as much as I disliked him. When he and I worked for Vollard our mutual dislike was so inflammable that Vollard had to keep us apart. Rouault was mad, bad—and religious.' Chagall expressed the wish to paint for a time in England, and I renewed my efforts to persuade him to make a series of views of London. The idea still seemed to attract him, but it was never carried out.

These two occasions had a slightly formal character. Next time we met Chagall he was at home and an altogether more casual atmosphere prevailed. Elizabeth and I visited Vence that autumn, and on the day of our arrival, 9 September 1954, we spent the afternoon at Les Collines, his house nearby. Even though a retrospective exhibition of his work had been held at the Tate six years before I did not fully appreciate his stature until I saw the paintings that he had repurchased or retained.

The paintings—of all periods—on the walls of Les Collines are the paintings of a master. 'I buy good examples when I can,' he said, 'but they're getting horribly expensive. Look at this bearded Christ I've just managed to get hold of. I did it in Russia before I'd seen any paintings at all, only photographs of them. But do you know that not for an instant in fifty years of painting have I been sure of myself? Everything for me has been uncertain, tentative and the way ahead unclear.'

Chagall's character is evidently one of extreme complexity, and above all of diffidence; he prefers an oblique approach to things, which appears to be in contradiction to the strong vein of naïvety in his work and to the simplicity of the first impression he gives. Admittedly my meetings with him have not been many, but he appears to me to be single-minded and benevolent.

Feeling that he was being a little too solemn, and in his preoccupation with his own uncertainties a little neglectful of his guests, he spoke, with a gentle smile, of Tate affairs in 1954: 'It takes talent to paint a picture, genius to sell one, but supreme judgement and courage', he smilingly said, 'to direct an art gallery.'

Chagall frankly expressed his continuing romantic love for Bella, his first wife, and the evident respect of his second wife for his feeling commanded our admiration. To Elizabeth she spoke of the agonizing doubts which Chagall suffered over his work and of the way these were exacerbated by the total confidence of their neighbour Picasso, who, when they met at the kiln where they both took their ceramics to be fired, even taunted her husband with his perplexities.

Chagall, more especially in his own home, has a friendly warmth and a wry fantastic humour, as well as a quick sympathy for the predicaments of his fellow human beings which makes his companionship a delight.

*

In the meanwhile I had paid a visit to one of the formidable objects of Chagall's dislike, when I spent some hours with Rouault in the afternoon of 23 June 1954—hours which for me passed all too quickly, for I revered him as one of the very few great masters of this century. Although 2 rue Emile Gilbert was the place where he both worked and lived I was not shown into the studio—I understood that almost no one was admitted—but was received instead in a perfectly tidy, very bourgeois drawing-room furnished solidly in Victorian oak. It might have been the waiting-room of a doctor. The only painting in sight, displayed upon an easel, was a newly-completed portrait of a woman, obviously not the work of my host. Here I was welcomed by Mlle. Isabelle Rouault; a moment later Rouault appeared and seated himself in a high-backed oak chair. The painter, eighty-three years old, was an arresting figure. His face, in particular the modelling of the square brow and the eyelids and the unusual pallor, seemed oddly familiar, until I remembered having been told that, especially in his early years, he made many studies from his own face, seen in a mirror, which he introduced into his paintings. The expression of the wide-open light blue eyes varied from vagueness to belligerence—a belligerence directed far backwards in time. He wore a white linen skull-cap, with a sharp central crease from crown to cranium, which at intervals he removed, crumpled on his knees and then replaced; a bright blue dressing-gown and a yellow scarf wound round his neck.

Being aware—reminded by his daughter perhaps—of my admiration for him, and that the Tate's first exhibition after the war was devoted to his work (and Braque's), he received me with marked benevolence, but he was preoccupied, unless his attention was momentarily arrested by some topic of special interest, by the past. To the present he seemed indifferent, as something unreal. The remembrance of events of his past life, on the contrary, quickly moved him to sardonic amusement or regret, to tenderness or anger —mostly to anger. Delivering his funeral oration, his friend the Abbé Morel spoke of Rouault's capacity for anger, 'which', he added, 'was always resolved in God's gentle pity'. This visitor, at least, saw much evidence of anger and none of resolution into pity. When I asked him whether he had ever been to England, he answered harshly, 'To England! No, never. You see, I've been in *prison* for so many years, a prison where the gaoler's name was Vollard.' The mention of the name of Vollard released a flood of bitter reminiscence: his voice was clear but he spoke with accelerating rapidity, often breaking into a Parisian argot which made him at times difficult to follow. I recall his saying that he was shut up from morning until night, a voluntary prisoner, by Vollard, who spied upon him and urged him constantly to ever greater output. Nothing of consequence, I fancy, was lost by my inability to follow the angry flood of Rouault's recollections, whose coherence suggested that they had been voiced many times before: he had no reason to treat a mere visitor with particular confidence. At the first pause I asked why he had entered into the agreement with Vollard that caused him so much distress. 'I was well-known long before,' he replied, shaking with rage, 'but when Vollard offered his terms, miserable as they were, I couldn't afford to refuse them. You see, I had my family to keep.'

Presently his rage was spent, and he had need of a subject which would evoke happier memories, and he talked of the master to whom he had shown an articulate, lifelong loyalty: Gustave Moreau. ' "A hermit", Degas remarked of him, "who knew the timetables of trains, the creator of Messalinas whose knowledge of woman was said to have been derived from the mother—latterly blind and deaf—whom he lived with and adored." He was a teacher of genius, a spiritual support,' Rouault continued, 'and life was a desert when he was no longer there. And when I call him a teacher of genius you must remember that there were certain standards in those days.

Bouguereau, Lefebvre, and the other academic greybeards, they were not such bad teachers either—especially by modern standards.' But after a time the need to express himself with love and reverence was satisfied and he began once again to need an object for the anger that came easily to him and he spoke at length of his lawsuits. 'You have forgotten', his daughter reminded him with a smile, 'the Vollard suits.' And he began to talk about the legal issues between himself and Vollard's heirs, but what he said about these issues, for someone who knew little about the matter, was confused, and presently his narrative petered out. If he could have forgotten Vollard, even for a moment! I thought he must be very tired, and I prepared to leave. I spoke about his work. 'You are very kind,' he replied, 'and I thank you, but I've had a hard, in many ways a bitter life, and the recognition that can mean much when one is young means little when one is old. Recognition came to me too late.'

*

From the previous year, when I was taken by Eugene Mollo, a White Russian former student of my father's at the Royal College of Art, to see Michel Larionov and Nathalie Goncharova, I rarely visited Paris without calling at the studio of this remarkable couple high up in a decrepit house, 6 rue Jacques Callot. At the time of my first visit, in June 1953, both were about seventy-two years of age but appeared even older. In spite of their age, their poverty and the manifold infirmities they suffered from, no one could have been more high-spirited. Partly because I was introduced by a common friend and partly because of the warmth of nature they shared, they immediately accepted me as a friend.

I was fascinated by this enclave of pre-revolutionary Russia. It was *haute bourgeoisie* (Goncharova's family was land-owning and her great-grandmother was the wife of Pushkin) but intellectual and radical. They lived together for most of their lives and refrained on principle from getting married until just before Goncharova's death in 1962. The studio was heaped so high with their possessions that the ancient floor might at any moment have collapsed beneath their weight; their disorder was so extreme, yet so full of an individual character, as to constitute almost a work of art, of a kind later known as 'assemblage'. But many of these possessions, so anarchically disposed—almost all of them pictures and publications—were of the most striking character. The profusion of paintings and drawings by both Larionov and Goncharova of a near-abstract rayonist and fully abstract order revealed to me something of the energy and assurance of pioneering painting in Russia before the First World War. In my ignorance I had supposed it somewhat tentative and exotic. (Kandinsky's early abstracts were of course painted after his departure from Russia.) Reading my thoughts, Goncharova said, 'Michel was making abstracts well before Kandinsky.' Larionov modestly disclaimed her assertion and pointed out household objects, difficult for others to discern, even when traced by Larionov's depreciatory finger, which, he claimed, figured in coloured drawings that looked entirely abstract to the innocent eye, made in 1906, 1907 and 1908. (The Tate owns one of these, 'White Drawing', made in 1907 and given by Eugene Mollo in 1958.) Almost as surprising as the paintings and drawings of these two was their collection of publications, which lay in dusty piles, some reaching almost to the ceiling, among them nearly all the avant-garde publications pertaining to Russian art before the Revolution—a collection, Eugene remarked, probably unique in Western Europe. Their vast disorderly accumulation of possessions, which they had long since ceased to attempt to control, had almost driven them out. So little room was there in the studio that on my first visit, when Goncharova regaled us with a strange-tasting drink from the bottom of a dusty bottle, she and I sat on a narrow bed and Larionov and Eugene each sat on a pile of publications, which, pulled forward like chairs, had evidently served as seats before.

When I had been there an hour I had the sensation that time had stood still: the Russian Revolution had yet to take place. I happened to remark to Goncharova that I was reading a newly published book on Turgeniev. 'Turgeniev!' she exclaimed. 'His family had an estate near ours', and she gossiped casually about a man who to me was as remote as an inhabitant of Parnassus. Neither on this nor on any of my subsequent visits was there any reference, however oblique, to the Revolution.

The gaiety of the household did not conceal its acute poverty, for which Eugene had prepared me. One of the purposes of our visit was to effect a modest amelioration of it, for he had offered to present one or two of their paintings to the Tate. I selected 'Nocturne' by him, and 'Autumn' and 'The Laundry' by her (the first two painted in 1910 and the third in 1912). Larionov later presented a drawing of Diaghilev. Their poverty and neglect, in a city famous for its recognition of talent, astonished me: they were greatly talented, they were pioneers of the by then dominant movement, most of whose pioneers—however inconsiderable—are acclaimed.

The paintings given jointly by Eugene and the artists were warmly welcomed both by the Tate Trustees and the British public, as distinguished examples of a movement entirely unrepresented in British public collections and negligibly elsewhere.

On a later visit Larionov and Goncharova told me, to my immense pleasure, that the showing of their first three paintings acquired by the Tate had brought them immediate recognition, of a kind that enabled them to find a ready sale for their work. A few years later I saw at a London dealer's a slight drawing of a kind that had littered the floor at 6 rue Jacques Callot: it was priced at £3,500.

Once they took me to a huge glass studio (which they had never mentioned to me before), derelict, but in a house with associations, they told me, with both Racine and Corneille, approached through a chaos of demolition and building operations. The place was packed with their early abstract and near-abstract work mostly done in Russia. It was among these dust-coated canvases, which looked as though they had suffered half a century's neglect, that I decided that there ought to be a Larionov–Goncharova exhibition in London. In principle they were delighted, but many difficulties presented themselves: the work of Goncharova was not shown until 1961 at the Arts Council Gallery; that of Larionov is still unshown. Larionov and Goncharova were gay and generous, candid and stoical and without vanity or malice: when Russians are good, how shining their goodness!

Only shortly before her death in 1962 and on the occasion of her long-deferred exhibition, Goncharova sent me a message offering an important example of her work, 'Spring Gardening', to the Tate. This was gratefully accepted.

*

Meetings with three other foreign artists whom I particularly admired always gave me pleasure: all were Italian, all sculptors, and all intermittently suffered criticism on similar grounds: Giacomo Manzù, Marino Marini and Emilio Greco.

Two years after making the acquaintance of Manzù in 1948, at the first Venice Biennale held after the war, Elizabeth and I visited his studio in Milan. It was as meticulously tidy and perfectly organized as that of Giacometti was anarchic. I found even more to admire in the sculptures I saw there than in those I already knew. There was a little dancer, a big figure barely finished, a new 'Cardinal', even finer than the one bought by the Tate, and most impressive of all, the Crucifixion studies in very low relief entered for the competition for the main doors of St. Peter's. Manzù told us that he had been stunned for a while by their rejection, but the nudity of the principal figures, the German helmets of the crucifiers, as well as the resemblance of a callously staring figure to a notori- ously fascist-sympathizing member of the Sacred College made rejection almost inevitable. These studies—expressing the unique momentousness of the event without sacrifice of naturalness, and with the utmost economy of means—I believe to be among the finest sculptures of the age. Manzù's designs were eventually accepted and he himself became a close friend of Pope John. Close friendship between a Pope and a major artist has of recent centuries been a rare phenomenon indeed.

On this same visit I also renewed acquaintance with Marino Marini—also first met at the same Biennale. These two sculptors, both so highly gifted and esteemed, with studios not far distant from each other, seemed to live in different worlds: each seemed sur- prised to be reminded by me of the existence of the other. They are very different kinds of men: Manzù is reserved, a little awkward and inarticulate; his highly original art, on account of its idealism, its elegance and its religious orientation—though he himself was losing his faith—has a deceptively traditional look. Marini faces life with an easy vigorous confidence, and his dynamic art, largely inspired by the sculpture of ancient China, sometimes looks a little more original than it is. To visit two sculptors of such stature within so brief a time was an experience not to be forgotten. Before the end of our visit the two of them met, briefly and, it seemed, almost as strangers, at a gathering of artists and collectors invited to meet us at the flat of Maurice Cardiff, British Council representative in Milan.

The immediate consequence of my visit was disappointing: at their October meeting the Tate Trustees declined to buy the Manzù 'Dancer' or the casts of the original models for the doors of St. Peter's (though they did buy three beautiful drawings, rather out of kindness for me, I suspected, than admiration); and 'Horse and Rider' and 'Horse'—both exceptionally fine works—by Marini were also declined. After this meeting as after so many others I felt desperately depressed by the inadequacy of my powers of persuasion. A little later I failed to secure a single vote for the Odilon Redon now in the Hulton collection: a highly original painter unrepresented in the national collections. Both Manzù and Marini, however, were represented before long at the Tate by admirable examples, and I even persuaded the Westminster Cathedral Art Committee to commission Manzù to make a bronze panel of Ste. Thérèse of Lisieux— a formidable undertaking!

Like Manzù, Emilio Greco suffers on account of the apparently traditional character of his work and its stylishness. Admittedly it has occasionally a distorting wilfulness and affectation about it, but there are very few sculptors alive capable of combining inventive range with intensity, expressiveness with harmony, as for example in the doors for Orvieto Cathedral which Greco had recently completed when we visited his studio in August 1963.

Manzù and Greco are conspicuous examples of artists sometimes regarded with reserve if not suspicion on account of the element of elegance in their work. I believe suspicion of elegance to be outdated, a survival of a prejudice that at the beginning of the century may well have served a useful purpose. At that time a revolution was in its early stage, when, like other revolutions, it was found convenient to reject more of the qualities of what it was supplanting than was necessary to enable it to fulfil its own long-term purpose: that of displacing an art that tended to be an expression of the artist's ideals with an art that was, whatever its imperfections, a direct revelation of himself. This, of course, is the roughest possible approximation to a common factor in the multifarious forms of twentieth-century art. It was inevitable that the fauves and the dadaists, and a little less positively the cubists, should have regarded elegance as abhorrent. Even so relatively traditional a figure as Sickert used to declare that taste was the enemy of art (an axiom he was apt to disregard when he had a brush in his hand). Elegance, however, is a fairly constant human aspiration, and for a revolution that has long since overwhelmingly prevailed to exclude it is to make a sacrifice without justification. Elegance is in fact gradually reappearing, but where it shows itself too frankly it still brings upon itself the disapproval of the 'Old Bolsheviks' and of many of those whose opinions were formed under their ascendancy.

Greco has given Elizabeth and me as much pleasure as a man as he has as a sculptor and draughtsman: he is perceptive, considerate, endlessly benevolent, and I believe without malice; he shows an ardent, almost unquestioning loyalty in friendship that perhaps owes something to his Sicilian heritage. I could not imagine his failing a friend in trouble.

*

Matisse I never had the privilege of meeting, but in Paris in mid-summer 1955 I found myself very near him. In response to an invitation from his daughter, Mme. Duthuit, I called at her house in the rue Miromesnil. 'If you've an hour to spare I've something to show you', she said, 'that I think would interest you,' and she drove me to an old studio of her father's by the Porte de Versailles. The studio was exactly as he had left it (he had died only the previous year). As we stood for a moment at the door, the place seemed so much a workshop in full production that we instinctively paused, as though to await the approaching footsteps of the master. 'This', said Mme. Duthuit, 'is what I wanted you to see', and she pointed to a series of six-foot high plasters of a woman's back, the celebrated 'Nu de Dos', on which Matisse had been periodically engaged between 1909 and 1929. The sight surprised me, for the series before me consisted of four, whereas three had long been familiar to me (indeed the Trustees were interested in their purchase) but I had never heard of a fourth. 'None of the family', Mme. Duthuit explained, 'had any notion of the existence of No. II of the series; we discovered it here a few months after my father's death. I was astonished, because during the last two years of his life I had been with him constantly, doing what I could to free him to devote all his failing energies to his work.'

We went back to the rue Miromesnil, where I was presented to Mme. Matisse, a very old lady with courtly manners.

The Matisse family, the two ladies explained, were willing to allow the Tate to buy the 'Nu de Dos'—including No. II which, made about 1913, added greatly to the intelligibility of the series—for £11,500—a most generous offer. 'We want to make sure', Mme. Duthuit said, 'that one set at least should remain in Europe—and where better than under your roof.' By 1957 all four had been bought.

Another visit I paid at the same time to a painter's studio set off a chain of circumstances which led to a development of the utmost consequence for the Tate. We lacked any representation whatever of the futurist movement. Noticing by chance Severini's name on the door of a studio I called in the hope of doing something to remedy this lack. Severini, who received me most kindly, was engaged largely on mosaics (to my surprise he said that he had never heard of Boris Anrep) and in writing his memoirs. Among his paintings was 'Madame S.' (a portrait of his wife), a splendid example of his futurist period. 'I've given an option to a German collector,' he said, 'but I'd rather it were at the Tate.' In the face of other commitments, and in spite of our utmost efforts, we were unable to raise the modest sum he named: £2,000. It was the loss of 'Madame S.', as I shall narrate, that inspired Robert Adeane, a Tate Trustee, to give effect to an idea that had been in the air for a number of years by founding the Friends of the Tate, a body which has brilliantly enriched the collection and over which he has continued to preside with dynamic energy and great personal generosity.

In the meanwhile 'Madame S.' was put up for sale by Severini— at a higher price than we had been asked—at a dealer's gallery in Paris. I asked the dealer how long a time had elapsed between the portrait's being placed on view and its sale. 'I suppose', he replied reflectively, 'about seven seconds.' Severini had allowed the Tate seven months.

CHAPTER SEVEN

CHURCHILL

IN *Brave Day, Hideous Night* I related the circumstances in which, at a private dinner at the Royal Academy on 16 February 1949, I received an invitation to lunch with Churchill at Chartwell four days later. In the early morning after the dinner he telephoned to confirm the invitation, and to tell me what train to take. I wondered at the courtesy of a man so burdened with responsibilities who instead of sending a message spoke on the telephone himself.

When I arrived at Chartwell no car stood in front of the house, and from the hall no sound was heard. Upon a table reposed an object familiar from innumerable photographs: a wide-brimmed, grey painting-hat. I was contemplating this celebrated object with respect, as though it were the hat of a king sent to represent him on some ceremonial occasion, when I heard soft padding steps approach, and presently, dressed in his sky-blue siren-suit and shod in soft black slippers on which his initials were worked in gold, there appeared my benignly welcoming host.

Before lunch we visited his studio, the long narrow room brightly lit by high windows along two walls, from which he moved to another later on. Upon a long narrow table standing parallel to the room were ranged tidy rows of paint-tubes; beside it was the great terrestrial globe, a gift, he told me, from the American Army. Except for this globe, there was throughout the whole house a conspicuous absence of any display of trophies, historic battle orders and the like.

During our first visit to his studio Churchill told me that he would be grateful for any criticism of his painting I might care to make. 'Speak, I pray, with absolute frankness,' he urged as we went in to lunch. As soon as we sat down he began to speak of Sickert: 'He came to stay here and in a fortnight he imparted to me all his considered wisdom about painting. He had a room specially darkened to work in, but I wasn't an apt pupil, for I rejoice in the highest lights and the brightest colours.' He spoke with appreciation of Sickert's

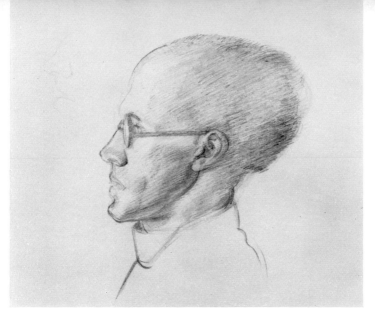

Father Vincent Turner, S.J., 1944, chalk, by
Charles Mahoney

Albert Houthuesen, 1927, pencil, by
Sir William Rothenstein

Richard and Lucy leaving Westminster Cathedral,
1959

knowledge of music-halls, and he sang a nineteenth-century ballad he had learnt from him; and he sang it from beginning to end. 'But I think the person who taught me most about painting was William Nicholson. I noticed you looking, I thought with admiration, at the drawing upstairs he made of my beloved cat.' During lunch his most memorable remark did not concern painters or painting. Upon his inquiring why I declined his offer of a cigar, I replied that every man should possess one virtue; the only one I could certainly claim was that I did not smoke. To which he instantly rejoined, 'There is no such thing as a negative virtue. If I have been of any service to my fellow men, it has never been by self-repression, but always by self-expression.' Back in the studio, fortified by half a bottle of champagne, I found less alarming his invitation to give my opinion of his work without reserve. In the course of the afternoon we must have looked at every one of the numerous paintings in the studio and the few that hung in various other parts of the house. Passing a bust of the young Napoleon, Churchill murmured, 'Those sublime features, the most beautiful in history.'

Churchill was so genial and so exhilarating a companion that before I had been with him long the notion of speaking with absolute frankness seemed as natural as it had earlier seemed temerarious. My first detailed criticism of one of his paintings had an unexpected, indeed a startling, result. About a landscape, a wood on the margin of a lake, I offered the opinion that the shore was far too shallow, too lightly modelled and far too pale in tone to support the weight of the trees with their massive boles and their dense, dark foliage, so that, instead of growing up out of the earth, they weighed it down. 'Oh,' he said, 'I can put that right at once; it would take less than a quarter of an hour,' and he began to look out the appropriate brushes and colours. 'But this painting, surely,' I said, 'must be among your earliest.' 'I did it about twenty years ago', he conceded. 'Well then,' I protested, 'surely it's impossible for you to recapture the mood in which you painted it, or indeed your whole outlook of those days.' 'You really are convinced of that?' he grumbled, abandoning his intention of repainting the picture with evident reluctance. This was the first of several occasions when I had to persuade him to desist from repainting an early work in consequence of some criticism of mine. 'If it weren't for painting,' he said as we left the studio, 'I couldn't live; I couldn't bear the strain of things.'

K

When I praised his portrait by Orpen for the closeness of observation it showed, he said, 'Yes, it's good; he painted it just after I'd had to withdraw our forces from the Dardanelles, and I'd got turfed out; in fact when he painted it I'd lost pretty well everything.'

It was an extraordinary experience, this first visit to the studio at Chartwell, above all because of the combination in the artist's temperament of extremes of humbleness and confidence. I learnt to refrain from too positively constructive comment in case he should impulsively put it into effect—he evidently splashed down paint without any inhibition at all, and used whatever aids he judged most appropriate to the work in hand. He preferred to work direct from his subject (and an open-air subject for choice) but he worked on occasion from photographs and even had negatives projected on to sensitized canvases. The paintings he showed me were energetic, yet they lacked intensity, and he was prone to an excessive use of acid greens. When I observed that the effect of these greens was sharpened by the chilly elephant-grey frames he favoured, he said that I must come to see him in London to discuss the whole problem of framing; but would I there and then choose some paintings for the Summer Exhibition at Burlington House. When I had done so he gave me a puckish look and said, 'Certain of your choices coincide with those of Sir Alfred.' Then we talked about prose style. 'People are sometimes shocked by my use of slang,' he said, 'but the shortest words are usually the best—and the simplest constructions.'

Churchill behaved as though I had done him a favour by coming to Chartwell. 'It was awfully good of you', he said, 'to have helped me by giving me so much of your time.' Then a double whisky was brought in to fortify me on my homeward journey and the arrival of the taxi to take me to the station was announced. 'There's plenty of time,' he said, 'and there are one or two more of my daubs I'd like to show you.'

When I asked the taxi-driver whether we were going to catch the train he said, 'It's always the same, so I give visitors a bit of extra notice.'

As I was leaving he asked me whether I would do him the honour of accepting a copy of his *Painting as a Pastime*. Upon my saying that I should be delighted, he sent his soldier servant to bring one from a place which he designated. On his return with a copy Churchill said irritably, 'No, not one of those; one of the *special* copies.' When it was explained to him that there were no special copies left at Chartwell, he did not offer me that which had been brought, but a few days later a 'special' copy, inscribed and beautifully bound, arrived for me by post.

At the Academy Dinner that year Munnings had associated Churchill with a storm of abuse he directed at 'modern art' in general and Picasso and Matisse, also Henry Moore, in particular, saying that he and Winston were walking in the street and Winston had said to him, 'If we met Picasso or Matisse we'd give them a running kick, wouldn't we?'

Not until the following spring did I pay another visit to Chartwell. In the meanwhile, at the suggestion of one of his friends, I had written a brief appreciation of Churchill as an artist.[1] In view of the privileged circumstances in which I had come by my knowledge of his work, it was of course out of the question to publish it without his consent. I accordingly sent him a draft, and shortly afterwards there came an invitation to spend 11 March at Chartwell. The prospect of going over the draft with the subject of it was one that I did not relish at all. I was not sure whether he had read it, but he gave me leave to publish it. 'I just hoped you'd come here for a talk and once again I'd be most obliged for your advice on what I should send this year to the Academy.'

I at once asked him whether there was any truth in the remarks that Munnings had attributed to him about kicking Picasso and Matisse. 'Quite untrue,' he said. 'I was angry. I wrote to Sir Alfred. All quite untrue, and besides, *I never walk in the street.* Speaking of Presidents of the Royal Academy,' he asked, 'what sort of man is Kelly?' (who had recently succeeded Munnings). 'I trust that you will find him easier to deal with over that vexed Chantrey matter.'

On my previous visit to Chartwell I had been alone with Churchill, but on this occasion there was a family party, Mrs. Churchill, their son Randolph, and Mrs. Esmond Romilly, besides his friend William Deakin (who had helped him with research in connection with his book on Marlborough). The conversation turned, for some reason, on my old friend John Strachey, who had been Secretary of State for War in the outgoing Labour Government. 'I don't impugn his loyalty,' Churchill said, 'but surely there are able men beyond suspicion of sympathy with communism: it's wrong to impose a

---

[1] Included in a collection of essays entitled *Winston Spencer Churchill, Servant of Crown and Commonwealth* (Cassell), published as an eightieth birthday tribute on 30 November 1954.

stricter security standard upon technicians, messengers and so forth than upon Ministers.' 'But you *should* impugn his loyalty,' said Randolph; 'why not in your next speech?' 'Curious as you seem to find it, Randolph,' his father replied, 'I write my own speeches.' I asked him what sort of notes he prepared for his speeches. 'Don't give me away,' he said; 'my secret weapon is a pair of long-range spectacles, which enable me to read the brief notes, with certain paragraphs written out in full, lying on the table in front of me. But if I were young and beginning again I'd first make five-minute speeches from memory, without any notes except of facts, and by practice be able gradually to lengthen the time.' Speaking of his occasional spontaneous oratory, he said, 'I let out a number of ideas, and before very long they are breeding among themselves.' When I asked him whether an oration, for example, to the United States Congress, with the weighty issues involved and the infinitely complex arrangements for its delivery and dissemination, did not make an alarming ordeal, he replied that for him to make a public speech was always something of an ordeal and that the attendant circumstances added little to it. (Not long afterwards, at the lunch given by Cassells for their authors after Churchill had laid the foundation-stone of their new offices in Red Lion Square, I was able to judge how nervous he could be. The lady sitting between us had tried to read the little sheet of notes he had made in preparation for his speech. As soon as he became aware of what she was doing he slapped it face downwards on to the table. It was evident that the prospect of delivering even a brief speech and on a relatively unimportant occasion made him tense; and his impatience with his neighbour was not the only symptom of nerves he showed.)

There was something deeply impressive about the immediacy and force of Churchill's reaction to injustice. When Mrs. Romilly described a bye-law requiring certain municipal tenants to get rid of their pet animals or quit their premises, and an inequitable and concealed property-tax, he said he was prepared to raise both matters in the Commons. When he discussed politics he showed no traces of rancour or even bias against his opponents. 'If social meetings between Government and Opposition continued as they had during the visit of the French President', he said, 'I told Attlee that there would shortly be a Coalition.' Towards the end of lunch he began to look tired and old, and his deafness became more evident, but all the time, on a certain level, he maintained an unsleeping alertness. When he was deep in conversation with Mrs. Churchill and myself either Randolph or Bill Deakin quoted something in Latin to the other. 'When I was at Harrow,' he said, 'that quotation went like this', and he gave a different version of it.

After lunch he took me off to his studio and we went through his pictures. 'There's nothing quite recent,' he said, 'as I've been unable to paint during the election' (the recently held election at which the Conservatives had been returned to power with himself as Prime Minister).

On the whole he showed little judgement about his own painting (which means no more than that his assessments differed from mine), and he seemed equally surprised by the objects of my praise and censure. There was a landscape we were agreed about in which he had tried, and with success, to capture 'the emanation of light over water', but about another canvas, a still-life with a figure of Buddha, which he called 'Life and Death', we differed sharply. He was pleased with it and told me that it was his firm intention to send it to the Summer Exhibition, to which I replied that it might win him popular success but it would not add to his reputation as a painter. Nothing I said diminished his satisfaction, and off the picture went to Burlington House.

It was in Burlington House at the Academy Dinner in 1950 that I next met Churchill. When I arrived he and Munnings were in conversation. Churchill greeted me and Munnings said irritably, 'You don't know Rothenstein!' 'Why not?' Churchill asked, and he said to me, 'I don't like this standing about; let's sit down.' I deliberately placed two chairs beneath Stanley Spencer's 'Resurrection, Port Glasgow', and in order to evoke his comments I pointed to the back-stretching arm of a figure in the left foreground, saying that if the adverse critics of the picture saw, for instance, such an arm on the murky wall of some church in Italy they would recognize it as masterly. 'But it is incorrectly articulated,' he objected, extending his own left arm in a similar position; 'you must admit that.' 'I don't admit it,' I had to reply, 'and I have the advantage of being able to see both arms.' 'I concede that,' he said sternly, 'but I still don't like the picture; and moreover, if that is the Resurrection, then give me Eternal Sleep.' At the banquet my immediate neighbours were Stanley Spencer himself and R. O. Dunlop. Stanley, in exalted spirits and oblivious of his surroundings, described a bathe in a clear pool in Macedonia in the First World War and how he saw the sun from beneath the surface of the water; he compared, most eloquently, our life to the water and truth to the sun. Poor Dunlop, already rather drunk, was moved by this analogy to the verge of tears. But Stanley was not at all amused when I repeated the comment Churchill had just made about his 'Resurrection', and never forgetful of any unfriendly criticism he irascibly recalled an earlier remark of Churchill's: 'If Mr. Spencer's work represents enlightenment then we should be grateful for our present obscurity.' This remark must have been a long time rankling, for Stanley added, 'I felt impelled, just before the Battle of Britain, to wire to Churchill, "How about our obscurity? Not so good now, is it?"'

In the second volume of my autobiography I mentioned a visit to Churchill at No. 10 Downing Street, on 25 March 1954, and described the part of our conversation that related to the difficulties which the Tate was undergoing at the time.

It seemed natural to find him in his blue siren-suit and initialled slippers at Chartwell but incongruous at No. 10—incongruous but none the worse for that. 'Once again,' he said, 'I should be much obliged if you would help me select four works for the Summer Exhibition. They're putting pressure on me to send more, but I won't.' Among the four we selected was an energetic landscape, made recently on the south coast of France. 'This, and one other, was done in oils over a tempera base,' he explained, 'in only two hours—after my stroke.' Among the works that I particularly admired was one of an orchard; my admiration, Churchill told me, was shared by Gerald Kelly, but he thought little of it himself.

In the meanwhile we were looking through stacks of canvases and once again we examined one of his two recent landscapes, two big trees blown about by a high wind, and a small tree between them: 'Look!' he said, 'they're hitting each other properly, aren't they? And there's the little neutral, or a child perhaps, his parents are fighting over. I think I'll call it "The Custody of the Child".'

I congratulated him on a recent speech, and he said, 'They can ring down the curtain whenever they want, but as long as it is up, I go through the appropriate motions.'

Before I left he asked me how I was getting on with the Royal Academy over the vexed Chantrey affair, and what sort of President Kelly would make. I answered that, although he would certainly at times be a difficult President for his fellow-Academicians, he was a highly civilized man and a perceptive judge of painting, and that he'd discourage the philistinism that Munnings continually whipped up.

Five days later I was again invited to No. 10 Downing Street. The Prime Minister was much preoccupied with the South of France landscape that we had discussed on my recent visit. He had carried out the modifications to the sea and the rocks which, under heavy pressure from him, I had suggested, and he had decided, on further consideration, to title it 'A Family Quarrel'—'just look at the way they are hitting one another,' he said gleefully, pointing to the boughs, tangling as they were bent by the wind. 'I might', he remarked suddenly, 'hold a one-man exhibition after I retire.' When I asked him how President Eisenhower painted he said, 'Ike paints pretty well: how I wish he and I might set up our easels side by side.'

Then he spoke of his deeper preoccupations. 'Compared with the problems posed by hydrogen and atom bombs every other is trivial,' he said; 'I've no great faith in negotiation, but it is' (and here he spoke with great emphasis) *the only possible course open to us*', but he alluded hopefully to a project of President Eisenhower's for the formation of an international atomic unit.

That day he was less averse to answering questions than on most other occasions. 'I've had so long an experience of responsibility,' he said, when I asked him whether the need for making great decisions affected him physically; 'only slightly: but it preys upon the mind. I experience fear and anxiety, often.'

As we looked together at his paintings he sought repeated assurances that those we had selected on my previous visit were fit to go the Summer Exhibition. He did not follow his usual habit of seeing me to the door, but instead bent over the first of the canvases to go in order to sign it. 'This paint,' he zestfully observed, 'is the blackest black.'

In the winter of 1955 a representative of the Parliamentary Press Gallery came to consult me about a proposed presentation to Churchill of a drawing of the House of Commons in session, in which he was to figure speaking, as seen from the Press Gallery, and he asked me to suggest an artist. I proposed that the commission should be given to Edward Ardizzone. This advice was followed, and it was for this reason no doubt that I was invited to the luncheon held at the Savoy on 28 February to celebrate the presentation. According to the Chairman of the Press Gallery some of the members

had misgivings about the drawing—indeed it didn't in the least conform to the pattern of the traditional 'political caricature'—but to
their relief the Prime Minister, 'after looking at it steadily for nearly
half an hour', approved it.

Before luncheon was served Churchill invited me to talk with
him. The President of the Royal Academy, Professor Albert
Richardson, it appeared, had made some proposals with which he
was thoroughly dissatisfied, about which he sought my opinion. He
then asked me whether I had seen his portrait by Graham Sutherland
(he alluded to the portrait presented to him by Members of both
Houses of Parliament which had provoked a violent controversy). I
replied that on account of the active part that Sutherland had played
in the attack on the Tate I had deliberately avoided seeing it, being
determined not to involve myself in the controversy in the slightest
degree. Rumours of his extreme distaste for the portrait were
widely current, but I was surprised by the vehemence with which he
spoke about it. 'I think the time has come,' he concluded, 'for an
artist to give some consideration to the *subject* of a portrait, instead
of looking over the wilderness of his subject hoping to discern there
some glimmer of his own genius.' This portrait was a subject to
which he often reverted. On a later occasion I must have suggested
that his feelings about it were disproportionate, for he said, 'Haven't
you noticed that the pain one suffers is by no means necessarily
proportionate to its cause?'

Churchill made a delightful speech, in which, although no names
were mentioned, he dealt with much the same theme, namely, the
prime importance in portraiture of respect for the subject. After
speaking at some length about the painting of portraits, he concluded
by saying that he would say nothing about painting in the presence
of such an authority as I!

While I was still in bed on the morning of 3 March, Churchill
telephoned to ask whether I would come to Chartwell the next day;
in order to be able to do so, I postponed until the following night a
projected journey to Scotland. Next morning I found him dissatisfied to the point of anxiety by Professor Richardson's proposals
for his representation at the Summer Exhibition that year. I was not
surprised, for all five canvases were trivial little bits of good taste,
none of them affording a hint of the energy and closeness of observation that marked his best work. One of the five Professor Richardson
had suggested should be trimmed, which further disturbed

Churchill. Together we chose instead some more robust and characteristic works, to his manifest relief.

Explaining that his chef was away, he said that we were going to have lunch with his daughter Mary and her husband Christopher Soames who lived nearby.

After lunch Churchill suggested we should look at his paintings (with all of which I supposed myself already familiar), but instead of taking me back to the house he led me—past a wall and a cottage which he had largely built himself—to an outbuilding where I had never been before. (For our walk he wore, over his siren-suit, a white overcoat with a light fur collar.) The interior walls of this place were entirely covered with his paintings, to which in our many conversations about his work he had never alluded. Among these were some of his most interesting canvases, including two pictures of trees seen through drifting mist, made at Roehampton about 1919; also a self-portrait, as well as portraits of Arthur Balfour and his sister, done from photographs. The two mist-veiled trees had a magical touch, to which he himself, however, seemed entirely unresponsive. Later we returned to the house to reconsider the works provisionally selected for the Summer Exhibition. He was eager to show the spirited wind-buffeted trees that I had seen the year before, and now definitely christened 'The Custody of the Child';[1] as well as an ambitious but, to my thinking, unsuccessful 'Bottlescape', of 1932.

Talk about painting was punctuated by comments, surprisingly candid, about Cabinet colleagues and other figures in public life. Press reports that when Lord Attlee had fainted at some function in Buckingham Palace he had ostentatiously offered help, he said, had greatly angered him; and with particular justification, I think, for he never in my hearing spoke of Lord Attlee without expressions of liking and regard.

Ever since I had come to know Churchill's painting I had been convinced that we should have an example at the Tate. I readily admit that the thought entered my mind that it would be an acquisition fascinating in the way in which, for instance, a landscape by the Elder Pitt would be, but the chief consideration was that if one of the very best could be secured, it would be an acquisition worthy in its own right. This last consideration was crucial, for Churchill was an untaught and often an impetuous artist, whose way

[1] This picture when shown in a retrospective exhibition of his work at Burlington House in 1959 was dated 1956 (instead of 1954) in the catalogue.

of life involved continuous interruption of his painting; only a small proportion of his pictures therefore seemed to me worthy of a place in the national collection. Up to that time he had retained by far the greater part of his production, and his best pictures were still almost all in his own possession. If for any reason this situation were to change, and his pictures to be scattered, it might have become impossible to obtain one of the very best, in which case I would have felt bound to advise against his representation. In May 1955 I submitted these considerations to the Tate Board, and it was agreed that I should explore the possibilities of making a purchase, the Board considering that his resignation as Prime Minister removed an obstacle to his representation. I accordingly wrote about the matter to Churchill, who invited me to Chartwell for 18 July.

My host welcomed me still wearing his dressing-gown, then left me to look through a long rack of his paintings, situated in an upstairs room recently equipped as a studio, the big room where he formerly painted having been converted into a drawing-room. At lunch he seemed at first apathetic and deaf. After a few moments his interest was aroused and he became cheerful and animated. I had told the Trustees that I had somehow formed the impression that he would either decline to allow the Tate to acquire one of his pictures, or else he would offer to present one. The Trustees proved wiser than I, for it quickly became apparent, if matters were to be brought to a conclusion, that it was essential that the Gallery should offer to buy a picture. It was not less apparent that he was unwilling to sell, but that, assured of the Trustees' willingness to buy, he would be happy to present one, provided that he was assured that extraneous considerations had no part in our interest in his work. I explained that while I believed he was aware of my own long-standing admiration, the Trustees had been naturally sensitive about making an approach to the Prime Minister to whom several of them owed their appointments. At this he grinned broadly and said, 'So you think it's all right, do you, now that I've been kicked out? Not,' he continued in a grimmer, almost challenging tone, 'that they could have forced me to go before I wanted to.' When asked whether there were not great compensations in freedom from public responsibilities that left little time for private pursuits, he gave a doubtful grunt.

The next instant I realized how trite and foolish my question was when he began to speak of his *History of the English-Speaking Peoples*; for of the many qualities that combined to make up this towering figure none was more extraordinary than his capacity to contemplate, to create, to study, to engage in numerous and varied pursuits, while playing a foremost part in the affairs of the entire world. He complained of the pressure exerted upon him by his publishers, Messrs. Cassell, to complete his *History* (their chairman had told me of the gigantic, the unprecedented scale of his proof-corrections). I asked him whether he looked forward to any degree of formal integration with the United States, and he said, 'No, our intimate union can be better preserved if we remain apart.' Towards the end of lunch he was told that there was a telephone call from Bernard Baruch in New York, and his soldier servant asked him if he wished to take it. 'No,' he said; 'I'm more interested in the sweet being served hot.' Immediately after lunch he showed me what was perhaps his earliest, at least his earliest surviving, essay as an artist, a little water-colour of a carriage, made when he first visited the United States as a young officer, in Jerome Park, New York. This must by many years predate the copy in oils of a Daubigny, belonging to his nephew, John Spencer-Churchill, who told me that he believed it was his earliest painting. Upstairs in his studio he declared his intention, however, of devoting more time to painting, and of working on a larger scale, and he showed me, with enthusiasm, a device he had invented, a cellophane cover with a narrow frame fitting over a canvas enabling trial passages to be put in, and so light that it could be carried to the site; also a new brand of tempera obtained from Switzerland. We chose three paintings from which the Trustees were welcome to any one they pleased, which he would regard it as a privilege, he said, to present to the Gallery. The selection made, he invited me to join him in feeding his swans.

On my way out he expressed his admiration for the Ardizzone 'House of Commons in Session', doubtless ignorant of my connection with the commissioning of it. As he showed me into his car he observed, lighting another cigar, 'It's a mistake for anyone who leads an active life not to smoke: it's a unique sedative.'

On the morning of the following Thursday, 21 July, I was deep in the complex preparations for the afternoon's Board Meeting, when he telephoned, asking me to go to see him as soon as possible at his London house, 28 Hyde Park Gate. I found him in bed smoking an immense cigar; a box containing others stood on his bedside table. He had been giving much thought, he said, to the selection of his paintings for consideration by the Tate and he asked me to tell the

Board of his own strong preference for 'The Loup River, Alpes Maritimes'. When I remarked on the absence of 'The Orchard', which he had promised on Monday that the Board should at least 'see'—though it was understood it was not to be his sole work in the Gallery—he said emphatically, 'I can't let that be seen in any circumstances.' It was most singular, this aversion to one of his most beautiful pictures. The reason for his change of intention may not have been aesthetic: I gathered that Gerald Kelly had tried to secure it for the Dulwich Gallery, but that Churchill had refused to part with it; and he possibly felt that to let it go to the Tate might have offended Kelly. 'I'll sign whichever picture your Trustees accept. And I should be most obliged if you would let me know their decision by telephone this evening.'

In his bedroom there was a green bird in a cage. Presently there was a tap on the door and Lady Churchill asked for the bird. 'Come in, my dear; I've Sir John Rothenstein with me.' 'But I *can't*,' she said; 'I'm in my dressing-gown.' On my way out I found Mr. Patrickson, who made Churchill's picture frames, and we had a brief talk about mouldings and colours while he drove the three selected pictures and me to the Tate.

After the Board Meeting I telephoned to tell him that 'The Loup River' had been accepted, and with the utmost pleasure. This painting, in my opinion one of his best, was made in 1930, the site lying about 500 yards from where the main Cagnes to Grasse road crosses the river, and it exemplifies his unusual perception of light effects over water.

On my return to London on 23 February 1956, from a visit to the United States, I found an urgent message from Churchill asking me to go down to Chartwell the very next morning.

Sir Winston seemed indifferent and infirm, but as on other occasions his spirits revived over lunch, and before it was half through he was alert and genial as ever. Always retentive of matters that had annoyed him, he referred, although without mentioning Munnings by name, to his association of himself with abuse of Picasso and Matisse, and as though by way of an additional repudiation he described how on a recent visit to France he had been studying books on Cézanne, Van Gogh and certain of their contemporaries and had even made some copies of illustrations of paintings by Cézanne.

For some reason (perhaps because President Eisenhower was

also an amateur painter) the conversation turned to politics, and he said he thought that Eisenhower would not run for President again. He showed a tolerant interest in my observation that whether he wished or not he was probably under heavy pressure to do so from the Republicans, his candidature offering their only opportunity of winning the election. 'I perceive', he said, 'that you're a *Democrat*', and when I asked whether it was not the case that British Governments got on better with Democratic than Republican Administrations he admitted that this on the whole was true but he added, 'I couldn't get on better with anyone than with Ike.' When I mentioned the increasing goodwill towards this country I had found on my recent visit to the United States, he said grimly, 'We need it all— every bit of it.'

We then walked across the garden to the outhouse where the majority of his paintings were kept, held in their places on the walls by moveable slats, a device of his own invention. There was the poetic 'Orchard', which I urged him to bequeath to the Tate. He made no promise, but smiled, evidently less displeased than formerly by my praise of it.

That afternoon his mood was new to me: it was one of gentle sadness. He was evidently much preoccupied with his *History of the English-Speaking Peoples*, the first volume being due to appear that spring, and he showed me an advance copy of the American edition, saying that he hoped it would unite Britain and the United States more closely, make the United States more aware of the extent to which she was the guardian of our common traditions and heritage, and that it might become a text-book for schools. When he spoke of having begun it fifteen years ago and been unable to complete it, he seemed pleased when I pointed out that the delay was providential for his purpose, as the United States was ready as she never was before to undertake such responsibilities. 'It isn't so much the writing of a book of such wide scope that presents the difficulties: it is the sheer weight of the organization involved—but I'm glad to have something such as this to occupy me.' The bitter weather, he complained, had compelled him to postpone a painting holiday in the South of France. He sent me back to London in his car, an extraordinary rug, a Union Jack made apparently out of thick bearskin, wrapped round my knees.

During his last years I had the privilege of Churchill's company less frequently, partly, I believe, because for one reason or another he had not been able, in retirement, to realize his ambition of giving more time to painting. Almost invariably after the Academy Dinner he sent to ask me to accompany him round a part of the exhibition. In the course of such a perambulation in 1956, when Munnings had embarrassed his fellow Academicians by releasing to the press a statement that this was the worst Academy ever, dominated by 'young brutes', and that he declined to attend the dinner, Churchill told me that he 'sharply disapproved', also of my inclusion in what Munnings called a 'satiric' picture—a harmless but silly caricatural conversation piece which he showed that year.

One of the paradoxical features of the private character of Churchill was his aversion—and it was a passionate aversion—to any aggressiveness, hostility, ridicule, unkindness or discourtesy that had not an imperative justification. Perhaps there is no paradox in the passion for peace in a man with an experience of war unique in his generation.

In the course of another such perambulation after the dinner the following year, he asked me abruptly, 'Are the President and Council *bound* to accept *any* work submitted by an R.A.?' I told him that I understood that they rarely exercised their right of exclusion. Then he began to speak about his portrait by Ruskin Spear hanging in the exhibition, which he obviously disliked, and when somebody came up to talk to him he evidently still had much to say about it; later on I saw him refuse to shake hands with Spear.

The key to the understanding of Churchill's own painting is to be found, I believe, in a few sentences in his essay, *Painting as a Pastime*. These explain the seeming contradiction between the known personality and experience of the painter, and the character of the work; between the man profoundly and consistently pre-occupied with human affairs, above all in their political and military aspects, and in the small, often sunny landscapes in which there is no intimation of struggle or tragedy, and in which, indeed, man rarely figures at all. For many people his gay, brilliantly coloured little canvases seem to bear no relation to their creator, but such people make insufficient allowance for the difficulties of the art of painting. Had the fairies stuck a paintbrush into his hand instead of a pen into one and a sword into the other, had he learnt while still a boy to draw and to paint, had he dedicated an entire laborious lifetime to the tempering of his powers, and to the disciplining of his visual imagination, he would have been equipped to express a large part of himself, instead of a few facets. He would have painted big pictures (it is significant that in his essay he calls pictures 'great' when the context shows that he means 'big'). There can be no doubt that he would have depicted human beings and their environments, above all great public events. Fully equipped, he would probably have been what in the age of Reynolds was called a 'history' painter. His circumstances were in fact entirely different. He was a very late starter; he had neither the training nor the leisure necessary to develop his talents to the full. He did not undertake heroic themes, figures in action—many figures, perhaps, in vigorous action—he did not undertake them because they demanded what the circumstances of his public life denied him: the long daily experience of painting culminating in technical mastery.

Churchill's precise awareness of his limitations is implicit in the sentences which give the key to his illuminating essay.

The painter must choose between the rapid impression, fresh and warm and living, but probably deserving only of a short life, and the cold, profound, intense effort of memory, knowledge, and will-power, prolonged perhaps for weeks, from which a masterpiece can alone result. It is much better not to fret too much about the latter. Leave to the masters of art trained by a lifetime of devotion the wonderful process of picture-building and picture-creation. Go out into the sunlight and be happy with what you see.

This awareness led him to cultivate the possibilities open to him with the utmost assiduity and resource. He was therefore able to do much more than enjoy himself in the sunlight. The skilful choice of subjects within his range to which he could respond ardently enabled him to paint pictures that convey and enhance delight and are distinguished by their painterly qualities; pictures, too, that have an intimate and direct relation to his outlook on life. In these there comes surging irrepressibly his sheer joy in the simple beauties of nature: water, still, bubbling, or agitated by wind; snow immaculate and crisp; trees, dark with the density of their foliage or dappled by sunlight; fresh flowers; distant mountains, and, above all, sunlight at its fiercest. The high peaks of his achievement, in my opinion, are 'The Goldfish Pool at Chartwell' (1948), 'Chartwell under Snow' (1947), 'Cannes Harbour, Evening' (1923) and, I am happy to add, 'The Loup River' (1930) now hanging in the Tate. These express, with insight and candour, his exultant enjoyment of living. 'I look

forward', he said, 'to a leisure hour with pleasurable agitation:
it's so difficult to choose between writing, reading, painting, brick-
laying, and three or four other things I want to do.'

The years did not diminish his eagerness to acquire new skills.
During the early 'sixties, when I was sitting to Nemon (one of the
very few living academic sculptors able to infuse life into their
creations), he described to me how, in the course of a sitting,
Churchill, of whom he had modelled several heads, seized some
Plasticine and, modelling Nemon's head, began to talk of taking up
sculpture.

I count this intermittent yet years-long association with Churchill
as one of the great privileges life has accorded me. It was in one
respect at least a singular relationship, in that in spite of his
extraordinary candour and the warmth of his friendliness I do not
believe that I ever came to know him very much better. His mannerisms, his way of life, as well as certain experiences that inflicted
lasting wounds, certain affections and aversions, I certainly came to
know, but about the deeper operations of his mind I understand
little more than I did at the end of that first day at Chartwell
in 1949. Of one of his attributes I would like to make particular
mention: his extraordinary and unvarying consideration and
courtesy.

*

On 24 January 1965 the news that Churchill had died shortly after
eight in the morning was broadcast at nine. We listened to this and
to Beethoven's Fifth Symphony that followed it. I found tears in
my eyes. We knew how very ill he was; that his memory had failed
and death was merciful. A few Sundays earlier Cyril Connolly had
written of T. S. Eliot, who died on 4 January, that he had liked the
feeling that he was around. I felt that about Churchill and so, I
imagine, did all Britain. A great presiding presence was no longer
there.

The funeral took place six days afterwards. Today so much of the
finest art, however widely appreciated, is of a private character,
addressed to a comprehending few. Churchill's funeral, on the contrary, was a superbly contrived public work of art, dignified,
splendid, tender, ingenious: the sudden unexpected singing in St.
Paul's of *The Battle Hymn of the Republic*; the bowing cranes on the
South Bank of the Thames as the boat carrying the body passed

by. By evening he was lying not many miles away in Oxfordshire earth.

Early in 1968 I went to Chartwell to appear in a short film *Churchill the Painter* of which I had written the script. The house had become a museum. The contents had been rearranged with scrupulous and loving care; innumerable trophies of Churchill's fabulous career placed on view; enlarged photographs covered some of the walls. It is a fascinating museum, but—although a number of the rooms are left exactly as they were—it was no longer the home it had so recently been.

CHAPTER EIGHT

THE TATE GALLERY 1954-1964

THE Tate Affair had done some damage to the public standing of the Gallery. But it was transient; indeed many people of influence, newspaper proprietors, journalists and private citizens, made special efforts to repair it. These honourably inspired efforts as well as a widely-shared revulsion—to say nothing of the shortness of human memory—combined to obliterate almost all traces of it. A few of the hostile participants maintained their hostility; a rather larger number maintained that 'there is no smoke without fire'.

My autobiography has amply illustrated, I think, the difficulties which lie in wait for—when they do not positively confront—the director of an art gallery, that oddly isolated figure, responsible to the Trustees, considered the institution's representative figure by the public, distinct from the rest of his staff, yet closely dependent upon them. Of the shocking shortage of senior staff and its consequences I have already written. One of the few positive results of the Tate Affair was the accelerated recognition of the risks inherent in administering, let alone reconstituting, the Gallery with so minute a staff, and its consequent strengthening by highly qualified graduates of the Courtauld Institute.

The Tate has not yet been able to rival for their comprehensiveness the splendid series of catalogues compiled by Martin Davies and his colleagues for the National Gallery, and one urgent need still remains unfulfilled: a catalogue of the Tate's unrivalled collection of Turner's oils. The new Tate catalogues were of the highest quality, and the time was long past when it was possible to attribute, for example, two works signed by Paul Nash, and manifestly by his hand, to his brother John, as was done in the Tate's British School catalogue published in 1937.

For a time the little team engaged on the compilation of catalogues was compelled to conduct a considerable part of its research in the libraries of the Victoria and Albert Museum, the Courtauld

Institute and elsewhere, wasting much time in travel, as the Tate had no library—worthy of the name—of its own. In the meanwhile intensive efforts were made to build up a reference library under our own roof. In the decade 1953-63 the library was increased from 1,400 inadequately indexed books and periodicals to 4,700 books and over 20,000 exhibition catalogues, all instantly accessible. This invaluable collection of catalogues as well as of books and periodicals was assembled by ubiquitous begging, and by a world-wide system of exchanges with kindred institutions. As a consequence our own staff, who had recently been compelled to look elsewhere for elementary information, was enabled to send informative replies to innumerable enquiries from scholars and other members of the public.

During the same period the administration was continuously improved as Norman Reid—who had joined the staff in 1946 as a Temporary Assistant and was appointed Keeper in 1959—came to play an increasing part in its organization, and its smoother functioning owed much to his versatile, confident practicality. Working with him, as in Leeds with Ernest Musgrave and in Sheffield with George Constantine, made me acutely aware of the limitations of my own capacities for administration. I demanded high standards; I am in general fairly quick to discern anything amiss; I am, I believe, fairly quick, too, to discern solutions to problems. But for the means of remedying the one and of 'implementing' the other I am often at a loss. To Norman Reid these capacities were second nature.

The companionship of my colleagues was a source of constant— or to be precise, rarely interrupted—pleasure: as I walked each morning down Vauxhall Bridge Road and along John Islip Street, I used to look forward to seeing them. Even now, I still miss my old associates.

Norman Reid was the colleague with whom my day-to-day dealings were continuous, but there were others—Ronald Alley, Martin Butlin, Dennis Farr—on the more scholarly and less administrative side of the Gallery's activities with whom my relations were not so close but whose company was precious to me. But naturally the colleague with whom I worked most closely was Corinne Bellow. When she came to the Gallery some ten years previously as a secretary, she seemed to me to be inhibited by shyness from initiative and from the necessary ease of communication with those with whom she worked. It was only later that I discerned the qualities of heart and mind that won her a unique measure of affection and trust. I valued her highly as my Personal Assistant; after my retirement I felt totally lost without her organizing capacity, her sense of proportion, her benevolent, reassuring presence.

In 1955 the Gallery gained incalculably from the establishment of its own Conservation Department under the direction of Stefan Slabczinski, a restorer of outstanding talent.

When I first came to the Tate I was shocked by much of what passed for 'restoration': commercial restorers, some of them working behind locked doors, were free in their use of hot irons, which had the effect of depriving paintings of their impasto and giving them the look of oleographs, so smooth and thin did the paint sometimes become under their remorseless pressure.

In those early days funds available for conservation were minute and I accordingly encouraged our own exceptionally skilful and conscientious craftsman John Lee—whose lack of training I helped to remedy by arranging that he should receive a course of instruction from Helmut Ruhemann, Chief Restorer at the National Gallery—to undertake the cleaning of a number of paintings.

Association with Ruhemann (who also treated Tate pictures from time to time) increased Lee's knowledge and confidence and enabled him to serve us well, but as soon as the necessary resources became available conservation was placed on a fully professional basis.

Slabczinski—Polish-born and a pupil of Ruhemann's—immediately proved himself a masterly restorer; also an engineer of unusual ability, able when necessary to design and even to construct much of the intricate equipment he required. He was presently joined by a group of able assistants: Percy Williams, John Bull and Lord Dunluce.

The Conservation Department was shortly recognized as one of the best anywhere and something of a show place for foreign and other professional visitors.

From the first I was determined to make the Tate a focus of various but cheerful life. Owing to its relative inaccessibility by public transport and the extreme scarcity of restaurants in the neighbourhood it was clearly essential that we should have a restaurant of our own, or rather under our own roof. The concession to run such a restaurant was first given to a very large catering firm of high reputation, but the café (the room embellished with Rex

Whistler's elegant and spirited wall paintings) no doubt played too insignificant a part among their enterprises to be worth their while to develop fully, and it languished. It occurred to me to adopt a contrary policy and to engage the interest of some small concern, to which the success of the Tate concession would be crucial, and I consulted a friend, Denis Mathews, the artist and, at that time, 1953, Secretary of the Contemporary Art Society, which has its offices at the Tate. A few days later he and I received an invitation to lunch from a friend of his who ran, with her husband, a small restaurant in Shepherd Place, Mayfair. Their names were Tondi and Douglas Adams. The quality of the food and service impressed me favourably; likewise Mrs. Adams' quick grasp of the Tate's special requirements. These were not easy to fulfil, as it was necessary to cater both for sophisticated and affluent visitors—many from abroad—as well as for students, young artists, school parties and others of limited means. But I wondered how Mrs. Adams (afterwards Barr) would adapt herself to an official environment. She had the dark, flashing eyes and the olive skin of a gipsy, but a gipsy fashionably dressed; she gave vehement and outspoken expression to highly personal, even anarchic opinions, and she was amused and entertainingly conversant with the seamier side of life in Soho. She was granted the concession, and my misgivings were proved unjustified.

Temperamentally I am not disposed to feel affection for people in the mass, but I should be ungrateful indeed if I did not feel something approaching affection for that no longer inconsiderable part of the public that visited the Tate—that visited it without even having been encouraged to do so except by the display of what we believed, rightly or wrongly, to be the works of the finest painters and sculptors within the scope of the collections—many of them, moreover, by no means easy to like, at least on first acquaintance. Whatever our errors of judgement, it is certain that the acquisition of no single work has been prompted in the slightest degree by a desire to court popularity. Everything that has entered the collection during the term of my own first-hand knowledge of the Tate I believe to have been acquired because the Board as a whole, a Trustee, or the Director has believed in its intrinsic quality as a work of art. Certain purchases have, I think, been ill-judged, but they have not been made with popularity in view. The overwhelming support of the public is something I have always valued deeply.

Of course, as a private individual I was aware, often painfully aware, of the truth of Edgar Wind's observation that 'we are much given to art, but it touches us lightly, and that is why we can take so much of it, and so much of so many different kinds. . . . When such large displays of incompatible artists are received with equal interest and appreciation, it is clear that those who visit these exhibitions have acquired a strong immunity to them.' But it is nevertheless the duty of those responsible for the conduct of art galleries, at least in pluralist societies, to organize and foster 'displays of incompatible artists'. Our hopes are not that these will in fact be received with equal interest, but that the work of one artist will afford the particular nourishment which certain temperaments require, and above all the inspiration and example without which certain young talents might never discover their own particular potentialities. In any case, it is the function of the art gallery, in a pluralist society, to make art of high quality—no matter how diverse—widely accessible; it is for the scholar and the critic to ennoble and refine and to clarify the responses of the spectators. The function of the art gallery is to ensure that the process takes place on the highest level.

Nobody would be likely to describe the London art world as kindly, but the art-orientated public—that part of it, at least, which visited the Tate—I found extraordinarily responsive and friendly, and appreciative when their written complaints and enquiries were promptly and carefully answered.

A 'public', on account of its diversity and its size, must be, as an entity, elusive. But every now and then I had unexpected contacts with members of it.

One evening in 1959 (we were living in St. George's Square, Pimlico) I had worked late, and it seemed not worth while to go further than a local pub in search of something to eat. A man of enormous size—a long-distance lorry-driver, it later appeared—was standing by the bar by himself. Presently we were talking about housing in Millbank. 'Excuse me,' he asked, 'but how do you come to know so much about conditions in these parts?'

'I've worked here for a longish time—at the Tate.'

'THE TATE!' he exclaimed hoarsely, bringing his fist heavily down on the bar, 'that's the place that those bastards in Parliament won't give enough money for!'

'True enough. Have you ever been there?'

'Never myself, but the two kids go there every weekend—every minute they can spare. Don't know what they'd do without it.'

For its first fifty years, as has been narrated, the Tate had no public purchasing funds and was entirely dependent on private generosity. It was not until 1946 that the Government allocated an annual grant: £2,000! The grant was increased to £6,250 in 1953 and to £7,500 in 1954. In 1959 a radical change in the Government's attitude towards the arts resulted in the grant's increase to £40,000. In 1964 (only six months before my own retirement) it was raised to £60,000 and a further annual grant was made of £50,000 a year, which was allocated for the next five years to help make good some of the gaps in the collection of foreign paintings of the period 1900-1950.

Until 1959, then, the Tate was without funds remotely commensurate with its heavy responsibilities.

There was no more than token representation of such movements as expressionism and futurism, and such figures as Kandinsky, Mondrian, Soutine, Balthus and Mirò were represented by no more than single examples. Even the British collection had shameful gaps: the representation of Wilson and Stubbs, for instance, was entirely inadequate.

The full gravity of these shortcomings, however, is not apparent unless it is borne in mind that the Tate is by far the National Gallery's most important single source of acquisitions. Between the end of the war and my retirement a major collection of paintings was transferred from Millbank to Trafalgar Square. Included were such masterpieces as Seurat's 'Une Baignade', and paintings of comparable importance by Renoir, Monet, Pissarro, Degas, Gauguin, Lautrec, Van Gogh, as they passed out of the category of modern, besides scores of others. The Tate acquired 'Une Baignade' in 1923 for £6,000: its value today far exceeds the total sum allocated to the Tate for purchasing in the entire course of its history. There were transfers, too, in the reverse direction, but only of paintings that the National Gallery did not wish to exhibit. In view of the high standard of the National Gallery's collection many of them were welcome, but they were, to put it bluntly, its cast-offs.

The increase in our grant from £2,000 in 1946 to £110,000 in 1964 was of course very substantial, but nevertheless it was grievously belated. Before 1959 the funds which the Tate had at its disposal from official sources were negligible; we had to let go opportunity after opportunity for the want of even moderate sums; and when at last funds were available, comparable opportunities no longer existed. The first painting purchased by the Trustees after the radical increase in our own resources in 1964 was Picasso's 'The Three Dancers', which cost far more than the £50,000 specially allocated for the acquisition of such master works. Had not Roland Penrose, a close friend of Picasso's, been a Trustee at the time, and willing assiduously to urge the Tate's suit for the better part of a year, 'The Three Dancers'—a painting on which the artist sets a particular value—would most probably never have entered the collection at all. It was the first painting, Picasso told Roland Penrose, that he had sold directly to a museum. The special grant which (with the help of the Friends of the Tate, the Contemporary Art Society and a private bequest) enabled the Tate to buy 'The Three Dancers' was imperatively needed—but already inadequate.

*

There were times when I suffered acute depression at missed chances of acquiring splendid works, mainly owing to a continuing and desperate lack of funds or, less frequently, to the indecision of Trustees. At others, particularly when the Tate was the target of criticism, I was conscious of pride, even of astonishment, at what between us—Trustees and staff—was in fact accomplished, and how, even in the foreign field where competition was at its most ferocious, we did buy or beg works by Degas, Cézanne, Matisse, Rouault, Picasso, Modigliani, Balthus, Soutine, Ernst, Giacometti, and numerous others whose works are a precious national asset. For instance a preliminary study for 'The Little Dancer aged Fourteen' by Degas—we bought a finished bronze in 1952 for £9,000 (a purchase made possible by a grant of £6,000 from the National Art-Collections Fund)—was sold in 1966 for over £50,000. The price of £9,000, it will be recalled, had been bitterly stigmatized as excessive. Few of these acquisitions—it must regretfully be admitted —count among the crucial, formative works of their time.

There must, of course, be grounds for criticism of the way in which the Tate spent its exiguous funds, but from early days it has exhibited one shining virtue: a strong disposition to help itself. Its friends Henry Tate and the Duveens, father and son, built it—no single gallery having been added at public expense; one of its Trustees, Samuel Courtauld, provided the funds for the purchase of the splendid collection of impressionist and post-impressionist paintings that for many years, with the Turner and Blake collections, were the Gallery's most brilliant ornament. During my own directorship a succession of honorary attachés gave their services; indeed there was hardly a time until quite recent years when somebody was not working at the Tate in some capacity or other without remuneration. But the most striking and fruitful instance of the Gallery's disposition to help itself during the period I am writing about was the foundation of the Friends of the Tate. It was an immediate consequence of our failure, already mentioned, to buy one of Severini's finest works, 'Madame S'. The Trustees shared my admiration for it, but at the same time an outstanding double portrait by Lely, 'Two Ladies of the Lake Family', which I had seen at Leggatt's in St. James's Street, was also available. Neither picture was expensive: Severini had reduced the price of 'Madame S' to a modest £2,000 and the price of the Lely was about £1,750, but our resources were already strained to the utmost by the prospective purchase of the great series of four bronzes by Matisse, 'Nu de Dos'. The Lely was purchased with the aid of a contribution from the National Art-Collections Fund.

Robert Adeane, a Trustee appointed that year, was shocked at our being compelled, by the lack of £2,000, to relinquish our option on a major example of an unrepresented school and at the fact that we would have lost the Lely also but for outside help—two splendid paintings at the total cost of £3,750! The shock he sustained from the realization of our intolerable predicament eventually resulted— as briefly mentioned earlier—in the formation, through his initiative and under his chairmanship, of the Friends of the Tate. The Friends did not come formally into being until more than two years later, but his intention of establishing some such body became ever more firmly fixed. The Friends were formally established, under the benevolent patronage of Queen Elizabeth the Queen Mother, early in 1958; its appeal for support was published on 1 May and by the following March nearly £19,000 had been subscribed by over 400 members, corporate and private. Over the following decade its membership grew to over 2,300; it raised more than £157,000, and the Gallery owes to its direct gifts or to its support works by Picasso, Matisse, Braque, Balthus, Permeke, Ernst, Stanley Spencer, Sickert, Lely, Jackson Pollock, seven by Moore and numerous others.

The Friends of the Tate, imbued with Robert Adeane's own purposeful energy and supported by his generosity, at once became the Gallery's indispensable benefactor. Two years later the American Friends of the Tate were established, who, it was hoped, would present works by American artists. In spite of the enthusiasm of its council its intentions were largely frustrated by the withholding by the United States Government of the tax-deductability status responsible for the spectacular spate of gifts to American art museums. We were naturally averse from accepting gifts from our American friends on terms less favourable to them than they would have received had they presented them to museums in their own country. The new body did not dissolve before it had enriched the Tate with a fine Mark Tobey and a few other welcome gifts.

Being closely concerned with the formation of the Friends of the Tate and a member of its Council I saw much of Robert. I was deeply grateful for his immensely effective efforts on behalf of the Gallery, but I did not regard him as a particular friend of my own. The way in which, while he conversed, his light blue eyes would focus, like a sailor's, on the horizon gave me the impression that he listened with reluctance or even—except when some practical information of immediate relevance was being imparted—not at all.

Before long I discovered that his far-away look was a mannerism not inconsistent with careful attention to what he heard, and I realized that, almost without my being aware of it, I had made a friend whom I particularly valued, a friend, moreover, who was a most unusual personality. Robert's zest for multifarious pursuits, voracious and untiring, whether for his far-flung and ever-extending business activities, for shooting and fishing, travel, agriculture and many others, included a new interest: collecting pictures. Trusteeship of the Tate and chairmanship of the Friends roused his latent enjoyment of painting.

He would have been bored by aesthetics and took only the most cursory interest in the history of art, but he enjoyed looking at paintings, especially when he had bought them and hung them at his house, either in Chelsea or in Essex. There are certain collectors who treat the works of art they own as sacred objects and they expect, even in a genteel way extort, a hushed respect for these objects, and for themselves, too, as their possessors. Robert is a collector of an entirely different kind. No mystique attaches to anything in his collection: if he gets bored with his pictures he sells them and buys others; if he finds that their places on his walls fail to do them justice he hangs them somewhere else or puts them in store.

I remember an occasion when a periodical planned to include Robert in a series entitled 'Six Great Collectors' or something of the sort, and a young art critic called at Cheyne Walk, analysed Robert's opinions, built upon his casual expressions of assent or dissent an intricate theory about his motives as a collector, making numerous notes about the pictures and their places on the walls in preparation for an elaborate, profusely illustrated description of the collection. A few weeks later I happened to be dining with Robert. We passed an enjoyable evening but as he said goodnight he added, 'I'm a bit worried about that young fellow—you know the one who's writing that piece on me for "Six Great Collectors". Well, he's coming tomorrow to take colour photographs of all the pictures in the dining-room and drawing-room.'

'But why', I asked, 'should that worry you?'

'Because I've just remembered', he explained, 'that he won't find a single one of the pictures he saw when he was here before. Some of them have been sold and the rooms have been completely re-hung with different things.'

At the time when we had high expectations of the American Friends we cultivated likely supporters. In order to discover whether it was a project worthy of support, a stockbroker and his wife, previously unknown to either of us, invited Robert and me to dinner. The conversation was pretentious, names were resoundingly dropped—'Jack's' and 'Jackie's' in particular. It soon became apparent that the occasion offered neither prospective support for the Friends nor amusement for ourselves. 'I'm sorry,' Robert suddenly announced, as soon as we could leave without positive discourtesy, 'but John and I have an appointment.'

'I hear', said our hostess, 'that the Italian Ambassador is giving a reception at the Sherry-Netherland. I suppose you're . . .'

'No, we're not,' said Robert. 'As a matter of fact we've a date with a girl at "Birdland".'

We were the objects of incredulous glances, but Robert had spoken the exact truth—only our appointment was for rather later. The 'girl' was the widow of Jackson Pollock, whom we had met earlier that day to discuss her husband's representation at the Tate, and she had suggested that we should continue our discussion at

'Birdland', where, she said, we would hear excellent jazz. This further meeting led to the presentation by Mr. and Mrs. H. J. Heinz, through the Friends, of Jackson Pollock's 'Number 23'.

*

The other private body of benefactors that had its offices in the Tate was the Contemporary Art Society, a benefactor to which the art galleries of Britain are deeply indebted. Since the Second World War the work of independent and pioneering artists has become widely accepted and often eagerly sought after. This was previously far from being the case. Visitors to most municipal galleries could hardly fail to note that the only works by serious modern artists to be seen on their depressing walls were those presented by the Society. The Buyers (in effect the committee in rotation), like all buyers, were susceptible to error, but how brilliantly their purchases stood out in the drab company which in those unregenerate days they were compelled to keep!

The Contemporary Art Society was founded in 1910—the year of Fry's fiercely controversial First Post-Impressionist Exhibition —to foster the representation, in the words of its founders, 'of some of the finer artistic talent of our time' which was 'imperfectly, or not at all, represented in the National and Municipal Galleries'. The Tate owes its first examples of many major artists—Rouault, Sickert, Epstein, John, Miró, Paul Nash, Moore and Ben Nicholson among them—to the beneficent activity of the CAS.

With the vastly increased response to 'finer artistic talent' the CAS is no longer a voice crying in the wilderness, an almost unique public buyer of serious modern art, but it has never ceased to make its invaluable contribution to public collections. It has been for- tunate in having its affairs handled by a succession of secretaries possessing, among other talents, acute visual perception and high social and administrative gifts: H. S. Ede, Robin Ironside, Denis Mathews and Pauline Vogelpoel. It was the two last-named who evolved the pattern of the celebrated evening parties at the Tate followed by the Friends and a number of other institutions.

The functions of the director of an art gallery are—or at least I found them—immensely satisfying: widely varied; carried out in mostly congenial company, and above all constructive. But regarded separately several of them are tedious: attendance at meetings that go on for too long, the composition of memoranda on peripheral matters and the like. Two of his functions were an unalloyed delight: the selection or discovery of works of art for the collection, and its arrangement. This last is comparable to writing art history. He is able to focus attention on those whom he believes to be the creative figures, to illuminate their relation with their predecessors, their contemporaries and their successors. He is able to give their due to shy neglected figures, remote from the mainstream of formative ideas—and he is able to exclude altogether those who imitate the mannerisms, the superficial attributes of the creative figures, the smart chameleons, the pretentious, the irredeemably dull. To demote such work gave me satisfaction, but rarely pleasure. Certain impressions derived from childhood and boyhood in an artist's household and a household frequented by artists never faded: above all of the difficulty of an artist's life—with the exception, perhaps, of the fashionable portrait painter's—of how much confidence, skill, fortitude, judgement and so much else it called for, and of how vulnerable were even the most successful. It was to my father or my mother—I cannot remember—that Burne-Jones exclaimed, 'If people only knew the immensity of the effort called for to be even a second-rate artist!'

The object of my complete rearrangement of the British collection was to show the development of the national school from the time of the Tudors to the present day with such regard to chronology, logic and proportion as to make it intelligible to a perceptive visitor without special knowledge of painting: to make it visible to him— as 'legible', so to say, as a lucidly written book on some aspect of British history. But historical sense and due proportion between the representation of major and minor figures would not by themselves suffice. I believe that pleasure is a far better introduction to any of the arts than instruction, and I accordingly did my utmost to ensure that the arrangement did full aesthetic justice to each of the works displayed by placing it in a harmonious context or else in significant contrast with its neighbours.

The delights of presentation are complementary to those of acquisition, but those of acquisition are the more intense, especially —but here I speak for myself—where the art of our own century is in question. Not, of course, that the acquisition of earlier works did not afford me immense satisfaction, partly for their own sake and partly because of the sense of their contributing to the eventual recognition of the British school as one far transcending—in spite of its wide fluctuations, its conspicuously barren periods—the mediocrity ascribed to it by many art-historians. (Now that not only its masterpieces but even minor works are being sought after eagerly by American collectors, a belated reassessment is in progress.) In this connection the assembly of the Tudor and Stuart collection, which included paintings by Bower, Fuller, Riley and a Van Somer that had belonged to Charles I and had been sold under the Commonwealth for £7 (which we bought, through the Friends of the Tate, for £160) and Michael Wright's splendid 'Sir Neil O'Neill', afforded me constant pleasure to a still greater degree the acquisition of works by the masters, Constable's 'Marine Parade and Chain Pier, Brighton', Stubbs' 'Mares and Foals', Whistler's 'Three Figures, Pink and Grey' and numerous Blakes, as well as that uniquely strange 'Fairy Feller's Masterstroke' by the inspired lunatic Dadd—all—and how many more—by purchase for scarcely more than nominal sums, or else by gift. This reference to nominal sums brings to mind a just but severe rule affecting the staffs of the national collections: namely, that if they buy anything within the scope of the collections they serve it must be offered to their Trustees. I bought 'Windsor Castle' by Benjamin West for £20, and 'Self-Portrait' by Lucian Freud for £120, and the Trustees exercised their option in respect of both.

There were two distinct reasons why the acquisition of the work of twentieth-century artists gave me such intense pleasure. One of these stemmed from my early environment. There was scarcely a painter or a sculptor recognized today as a creative figure whom I did not, at one time or another, hear express his bitterness at neglect, slights, or even persecution, by the Establishment and neglect by the public, or else I heard such expressions credibly reported. It was therefore exhilarating to have the power to give support—sometimes highly effective support—to those whom I believed to be the truly creative figures.

Renoir, as late as the 'nineties, when my father attended a private view of one of his exhibitions, he found alone and deeply discouraged, and when my father went up to him and voiced his own ardent admiration for his work, he replied, in effect, that he supposed it ought to be enough to delight in doing one's work and to have a modest confidence in what one was doing, but there were times when it was hard not to feel neglect. Even Sargent, who could reasonably be described as the most successful painter of his time, used to complain to my father of the pressures exerted upon him that confined him to portraiture to a far greater extent than he wished.

My sense of being among the first to occupy official positions determined to rectify the prevailing neglect or at best the belated and often grudging recognition on the part of the old Establishment is not, I think, the product of conceited fancy. I have earlier related that in the late 'thirties Henry Moore had scarcely considered the representation at the Tate of his own work and that of his contemporaries as a practical possibility. No less significant, perhaps, was the attitude of Clive Bell. When we met (which was by no means frequently) he made no disguise of his interest in the circumstance that a person of my anti-Establishment opinions and antecedents should, as Director of the Tate, occupy a position of some official influence, and he used to question me about what seemed to him a curious anomaly. I gather that he questioned Kenneth Clark, with whom he was on much closer terms, in a similar sense.

The other circumstance that makes modern art so inspiring a field of operations is its openness. The ultimate assessment of the masters, or of any artist, for that matter, who for one reason or another has been the subject, over the centuries, of intensive study, is the work of time, that is, of the ultimate consensus of the opinion of generations of scholars and connoisseurs. But those early in the field may achieve much for the artists in whom—justifiably or not—they believe. They may, by their writings, by their acquisitions for public collections, bring their paintings or sculpture into the forum of informed opinion; they may even help the artist himself at a moment of self-doubt or despair. In short they may determine events in a way impossible for their remote successors. That their influence may be misused with regrettable or even disastrous consequences few directors of collections of modern art, or few writers concerned with it, need to be reminded.

I would like to believe—what director would not?—that during my term of service at the Tate, the Galley rclearly proclaimed the values of dignity and order, of originality and dynamism—the very qualities most conspicuously affronted by the environment, so largely anarchic and squalid, that modern man, in spite of the unprecedented resources at his command, has created for himself. Whether these values have in fact been upheld or ill-served only posterity can judge.

The Tate building, which in the light of day reveals many defects, at night, its interior candlelit and embellished with flowers for receptions, assumed a mysterious grandeur. At these candlelit and beflowered gatherings I used sometimes to wander by myself watching the crowds of artists, writers, collectors and their friends, talking cheerfully and looking at fine painting and sculpture, and I would feel happy at having played some part in bringing into being this life, so engaging a blend of the serious and the sociable, in a place once redolent of decay, where solitary footsteps echoed.

*

From time to time the even tenor of our lives was interrupted by untoward events, of which the most dramatic occurred on Wednesday, 11 April 1956.

At ten minutes past eleven that morning the telephone rang and someone describing himself as Mr. Guinane of the Irish News Agency told me that an Irish student had just telephoned him to say that he had stolen from the Tate one of the paintings from the bequest of Sir Hugh Lane, and intended to give it to Dublin. (This bequest was still recurrently a bitter issue between Britain and Ireland—later resolved—owing to Britain's retention of them on legal grounds in spite of Ireland's superior, though perhaps not conclusive, moral claim.)

An immediate check of the pictures in the Lane Bequest revealed that one of them, 'Jour d'Eté' by Berthe Morisot, was missing from its place on the wall, and I immediately telephoned to Scotland Yard. Police arrived within a few minutes, and, to my surprise, about sixty press reporters. The situation was slightly complicated for me by the fact that Elizabeth and I were entertaining Marc Chagall and his wife to lunch at the Tate restaurant. Chagall, in high spirits, said he was jealous that a Morisot had been stolen instead of a Chagall, but he offered to lend any of his works to the Tate, inviting me to stay with them at Vence to choose it.

Lunch finished, I resumed my conference with the police. By the end of the afternoon it was possible to reconstruct the theft, which had been planned and carried out with skill. A young Irishman from Dublin, with forged credentials for copying at the Gallery, with accomplices who masked his movements at the critical moment, had lifted 'Jour d'Eté' from the wall, placed it between sheets of cardboard and, choosing the moment when one shift of attendants was replacing another, slipped out of the main entrance and down the steps. Altogether, the timing could not have been better, for the attendants were not only changing duty but their numbers were depleted as several of them had gone to the docks to help unload German paintings, shortly to be placed on exhibition, and some Matisse bronzes.

The process of reconstruction was made easy by the fact that the theft was a propaganda gesture. The thief had informed a photographic agency that there was to be an Irish demonstration outside the Tate. Their photographer took a prize-winning picture of the thief carrying the painting down the front steps. Something aroused his suspicions, and prompted him to photograph the back of the car, with its registration number, in which the picture was being driven away. Both photographs were placed almost instantly in the hands of the police. The police identified the man carrying the picture as Paul Hogan, aged twenty, of Mount Street, Dublin, and one of his accomplices, standing in the doorway, as William P. Fogarty, aged nineteen.

During the next few days—the Irish National Students' Council claimed the theft had been organized with the intention of presenting 'Jour d'Été' to Dublin; they also claimed that the picture was already out of England—the incident was widely reported and discussed in the newspapers.

The day after the theft the Irish Ambassador, Mr. F. H. Boland, telephoned to me to express the regret of his Government and their hope of the picture's recovery; he also repudiated the statement attributed to Patrick O'Connor, Curator of the Dublin Municipal Art Gallery, that he 'would not refuse to take the picture'. Anybody who brought the picture into Ireland, the Ambassador added, would be arrested, and a statement to this effect would be issued by the Minister of Justice; his Government would not consider securing the return of the Lane pictures by such means. Lionel Robbins called at the Gallery to hear details of what had occurred; strangely, he was the only Trustee to do so.

The following Monday was largely taken up with writing replies to questions about the theft put down in both Lords and Commons, and the tightening up of security measures.

Soon after six, on going down to the rooms I rented at the Tate, I was met by Lucy, who said that the Irish Ambassador had just telephoned, asking me to call him. I did so and he told me that a flat parcel had just been delivered at the Embassy by a woman, which

M

he had opened and found to be 'Jour d'Eté'; he had informed his Government and the Commonwealth Relations Office. Taking Lucy and Norman Reid, I drove immediately to the Embassy. The Ambassador opened the door himself and handed over the picture. He was most warm and cordial, saying that he would now try to get the picture from us by legitimate means. It appeared that the two young Irishmen had left the parcel with a woman friend, who as soon as she discovered what it contained took it to the Embassy.

On the way back to the Tate we stopped at Rochester Row Police Station to show the picture to the officer in charge of the case, Superintendent McGrath. At the Gallery we found the expected representatives of the Press, to whom I was able to express my appreciation of the care with which the picture had been handled.

I believe that the consistently admirable conduct of the Irish—the promptitude with which the Ambassador and the Minister of Justice condemned the theft, the equally prompt declaration of the Corporation of Dublin that they would not accept a stolen picture, the ready co-operation of the Irish Police, the dignity of the Students' Council's public statement and the thief's careful handling of the picture—all this contributed decisively towards the creation of the climate in which, only a few years later, the Lane controversy was amicably resolved. It would have been easy for the Irish to make the theft an occasion for noisy propaganda; instead they behaved with a scrupulous correctness and the utmost courtesy.

'I am so pleased to hear', said Churchill, when I met him a few days later, 'that after four disturbed and anxious days you've got your picture safely back.'

A few years earlier, however, he had taken a different view of an intrusion.

In mid-March 1953 there was held at the Tate an international sculpture competition on the theme of 'The Unknown Political Prisoner'. Anthony Kloman supplied much of the driving force and served as chairman of a central committee of which Henry Moore, Herbert Read, Roland Penrose and I were among the members. The exhibition consisted of maquettes selected by an international jury on which Georges Salles, then Director of the National Museums of France, Alfred Barr of the Museum of Modern Art, New York, and other eminent representatives of various countries served. To this jury was entrusted the selection of four prize-winners. The winner of the Grand Prize (of £4,525) was Reg Butler.

On Sunday 15 March Norman Reid and Tony Kloman telephoned to me at Beauforest to tell me that somebody had smashed the winning maquette.

Laszlo Szilvassy, a stateless man of Hungarian origin, was detained by Tate attendants and shortly afterwards arrested, and remanded.

Reg Butler, in a public statement, observed, 'I think it shows the model had something. You take about a shilling's worth of wire and bend it about in a certain way, and it becomes a symbol powerful enough to make someone want to destroy it'; he would reconstruct it, he added, in two or three days, saying that the finished work would be built and erected on a public site—in a London square or on the cliffs of Dover. The sculptor's mention of the Cliffs of Dover was spontaneous—I do not recall that any consideration had been given to the site of the completed work—but it provoked a minor storm in Parliament. Mr. John Arbuthnot, Conservative member for Dover, with the support of forty-one other members, tabled the following motion: 'Protection of the Cliffs of Dover: That this House views with dismay the proposal to erect . . . an enlargement of the winning entry in the international sculpture competition under the title "The Unknown Political Prisoner".'

Another group of members, headed by Mr. Desmond Donnelly, Labour member for Pembroke, tabled a rival motion. This read: 'Protection of British Art: That this House regrets the use of the order paper for aesthetic criticism and in particular to disparage a work of art that has won the admiration of men and women of many nations who have devoted their lives to the study of sculpture; and regrets that philistinism should be thus advertised.'

On the afternoon of the 30th, returning from judging another competition, 'Football and the Fine Arts', I saw Churchill staring, in glum silence, and for about two minutes, at Butler's reconstructed maquette. His evidently unfavourable opinion formed, he walked briskly out. A few hours later, at the Royal Academy's annual dinner, in the course of his speech, in allusion to the maquette, he said, 'I am not going to attempt to pronounce on the artistic merits or otherwise of this work, but if it is to be erected three hundred feet high on the Cliffs of Dover I feel that my duties as Lord Warden of the Cinque Ports might well force me to give a direct measure of attention to it.'

CHAPTER NINE

LIFE IN OXFORDSHIRE

LUCY'S return from Kentucky had immeasurably enhanced our lives, although it had added, from time to time, to our anxieties. At first she attended an Ursuline Convent near Wallingford, then Rye St. Anthony, a day-school, at Oxford. Later she was at home only in the holidays from the Convent of the Holy Child at Mayfield. Paternal duties, it seemed to me, chiefly consisted in holding the bridles of restive ponies at gymkhanas, or attending, on foot, meets of the South Oxfordshire Hunt. But from the age of sixteen she began to lead a more varied way of life. Elizabeth and I thought that Lucy should equip herself to follow a profession, and knowing what a shortage there was of reliable picture-restorers we suggested, while she was still at the convent, that she should join their ranks. In the holidays she studied with John Lee, a former member of the Tate Gallery staff, and on leaving school she went for three years to the Ruskin School at Oxford to master the rudiments of drawing and painting, necessary prerequisites to the practice of picture conservation. Later on she studied for over a year with Helmut Ruhemann, Chief Restorer at the National Gallery. For some time she maintained a studio at Beauforest and eventually founded, together with an Oxford friend, Lord Dunluce, the picture-restoring firm of Dunluce-Rothenstein. In 1964, to my pleasure, Alexander Dunluce joined the Tate's Conservation Department.

Lucy's attendance at the Ruskin transformed our house into a kind of country club for junior members of the University. The men closely resembled my own contemporaries, but the women, instead of being bookish, shy and somewhat on the defensive, were lively and confident, and they mingled with the men with a freedom inconceivable—except at the price of being 'sent down'—in my day.

But we were not to enjoy Lucy's company—at least under our own roof—for much more than six years. Towards the end of 1957 she gravitated to London, taking a studio—the workshop of Dunluce–Rothenstein—at 410 Fulham Road, early the following year. In this complex of studios she made many friends, among them Richard Rhys, who came to spend a weekend with us in August of 1958. He was an attractive blend of the imaginative with the practical, though he seemed to us uncertain how to give effect to his passionate interest in the performing arts, above all in drama. His seriousness did not interfere with a highly developed sense of the comic. I remember a story he told us about an incident in the part of Wales in which his family lived: a very popular man had stolen a pig from an extremely disagreeable one, who had sued him, and the verdict of the court was 'Not guilty, but the pig must be returned'. On 7 October—Elizabeth's birthday—Lucy called at our flat and told us that she and Richard were engaged to be married.

Richard had become a Roman Catholic while he was at Cambridge and I asked Monsignor Gordon Wheeler, then Administrator of Westminster Cathedral (I had been on the Advisory Committee for its decoration for the previous six years), whether the marriage might take place in one of the side chapels. From that moment the wedding, which was intended to be a modest affair, suddenly got out of hand. The ceremony, said Gordon Wheeler, must take place at the High Altar, and Cardinal Godfrey would officiate. The Tate Trustees generously proposed that the reception should take place at the Gallery. Lord Robbins and Sir William Coldstream said to me that they intended to give up the entire day of the wedding, 7 January 1959, to enjoying it. The ceremony was assisted by Monsignor Alfred Gilbey, Catholic Chaplain at Cambridge, who had received Richard into the Church; Vincent celebrated the nuptial Mass, *coram Cardinali*. Lucy and I persuaded the Cathedral authorities to leave the huge building almost in darkness and have only the Sanctuary brilliantly lit.

There were some six hundred guests at the reception: every friend of any member of either of our families seemed to be present. For us it was a uniquely happy evening, which the guests also seemed really to enjoy. I saw T. S. Eliot laughing: it occurred to me that I had never seen him laugh before. Lucy had shown since early childhood a marked and enduring response to the poems of Eliot, especially to the *Four Quartets*, which Vincent used to read to her. It so happened that not long before the marriage Eliot had lunched with us at the Tate; she took the occasion to invite him herself to her wedding. His presence afforded her particular delight. It was so noisy an assembly that when Robert Speaight read out the Apostolic Blessing from Pope John, and a message of goodwill from President Eisenhower (a friend of Richard's parents, Lord and Lady Dynevor), he was scarcely heard.

Towards the end of April we drove down to Carmarthenshire with Lucy and Richard to stay with his parents, and had our first sight of Dynevor. The Castle is mostly seventeenth century, with a fantastic but endearing Victorian Venetian gothic exterior. Some half-mile away in the park on a small hill-top are the massive ruins of the family's thirteenth-century castle, built on the site of one still earlier. This had been the capital of Deheubarth, the last independent kingdom of the Britons. Early in the thirteenth century Dynevor was referred to by a Welsh prince as a castle 'once famous, now ruined'. The Rhys family began to play a part in English history when Rhys ap Thomas supported Henry VII, with whom he fought at Bosworth, and the family fortunes were involved with those of the Tudors, though not always harmoniously. Charles V's ambassador reported to the Emperor, for instance, that Henry VIII 'has sent to the Tower a Welsh gentleman named Ris—where he was executed'.

The most movingly beautiful feature of Dynevor is the park, a place of small wooded hills, bounded on one side by the river Towy. Of this park 'Capability' Brown wrote that 'Nature has been truly bountiful and art has done no harm'.

In 1962 Charles Dynevor died. Richard, his heir, in the face of an almost intractable complex of difficulties, began to realize his aim with regard to the performing arts (which had clarified in the meanwhile) and only four years later transformed Dynevor into a centre where music was performed (sometimes specially commissioned), films were made and shown. But as I write much is still being done: the history of the new Dynevor is still in the making.

Newington is on the way to London from South Wales and Lucy occasionally comes for the day, so that Elizabeth and I often have the delight of seeing her and her children Miranda, Sarah, Susannah and Hugo, and, less frequently, Richard. One such visit in particular remains with haunting vividness in my memory (Lucy brought with her a collapsible swimming-pool): the four children splashing and running as white against green lawn and dark foliage as the white unicorns against grass or woodland in an illuminated mediaeval manuscript.

The year of Lucy's establishment in Fulham, 1957, brought another radical change in my life.

It was, I think, Proust who said that it is not very difficult to foresee what is going to happen; the real difficulty is to foresee *when*. In the middle of June I suddenly became anxious about my mother (understandably, as she was ninety years old and ill) and I wrote her a long letter and suggested going to see her in Sheffield, where she was staying with my sister Rachel. My apprehensions were justified but belated, for my mother was not able to read my letter. My sister telephoned to me at Beauforest on 15 June—the most brilliantly sunny day of the year—to tell me that our mother was dying—and I went straight to Sheffield. She was a 'born' Catholic but a lapsed one since her early womanhood. The only minister of religion who was a close friend was the Benedictine, Dom Wilfred Upson, Abbot of Prinknash, and she had expressed to Elizabeth her wish not to die without seeing a Catholic priest. She made no mention of this wish, however, during her last illness, so that nothing was done and she was buried according to the rites of the Church of England, to which she never belonged: a family compromise.

The flat where she mostly lived since my father's death twelve years before, 10 Devonshire Place, Marylebone, had been a family gathering place, and after her death the link between her children was broken: we saw each other far less frequently, by unfortunate chance rather than intention.

My mother was a larger-than-life Balzacian character. Reason had for her no validity; she was moved by violent loves and violent, contemptuous antipathies. For Rossetti (her father's master and friend), whom she had met only as a child, for Swinburne, for Oscar Wilde—none of whom she had seen in the present century—and for her family and a few friends of her own generation, she cherished a tigerish devotion. No word must be uttered to their disparagement. Of the objects of her contemptuous antipathy she made no secret. She suffered intensely from the misfortunes, especially the illnesses, of those whom she loved, but she was as far from fear as she was from caution—which was very far indeed.

*

Inclined though we were to be unsociable in the country we continued to see our friends and many others besides. Whether it was due to the proximity of Campion Hall, which had become an

extremely lively focus of Catholic life, or simply to chance I do not
know, but it was the case that in Oxfordshire we saw much of our
Catholic friends and acquaintances. It was on Easter Sunday 1945,
when Lucy received her first communion from Father Martin
D'Arcy in the chapel at Campion Hall, that I met Graham Greene,
who was living with his wife Vivien in Oxford. At that time aged
forty-one he was a tall rangy figure dressed usually as though for
country rather than town; even then the blue eyes in his smallish
round youthful face seemed, in startling contrast, the rheumy eyes of
an oldish man. Because he wrote fast and early he had often finished
his day's work by the time others had scarcely begun theirs, and
this made him restless and liable to boredom, which provided, I
fancy, much of the impetus for his far-ranging travels. We met
Graham and Vivien on a number of occasions, at their stylish house
at 15 Beaumont Street—to the small-scale and slightly self-conscious
elegance which it owed to Vivien Graham was manifestly ill-suited.
It was a very feminine house, containing a high proportion of miniature objects, most conspicuously a fully furnished and well populated
dolls' house. Upon this multitude of little things he looked with a
detached eye. Graham could hardly have been a more incongruous
figure than he was in the house in Beaumont Street; with Vivien,
wearing the neo-Victorian clothes which expressed so much of her
personality, attending to the needs of multifarious tiny fragile
objects, by her manner reprehending the faintest unseemliness;
Graham discoursing with a fair measure of candour of his visits to
nude shows and other places even farther beyond the range of his
wife's approval.

Graham is apt to show a benevolent interest in the business
problems of other writers, and over lunch at Rule's (the restaurant
near Covent Garden much favoured by him at the time) he took me
severely to task because no two books of mine bore the imprint of
the same publisher. 'It's not worth any one publisher's while to take
trouble over you if your rights are mostly held by others: to produce
your "collected works" would be out of the question', he said, 'so
let Eyre and Spottiswoode [the publishing firm of which he was a
director] sign you up for life: we'll publish anything you write and
we'll gradually collect what you've already published.' Greatly
touched by this offer I told him that I had just begun my *Modern
English Painters*. When the book was farther advanced we had some
discussion about it. 'Perhaps you'd care to look at this,' he said,

pulling the proof of a novel out of his pocket; 'I would be most interested in any suggestion you cared to make.' The novel was *The Heart of the Matter*, and it was so extremely successful that Graham was freed from the necessity of earning his living otherwise than by his pen. When the first volume of my own book was finished I had to explain to Eyre and Spottiswoode, from which he had in the meanwhile resigned, that I appreciated that the agreement between him and myself was a personal one and their firm must not feel bound by it, but they cordially endorsed it. It was on this same occasion that Graham tried to account for the elements of aridity and defensiveness in T. S. Eliot by relating them to his refusal to accept the logical consequences of his own religious belief, owing to a shrinking, social rather than doctrinal, from the many vulgar manifestations of present-day Catholicism. Unlike Eliot, Graham himself took them very much in his stride and even enjoyed them as he enjoyed much else that was shabby and vulgar—an expression of his own revulsion from the refinement whose absence made Catholicism unacceptable to Eliot, and from accepted 'good taste' in general. I even heard him flatly declare himself satisfied with current Catholic art 'even at its worst'. This disposition was more closely related to his art than to his life, for Graham's own choice of possessions is distinguished by acute discrimination. Sleaziness and vulgarity have an important place among the stimuli of his art, in the same way as Salford and its neighbourhood, for which he has no personal liking, furnish the stimulus of the art of L. S. Lowry, which tends to lose its quality when he leaves it. I recall Graham's zestful and amusing description of attending the lunchtime performances at the now defunct but then well-known Windmill Theatre, which specialized in nude shows, in particular of his regular fellow spectators, wearing, almost all of them, mackintoshes, and not attempting, like tyros, to secure front seats but posting themselves in various strategic positions all over the house. A fair number of men of 'position' occasionally frequented the Windmill Theatre for lunch and did much else that would provoke the censorious, but Graham made no secret of such activities, not only, I think, on account of his innate candour and impatience of hypocrisy, but deliberately, as a sign that he participated in conventional social life on his own terms. Graham's dislike of the conformities is almost as fierce as Francis Bacon's and scarcely less frankly advertised. But his fiercest antipathy, I think, is reserved for the formalities, hypocrisies and the conventional pieties that obscure and even falsify ascertainable truth—current in the public life of the Church. The vulgarities of many popular cults, the banalities, even the enormities, that meet the eye in innumerable Catholic churches do not affront him. Contrariwise, of Moore's Northampton 'Madonna and Child' he said to Elizabeth and me, 'It reeks of Comparative Religion.'

Early in 1947 Graham invited Kathleen Raine and me to lunch with him at Rule's to discuss the foundation of a Catholic quarterly, to be called, perhaps, *The Well*, which, he said, would be devoted to the truthful and unambiguous treatment of literature, the arts and sciences, in a manner entirely free of the concessions and clichés that frequently marked Catholic journalism and which would seek to show the relation—and where need be the absence of it— between the specifically 'Catholic' truth of pulpit and confessional journal and ascertainable truth. 'It would be spirited and gay,' he said, 'but all who wrote for it would have to be prepared for censure.' *The Well* never got beyond the stage of discussion, although Graham continued for some time to speak of it, and he went into the question of its probable cost: £250 an issue. Such a publication would serve a useful purpose even now, although, since the Pontificate of John XXIII and the Second Vatican Council, its contributors would have far less cause to anticipate censure.

An incident which took place a few years later at a Catholic congress in Paris illustrates more pointedly than the projected quarterly Graham's attitude towards the conventional pieties. Delegates on the platform included archbishops, bishops and eminent laymen. At a certain point one delegate after another delivered a message of greeting from 'the Catholics of Brazil', 'the Knights of Saint Columba', and the like. When it was Graham's turn he said, 'I bring you greetings from the almost-lapsed Catholics of England'. But Graham gives whole-hearted support to Catholics whom he admires. He had some part in Oxford's conferring an honorary doctorate on Mauriac not long after the war. In the evening a party to celebrate it was given by him and Vivien in their Beaumont Street house. Owing to a throat affliction Mauriac spoke French only in a hoarse whisper and the guests assembled in his honour were reluctant to tax his voice. Vincent found him standing alone. He congratulated him on his degree, remarking on what a lovely summer day had graced it. As it happened it was the first day of warm sunshine after some weeks of cloud. 'That is as it may be, Father', responded Mauriac. 'But have you reflected on how many people have today had their first experience of mortal sin?'

Of Graham I eventually lost sight: a chance encounter at the Walstons' or in the street, the occasional arrival of an inscribed copy of a book marks the limits of our intercourse. My friendship with him was never intimate and so our gradual drifting apart made little impression at the time, but I regret it now, because, although often bored himself, he is never a bore, never utters the expected opinion. The unexpectedness of his attitudes and opinions was due only partly to his possession of a highly original mind; for there are many original minds whose general orientation makes their utterance more predictable rather than less. Graham's unpredictability is due to the radical ambivalence of temperament which disposes him to 'love-hate' attitudes towards the people and the things he cares for most. Certainly I can recall no instance of his championing authority against liberty; otherwise his talk abounds both in perceptive appreciation and in searching criticism of the self-same people and things. Sometimes he talks like an anti-clerical, yet some of his warmest friendships have been with priests and I know few Catholics who would lose more of themselves if they were to lose their faith.

*

To the company of friends who visited us in the country was added by a chance encounter in London the august shade of Henry James. Ethel Sands, a painter and a member of an American family long settled in England, told me over a cup of tea that she had once owned Newington House (the 'big house' of the village) and that it had been a favourite resort of Henry James, who had learned to paddle a canoe on the reach of the Thame that bounded our adjacent gardens. I revered the writer and was delighted that he had shared my taste for the only exercise—walking apart—that I cared for and had indulged it on the same reach, exploring the channels and learning the shallows just as I had. Miss Sands and the rector of the time, Mr. Pendlebury, were on very friendly terms; she had a postern made in the high wall between the adacent gardens so that each family had easy access to the other. She kept her boat in the small dock at the bottom of our garden; here, then, it was that Henry James embarked on his canoeing.

Miss Sands reported a snatch of his conversation. E. S.: 'Berenson's a remarkable talker, but too acrobatic for me.' H. J.: 'Yes, dear child; every trapeze.'

'How well I remember', Logan Pearsall Smith once said to me, 'the way he used to say "Now, Logan, let's *do* so and so", and how we would spend half a day analysing, *doing*, one of our friends or acquaintances. One day I said to Henry James, "You *do* George Moore." "Logan, I will", he replied, "but not now, as that would take a *whole* day." But he never did. His analyses were a delight—they even exceeded in their marvellous fulness and subtlety those in his books. His eagerness to hear even the most trivial fact about somebody he was interested in was extraordinary; he would listen to a description of some mannerism, some trifling incident, as though it were momentous—for him it *was* momentous. People of your generation suppose that he was always regarded as a master, but he wasn't, without reservation, even at the end. Henry James took such an infinity of trouble over such a long span of years; then everything he did just went out into the fog, and for so long with no answering voice coming back. After his death I asked a director of Macmillans how many copies of his books they'd sold. "For the honour of literature", he replied, "I'm not going to tell you." '

Nan Hudson, who occupied Newington House with Ethel Sands, used on Sunday mornings to cross the Thame over rocking stepping-stones and walk over the fields to Mass in Dorchester, in order to avoid hurting the susceptibilities of the rector. One day she said to him, 'Tell me about our predecessors.' 'There's really nothing to tell,' he replied; 'you see, *she* was mad and *he* was a Roman Catholic.'

*

Friends associated chiefly with our country life were John and Penelope Betjeman. He shared my delight in our reach of the Thame. Few things give me more pleasure than drifting downstream between the high banks, beneath overhanging branches, so silently that the waterfowl, the herons and kingfishers, the water-rats and even the fish are scarcely disturbed. Because this reach is rarely frequented the wild-life is exposed to one's gaze in close-up. The swans pass like other boats; if strangers, with warning though unaggressive hisses; if friends, with graceful lowerings of their heads and quiet expiratory sounds. It is tragic that in 1968 there was a disposition to convert this river into a drainage ditch and a heedless (and according to our Oxford scientist friends, mindless) bulldozing of its ancient willows. It will be many years before its magic returns and its intelligent ecology is restored.

When the Betjemans first came to see us it was autumn, and John, looking up at the scarlet and tawny leaves of a copper beech turned to sudden brightness by a pale sun, said, 'They are like medieval stained-glass.'

I have never known him otherwise than witty and warm, yet as with many others wit and warmth, however spontaneous, also mask a liability to depression, with its attendant melancholy preoccupations. When he first came to Beauforest and we walked together along the river bank, he said, 'I imagine you'll breathe your last beside this Thame.' I suspect that death is constantly in his thoughts; and I know that literary success is liable to evoke in him the contemplation of the eventual failure that is sometimes success's sequel. More than most people he is haunted by the transitoriness of success, of happiness, of life itself. Penelope, on their arrival for this first visit, made no comment on house or garden; all her attention was focused upon the quality of the grass, and she said to Elizabeth, whom she had been persuading to keep geese, 'With this grass you'll soon be as famous a goose-breeder as I am.'

John's advocacy of Victorian architecture has become so familiar, has awakened so many sympathetic echoes, that its revolutionary impact first upon his friends and a little later the public at large is difficult for younger generations to imagine. Among my own university generation the generally held opinion that Victorian architecture and painting (Stevens, Watts and the pre-raphaelites and a few of their followers apart) were the only irredeemably ugly architecture and painting known to history was scarcely questioned. I remember John Strachey remarking that Victorian architecture was not only hideous but, on account of its redundant ornament and wilful complexity, it was also morally perverse, and I— although brought up in a house where the Victorian achievement in the arts was accorded a wider measure of respect than in most— thought his indictment justified. Compared either with the brothers Adam or with Corbusier it seemed to us hag-ridden and fusty. The general assumption, on hearing these grotesque arts ardently praised, not by a survivor of the Victorian age but by a young man of unusual attainments and otherwise sane, was that an immense joke was being perpetrated. Of course his advocacy was at times indiscriminate; but had he praised a few selected masterpieces his listeners and readers would no doubt have been persuaded—and thought no more about the matter. Had he not at times been indiscriminate—had he not eulogized, for instance, All Saints, Swindon in a series of talks on great buildings which included the Parthenon, Chartres, Sta Sophia and a temple at Ankhor—he would not have won an audience half so quickly. Gradually an incredulous generation came to realize that John Betjeman was in earnest, and his opinions began to be given serious attention. His achievement was not to persuade people to admire Victorian architecture—relatively few do, even today—but to *look at* Victorian buildings, instead of condemning them with averted eyes, and to try to distinguish between the good and the bad. By extension he taught people to look with especial sympathy at buildings (and much else besides) hitherto considered ugly. Of course there had been earlier advocates of Victorian architecture, some of them more learned than he, but none had awakened the perceptions of so wide a section of the public.

It needs no saying that his enthusiasms range over other centuries as well. In January 1970 Elizabeth and I took two American friends who were ardent admirers of John's—Floyd McGowin, the fastidious bibliophile from Alabama, and Elizabeth Coker, the novelist from South Carolina—to visit him in his ancient quarters in Cloth Fair in the City, overlooking St. Bartholomew the Great. John was in exuberant spirits. He asked us whether we had seen the most beautiful sight that London had to offer: St. Paul's floodlit with St. Augustine's silhouetted against it. When we confessed that we had not he instantly ordered a taxi, which put us down in Watling Street, where he insisted on our keeping our eyes averted until we had reached the spot where the slender tower and pointed spire of the church could best be seen against the cathedral's noble and radiant mass.

When we first became neighbours John and Penelope lived in a beautiful rectory at Farnborough, Berkshire, but on his insistence they moved to an Edwardian villa on the outskirts of Wantage.

Penelope is no less remarkable a person than John. I know nobody, at least no woman, who leads so independent a life as she; her case is the more striking in that she is a devoted wife and mother, as well as ardently religious. Although unusually intelligent and even scholarly (my father said that nobody in England had a better understanding of Indian painting), she is happiest with outdoor pursuits, among horses and geese.

Two related incidents serve to show both her toughness and her humanity. In order to dissuade her from becoming a Catholic a group of her friends and relations arranged a lunch party to which was invited an Anglican priest who had formerly been a Catholic priest, and who was to give testimony at first hand of the error of her intended course. As arranged, the conversation was directed to the question of religious allegiance, and at what seemed an appropriate moment the parson began, 'I was once ...' Penelope, aware, of course, of what was intended, turned and looked him in the eye and said, 'I don't care a bloody damn what you once were.' A few days later, seeing Penelope in the street, the parson turned to avoid her. She pursued him, making it plain that her words were not intended as a discourtesy to him but as a warning to her mistaken well-wishers, and the two of them became close friends from that time on.

After her conversion she sought out the Catholic families who lived on the downs in places too isolated to permit of their attending Mass, and armed with a Catechism rode on horseback to their homes and instructed the children—and on occasion the parents also—in the elements of their faith.

Elizabeth and I happened to be driving one day through Wantage. We stopped to see Penelope at an eating house called King Alfred's Kitchen, which John had bought. It proving impossible to find a chef, the venture was threatened with failure. We were shown up-stairs into the kitchen, where we found Penelope mixing mayonnaise. At the back of the old-fashioned iron stove simmered a vast stock pot. In spite of her other passionate interests—horses, geese, travel, Indian art, her religion, and much else—she had undertaken to do the cooking herself, and this she did for several years, and with the utmost zest. On our way out we noticed, among the rows of crumpets and rock cakes in a glass display case, a richly jewelled family tiara—also for sale.

In appearance they were a disparate couple: John, languid in voice and gesture and dressed in Edwardian style, straw 'boater' worn at a rakish angle and loose-fitting tweed suits which served as constant reminders of his delighted obsession with the recent past: Bedford Park, popular marine painting of the century's turn and the like; Penelope, robust, with a perpetual air of having just left a

stable yard—the muddier the yard the happier she—wearing
clothes of a conspicuous roughness, but with a mind unblunted by
her dedication to bucolic pursuits, and ever ready for a 'set to' on
theology or oriental art. Penelope is the less inhibited but John the
more eccentric. At a party one evening I remarked on his persistent
pursuit of a woman without evident attraction, and he reproachfully
replied, 'Don't you realize, John, that she's the most distinguished
lady balloonist in England?'

*

Another friend, although not an intimate one, who belonged to our
Oxford rather than our London life was Evelyn Waugh, who was a
fairly frequent visitor to Campion Hall. In nothing was he more
unusual than in the welcome, the acclaim almost, he accorded to
middle-age. Until the war he looked younger than his years.

During the war he was at one point removed from combatant
service—he was a combative man—to some sedentary post at home.
When his brother officers said goodbye to him he told them he
would rejoin them shortly. The first two nights in his new mess he
got deliberately drunk and behaved as scandalously as he knew how
—and he knew how. 'I will not tolerate my officers getting dis-
gustingly drunk in the mess', his commanding officer said. 'What
have you to say for yourself?' 'If you suppose that I am going to
break the habits of a lifetime on your account, Sir,' he replied, 'I
am afraid you are under a misapprehension.' Almost at once he was
back where his combative temperament had full scope. That was the
conduct of the young man. After the war he exaggerated his deafness, eventually affecting a vast ear-trumpet of a kind disused, I
would have thought, since the eighteenth century, which served not
only its ostensible purpose but as a weapon of conversational war-
fare; when, for instance, he asked a question he would bring it to
bear upon his victim, making impossible any mumbled or evasive
reply. Although I was slightly his senior he would affect towards me
an avuncular mode of address, and his wardrobe was of severe
formality. These and other changes in his demeanour corresponded
to a change even more conspicuously reflected in his writings, in
his outlook, a change from satiric 'outsider' to 'insider' defending
traditional social *mores*, although without hope that their effective
defence was possible, defending, in fact, what was not only doomed
but already disintegrating. It is characteristic of these conformist

times that although the term 'with it' is in constant use, there is no corresponding negative term. Were there such a one, it would precisely define the attitude of Evelyn Waugh. He was apt to be particularly incensed by such concepts as 'the People'. 'I'm not at all sure', he said, 'that it isn't one's duty to put a spoke in "the People's" wheel.' One afternoon, walking along the tow-path at Oxford, we discussed the intended substitution for the ancient barges, which served most colleges as the headquarters for their rowing, of new, luxuriously appointed pavilions. 'The Oxford rowing man of today', Evelyn contemptuously observed, 'requires all the comforts of the pit-head.' A visitor to his house told me that Evelyn, like some Victorian parent, saw his older children once a week and had said of those under ten that 'they wouldn't know me if they saw me in the street'.

As the years passed, however, the impulses to shock and to wound, at times irrepressible, diminished and Evelyn's attitude towards his fellow-men became increasingly benevolent and his religious sense seemed (to me, at least) to deepen. I wonder whether he had his own development in mind when he said to me, speaking about Belloc, 'For all his active life he had no personal religion. For him Catholicism was simply a *cause*: only when his active life ended did he find in it a personal religion.'

Evelyn was an unusually visual man. His growing conservatism caused him to chide me for signing a letter to *The Times* protesting against certain work carried out in Westminster Cathedral, especially 'in company with pagans and agnostics', but he told me that, after I had said that I thought Stanley Spencer's work at Burghclere was the finest religious wall painting made in England since the Middle Ages, he had journeyed there to look at it and come away deeply impressed. On another occasion he described a painting in his possession of a coach being robbed by highwaymen and asked me to recommend a painter who would make a companion piece of 'a Dakota crashing in flames'—a scene he commissioned Richard Eurich, with whom I put him in touch, to paint for him. Not many writers commission paintings except on occasion portraits of themselves. Nor is this an isolated instance of his acting as patron of a painter. He gave to Campion Hall the royalties on his *Edmund Campion* and enabled the Lady chapel to be decorated with paintings by Charles Mahoney. The resulting ambitious project, which took many years to bring to the verge of completion—it never, owing to

N

some misunderstanding, received its final touches—deserves a high
place among the small group of fine religious paintings of the time
Partly because, through the lapse of years and its painter's reluctance,
it has never been formally 'unveiled'; partly—and this is a far graver
drawback—because it belongs to the rare and least appreciated
category of art, namely the truly academic, it has suffered almost
total neglect. That revolutionary movements, by compelling the
reassessment of accepted ideas, by opening up new spheres of
experience, fructify the arts, is of course beyond question, but artists
with sufficient personal conviction to oppose or ignore the prevailing
tides deserve far more attention and respect than they receive. Those
who every morning find on their desks catalogues and private-view
cards from Tokyo to Buenos Aires, from Stockholm to Cairo,
illustrating the works of artists who have tended to adopt the idiom
of Dubuffet, Kline, de Staël, Vasarely, Newman or Rauschenberg
must surely experience moments of nausea that should dispose them
to greater sympathy with the solitary nonconformist, such as the
creator of the images brought into being by Charles Mahoney
through the generous patronage of Evelyn Waugh.

The politeness of many people masks more cruelty and indifference than they care to disclose. The aggressive unblinking stare
of Evelyn's protuberant blue-grey eyes and his abrupt, even trucu-
lent, utterance masked a heart which, although not unusually warm,
was nevertheless warmer than most. His occasional acts of compul-
sive rudeness were prompted, I believe, by unhappy moods, and
not by any sort of malevolence. A common friend said of him, 'Poor
Evelyn, he no longer enjoys his rudeness.' Several people have confessed to a certain fear of him, even Graham Greene, who is not
particularly subject to fear. In spite of his own proneness to boredom, I never knew Evelyn to bore, but on the contrary the inflexi-
bility of his attitudes and opinions, their expression in pungent,
'hard-edged' utterance, exercised a bracing influence on conversation and discouraged the vague sentiment and the loose phrase. But
he could be extremely benevolent. He called one evening when Lucy
was a little girl and took her on his knee. When asked if he would
stay to dinner he said, 'Only if Lucy is allowed to stay up.' The review
he wrote for *The Month* of Robert Speaight's biography of my father,
on account of the sympathetic insight it showed, gave me more
pleasure than all the others together.

On account of *The Loved One* he had been 'black-listed', he told

me, by the American Society of Morticians; 'so if I die in America
my body will be thrown into a ditch. Fortunately I don't want to *go*
to America.' Evelyn and I thought that Ronald Knox, the close
friend whose biography he wrote, as the only Englishman (the
eccentric Fenton apart) to translate the whole of the Bible single-
handed, as a great man and a great scholar, should be made a
cardinal, and we approached various influential people, but we
received little encouragement. Douglas Woodruff said, 'Wait until
his *Bible* is published, and see what the Protestant reviewers make
of it.' It was absurd, of course, to suppose that two uninfluential
laymen could achieve such an aim, however justified.

During his last years Evelyn was a very occasional visitor to
Oxford and London and our meetings, never frequent, became very
rare occasions. The recollection of the last, when I read of his death,
gave me a sharp pang of regret. It was at a Low Week Reception
by the Hierarchy of England and Wales. Giving me what seemed
a chilly stare, he suggested that I have dinner with him and we
spend the evening together, but I was already engaged.

Elizabeth and I had the good fortune to receive a visit in April
1951 from Ronald Knox himself, in company with our friend Father
Thomas Corbishley, who succeeded Father D'Arcy as Master of
Campion Hall. Like most of those who met him we were charmed
by this melancholic, patrician scholar-wit, but, considering how
much of the secular world he knew, how great the multitude of his
laymen friends, we were surprised to find how profoundly clerical
he was. I have met seminary-trained officials who have spent their
lives within the walls of the Vatican but who seemed nearer to the
secular world than this Eton and Balliol man, this former Fellow
of Trinity. He was indeed the son of a bishop, and Anglicans can
be very clerical. It was not that the talk of Monsignor Knox was
in the least degree confined to clerical topics: he showed a highly
informed interest, for instance, in an exhibition of Eton portraits
currently on view at the Tate.

Disturbed by the failure of the Athenaeum Club to recruit, as
was the case in earlier times, the most eminent men in the various
professions, I sounded our illustrious guest about whether he was
disposed to allow his name to be put forward. His first response was
favourable, even enthusiastic. 'My friend Geoffrey Fisher' (Archbishop of Canterbury)—'we were friends at Oxford—might perhaps propose me,' he said. He was a gay and witty guest. Four days

later two paragraphs in a letter showed that his enthusiasm for my suggestion had cooled.

> The more I brood on our conversation of Saturday afternoon, the more I am got down by the feeling that it would be rather fantastic of me to join the Athenaeum, on whatever basis elected. I really am not a clubman, and haven't the makings of one; on my rare visits to London I am always a guest, not a host, and I don't write letters to the papers. If the Athenaeum had a rule 666 under which would-be celebrities could be elected, on the understanding that they paid a small fee and never used the club at all, that would just suit me. But the existing arrangement seems to me, on reflection, a bad bargain for a person in my position. Is it worth while gratifying a vanity which I ought to have outgrown, at the expense of making a charitable gift to the Athenaeum? True, I am very rich; the only rich person I know. But, between drinks and alms and the income-tax, I find it possible to keep my current account within decent limits without making paper boats out of Bradburies.
>
> I am enormously grateful to you for wanting to get me put up. But if you haven't, so far, taken any irretrievable step, I'd rather retract my acceptance of your suggestion after all. If the thing has already gone so far that you can't stop the wheels turning without considerable effort, let the acceptance stand. I'm sorry to be a nuisance.

The wheels had not begun to turn and the Athenaeum was the poorer.

We corresponded briefly but I saw him only once again, at a lunch in celebration of the publication of his *Bible*, an occasion when tribute was paid to him by the illustrious in many fields (and a number of the less illustrious) at the Hyde Park Hotel. In his speech, but even more in his demeanour, I noticed an acute conflict between a temperamental modesty and shyness that allowed the tribute to overwhelm him, and an abundantly justified consciousness of achievement that allowed him to accept it as his due.

*

Another man of high talent whom we saw only in the country was C. S. Lewis.

We had heard much about Jack Lewis before we met him from

a close common friend, Robert Havard, a man who had he chosen could have made a career as a specialist but who instead turned to general practice from the conviction that this would enable him to give more effective service to his fellow men. We always looked forward to his return from his holidays, spent in one of two ways: in Conradian adventure in small sailing boats or in monastic retreat. Lewis and he were neighbours at Headington, and an emotionally relaxed but intellectually strenuous intimate 'bachelor' friendship (although Robert Havard was a widower and Jack Lewis eventually married) existed between them. With Hugh Dyson, J. R. R. Tolkein, Charles Williams and Lewis himself Robert Havard had been a foundation member of 'the Inklings'. I rarely heard a book mentioned that he had not read.

Early in 1952 Father Corbishley gave a party at Campion Hall to celebrate my knighthood. Our host asked Elizabeth whom she wished to meet and she indicated a gaily intelligent oval face, a high-complexioned man who had just come in. 'Oh, that's Jack Lewis', said our host, and from that occasion we became on increasingly friendly terms. Nothing about him ever suggested to us the antipathy for women we had heard imputed to him, but he bore, very conspicuously indeed, the marks, as impossible to mistake as difficult to describe, of the man whom taste or circumstance has deprived of the society of women, most commonly found upon dons and school-masters, less often upon soldiers. The notion of a man of such positive benevolence disliking half the human race was not to be credited: some who knew him but slightly had been misled, I think, by his 'senior common room' formation. His conversation was bracing; he was uninterested in trivialities or even the graver elements in gossip, but came straightaway to grips with religious and literary themes of the type expounded in his writings with persuasive logic and a disarming blend of authority and charm. After his appointment two years later to the Professorship of Mediaeval and Renaissance English at Cambridge we saw him more rarely. One evening in November 1963 Elizabeth met me at Oxford station and as I put my suitcase into the car I noticed that she was very tense. 'Jack . . . has been assassinated', she said. She repeated the dreadful news. 'I thought at first', I said, 'that you had said something dreadful had happened to Jack Lewis.' 'He is dead too', she said. In our dining-room the table was already laid for the lunch party arranged in his honour for the following day.

Occasional but very welcome visitors were Edgar Wind, Professor of the History of Art at Oxford, and his wife and close collaborator Margaret. Edgar's learning is prodigious and as an art-politician he can show a pertinacious militancy that has left opponents (victims is how they would be likely to describe themselves) severely scarred. But away from the study and the arena he can be gay to the point of flippancy. I suspect that flippancy is a quality of which he approves as the most effective antidote to the stresses and strains of scholarship. He enjoys both talking with candour about common friends and colleagues and listening to candid talk about them. Preoccupation with Pagan Mysteries of the Renaissance does not inhibit him from keeping a sharp perceptive eye upon the present. 'The whole conception of what constitutes an original work of art is changing', he said, several years before the change had become obvious. 'What artists paint or draw today are *pre*-originals. The true originals are the colour reproductions in the catalogues of their exhibitions.'

The foregoing brief pages about people whom over the years we met at our house or else in Oxford suggest that our lives were more sociable and more varied than they were. In spite of the discomfort and tedium of the travelling involved—the only sense in which I feel physically different from the way I felt when I was young is detestation of short frequent journeys—I would find it the gravest deprivation not to be able to live in both London and the country. For the pleasures offered, though equally gratifying, are in the main exact contraries. In London, although arrangements had to be made ahead, especially for someone for whom official duties continually displaced meetings with friends, one wondered what each day would bring of illumination or pleasure, encounters with interesting unknown people, of possible turns of events to be dealt with and the like. My enjoyment of London was enhanced by the acquisition, in 1962, in place of the one-room flat in St. George's Square, Pimlico, to which we moved after leaving our dungeon-like quarters at the Tate, of a minute regency house in Tryon Street, Chelsea. In the country one looks forward—this at least is Elizabeth's experience and mine—to the next event in a series precisely preordained, to the customary instead of the unexpected. Having no understanding of the higher problems of gardening, of the ordering of plants suited to the soil, but above all of the planning that may make of a garden a coherent work of art, I am fit only for the rudimentary tasks, such as weeding and mowing lawns, stripping ivy from trees and preventing nettles from gaining more than the most temporary foothold. Weeding for me has a therapeutic value: when I am baffled by a refractory sentence, which I cannot coerce into a precise expression of my meaning, or by doubts about a far more perplexing question, namely the presentation of ideas in their most logical sequence, I go into the garden and weed intensively, an activity which, by fully occupying the attention, obstructs consecutive thought, and when I return to my desk my mind has cleared and I am able to make a new beginning. This regime is to Elizabeth and me enthralling, and we are very reluctant indeed to suffer its interruption, except by visits of close friends.

Unless I had been able to live this kind of life, I should have been able to think very little indeed except in terms of response to immediate problems as they presented themselves. But gratuitous reflection or long-term planning, such, for instance, as related to the arrangement of the various collections at the Tate or to the general scheme for the decorations of the galleries, I could pursue only at home. In London, at the Tate, one circumstance calling for decision or for action followed too closely upon another to leave time to allow for concern with any but day-to-day issues, and by the evening I was too tired to think, let alone to write, and fit only for sociability and the reading of a chapter of a book before going to sleep. I envy my friends with greater powers of concentration and the capacity for making positive use of every waking hour, however distracted. Robert Speaight, for instance, writes his articles and book reviews and indeed portions of his books on his all but continuous travels, and he worked on his life of Belloc in his dressing-room between appearances on stage in T. S. Eliot's *The Confidential Clerk*.

Robert Speaight is a friend apt several times a year to materialize suddenly from some remote region of the globe, from playing More in *A Man for all Seasons* in Australia or from judging drama in Kansas City. Although, being of a zestful nature, he derives some pleasure from his peripatetic life—he is almost always on the move —and from the variety of his assignments, as actor, drama teacher and judge, writer and lecturer, he says that he is first and foremost an actor. But he has never become a career actor and taken whatever reasonably well-paid part has offered itself; he has accepted parts only in plays that he believes are well worth performing. Being without a private income he has been compelled to undertake other work, which, whatever satisfaction it provides, is modest in comparison to what he would derive from a series of leading parts in plays by Shakespeare or Eliot. There is an element of heroism in his eclecticism, as indeed in his character as a whole. He has had more to bear in the way of private griefs than most and I have never heard him complain. Even more ordinary misfortunes he views with amused detachment. I remember his describing how, owing to the theft of his luggage on a train, he found himself in the middle of the United States without any possessions except the clothes he was wearing, and deprived of the notebooks needed for the work he had come to do. This misfortune, as he told it, might have befallen a stranger, or himself long ago.

Acting is his chosen pursuit, but it is difficult to believe that the author of *Belloc* and numerous other works would not also have been a writer whatever his circumstances.

One of his conspicuous characteristics results from his being innately an actor, namely the playing of certain parts in life with a professional's bravura. These parts are always parts natural to him. He would no more stoop to pretence than he would accept a stage part that he considered unworthy. At his attractive house at Benenden in Kent he is the country gentleman, handsomely tweeded. He once telephoned to a friend in Oxford saying that he wished to see him about an important matter. It happened that Bobbie was facing an extremely serious problem; the friend, whose advice he was seeking at this critical time, awaited the arrival of his train with anxiety. Bobbie took him straight to the Mitre Hotel and ordered dinner. Coffee served, he asked 'Do you advise a pipe with a *straight* stem?'—he made a vigorous gesture of drawing and handling such a pipe—'or one with a *curved* stem?'—the gesture was repeated with the relevant variation.

Throughout his life Bobbie has been an ardent lover of France and of French culture; perhaps it is in France that he is most at home. From this love his epicureanism derives, and the special flavour of his hospitality. Entertainment of his friends in an hotel or at a restaurant or at the Garrick Club is always preceded by a detailed discussion with the chef.

As a public speaker and lecturer, his combination of fine voice and presence, enhanced by his actor's training and experience, with learning and sensibility and meticulous preparation makes him an impressive performer. Some years ago he gave a series of lectures on Shakespeare to a summer school in Oxford. A don at St. Anne's

College, a highly respected authority on Shakespeare and known as
a severe and astringent critic, exclaimed after them, 'Far beyond
anything I could aspire to.'

The versatile man is sometimes listed as a jack of all trades. Had
Bobbie been only an actor or only a writer, he would be more widely
admired in his own country than he is. But instead of enhancing,
one half of his notable achievement has diminished the full appreciation of the other. 'People like to put a man into a clear category,'
he once said with reference to a third person, 'and if they can't, so
much the worse for him.'

*

It is comparatively rare, I think, for character to be seriously
altered in the middle years of life. After the last rumblings of the
Tate Affair Elizabeth returned with immense relief, though with a
new cynicism about much of human nature and the workings of
procedures in public affairs, to the life that she loved. This was a
private life of creative aesthetic activity in house and garden, totally
satisfying, within our own perimeter. Though she is generous to a
fault with her time towards anybody she encounters in distress and
solicitous beyond reasonable self-sacrifice, her deepest gratifications
are aesthetic. But for marriage she would have been a painter.
Ideally—and had I had no life in London that required her participation—she would have preferred only rarely to pass beyond our
gates. She was and is essentially a private person, and indeed by the
summer of 1959 with such deep relief had she engrossed herself in
the calm and contemplative life of Beauforest that an American
sister of hers, staying with us at the time, was distressed at her
avowed distaste for public and community affairs. But it was in that
same summer that Elizabeth herself was shocked into a change of
direction whose consequences still disturb the Beauforest peace that
she longs for.

Radical change is as often as not occasioned by shock. It came in
the form of shattering noise. Out of a blue and quiet summer sky
there flashed, again and again, a jet fighter flying at a speed not
much below that of sound and at little more than tree-top level.
Enquiry from the nearby R.A.F. training airfield at Benson elicited
the information that the plane was based on an airfield at Chalgrove
and was used by the Martin Baker Aircraft Company in the testing
of ejector seats. Lucy was ill at Beauforest and Elizabeth was

nursing her. She stormed into her car and over to Chalgrove; she refused to leave until the plane had landed and she had interviewed its pilot. The consequence was a promise from the aircraft company to reroute the plane away from Newington and over other villages in the direction of Tetsworth. She saw no reason why she should be a beneficiary of the subjection of other villages to such violence and made enquiries of the then Ministry of Supply. A curt letter from the Parliamentary Under-Secretary of State informed her that the Martin Baker Aircraft Company had been granted permission to fly their test planes at very high speeds and at a height of fifty feet. We were little more than a mile from the runway. The arrogance of this letter, the take it or leave it attitude of the Minister, its inhumanity in blandly inflicting so acute a misery on hundreds of people provoked Elizabeth to further enquiries. Scores of men and women, she found, were having their lives made wretched by this ear-splitting din, and there was much talk about fraud and injustice done to local farmers on whose land the airfield had been established, but there was no one, she came sadly to recognize, who was prepared to do anything about it; either they did not know what to do, or they were too lazy to try, or they were too much afraid of what the repercussions might be for themselves. She set herself, therefore, to find out the facts and to see what she herself could achieve. The consequence was that for some five years her name was virtually identified with Chalgrove. She played her hand with a flair that a professional politician might well have envied—so well, indeed, that one or two members of the Government made no secret of their displeasure.

Until the summer of 1959 we had been entirely unaware that there was an airfield in use at Chalgrove. Elizabeth found that some 700 acres of excellent farming land had been requisitioned for an aerodrome early in the war—in wartime such requisitioning was, of course, legal—and that after the war's end the Martin Baker Aircraft Company, being engaged in work of national importance, had been allowed to use it for research and development of ejector seats and for test dropping. But it also appeared that the aircraft company was insisting on owning it. The consequence was that between 1950 and 1953 there had been dealings and pressures for outright purchase. Since the owners of the land all wanted to recover it, these transactions had involved no little duplicity and mendacity on the part of the Air Ministry. They had, however, been suspended.

In the summer of 1954 the Crichel Down affair had broken on the country and had entailed the resignation of the Minister nominally responsible. The then Ministry of Supply and the then Air Ministry would appear to have taken fright; there was no more talk of sale. But five years later, with the memory of this affair growing dim, the interested parties were beginning to move again.

So she began to move herself. In September she attended a meeting at Chalgrove about the future of this old requisitioned airfield. She discovered that instructions had been issued to the chairman of the parish council to circumscribe public interest: only parish councillors, members of the Oxfordshire County Council and former owners of the airfield were supposed to be given access; the press was explicitly excluded. No fewer than three Junior Ministers came down. The owners were asked whether they wished to recover their land. Reply being given in the affirmative, they were informed that the decision to sell to the aircraft company had already been taken.

Elizabeth found the ministerial tone condescending and overbearing. One of the trio was the local M.P., who took the view that solidarity with government policy prevented his upholding the interests of his constituents. The fraudulently dispossessed farmers, in her opinion, were being not only outwitted but also disfranchised. Her decision to do all in her power to help them was confirmed when, shortly after beginning to probe what had been and was afoot, she found herself the recipient of several threatening telephone calls.

Her pertinacious questioning very soon brought relative peace to our airspace; the permission for low flying was revoked. But her interest in Chalgrove airfield had by now widened. A close study of the text of the Crichel Down debate in the House of Commons and of the transactions already completed or impending with regard to Chalgrove disclosed that the fairly clear principles concerning individual freedom and justice formally enunciated by the Government in 1954 as an element in its surrender of wartime emergency powers, and endorsed by Parliament, were being systematically manipulated by a Service ministry in the interests of a private aircraft company, engaged though this was in work of national importance. Indeed the importance of this work was constantly used, in those distant days of flag-waving for such companies, as a cudgel to beat her with, though it had manifestly no connection in logic with what was happening, the farmers having formally indicated their readiness to rent their land for as long as it would be needed. But what was afoot was that as the farmers would in no circumstances have freely sold their land to an aircraft company, the two ministries concerned were using compulsory powers to acquire it—in peacetime and not for governmental purposes—on the quiet understanding that its freehold should thereupon pass to a private aeronautical enterprise. The degree of complicity of the Oxfordshire County Council was also a matter of much interest; the future of these acres had been discussed and an understanding reached between Ministry of Defence officials and County officials at a very early stage. Elizabeth found it ironic that Crichel Down (compulsorily purchased in wartime for wartime purposes) was a symbol of the wilful erosion of liberties, whereas, comparatively speaking and however deplorable, the affair was largely a consequence of bureaucratic red tape and blunder.

She pursued the matter as long as she could by private correspondence with the ministries involved. Nothing was achieved. She proceeded to take it up with various parliamentarians. Every M.P. to whom she showed the steadily growing file of documentation was profoundly disturbed by its contents, but it began to appear that many were inhibited by extraneous factors, among which were, for example, pressure lobbies. In Mr. John Hall, however, the Conservative Member for the Wycombe Division of Buckinghamshire, she found a man entirely to her own heart, a man prepared to do what was right and damn the consequences; he was a staunch and unflinching ally. In the Commons Mr. Hall secured and conducted a lively Adjournment Debate on the topic as well as a long series of Parliamentary Questions that elicited a sequence of mutually inconsistent replies from an equally long series of Ministers and Junior Ministers, who at the time succeeded one another with astonishing rapidity. Their wrigglings were watched with absorbed delight by many senior members of Oxford University. She activated the public press. The local press, especially the *Oxford Mail*, was more than interested. The editor of the newspaper, Harford Thomas, now managing editor of the *Guardian*, personally investigated the affair and devoted much space to a careful, detailed and critical discussion of the issues involved. In the national press there were letters and features; among the daily newspapers, in spite of the Government's being Conservative under the (at that time) confident leadership of Mr. Harold Macmillan, the most lavish of its space, as well as the most conscientious and painstaking in its collection and assessment of the evidence, was the *Daily Telegraph*. Reporters who at various critical junctures telephoned the Air Ministry for information reported confusion and alarm.

In the event the entire matter was shelved, that is to say put into cold storage for further consideration. The consequence was predictable. After a couple or so years of silence an announcement was made that the 700 acres were to be leased to the Martin Baker Company for ninety-nine years. Public control was ensured. There was no strict illegality. Injustice was done and an aircraft company allowed by an Air Ministry (with the backing of the Cabinet) to take possession for a very long time of other people's property. The restoration of peace-time usages endorsed by the Commons in 1954 was frustrated. There was no comfort for farmers dispossessed beyond their own and their children's lifetime. It is not inappropriate that John Hampden's memorial looks out over these acres.

The Chalgrove affair had directed Elizabeth's unwilling eyes to public affairs that threatened the well-being of the neighbourhood. She had come to appreciate that much of what made life worth living, her own contemplative quiet and fertile creativity within our garden gates, depended on vigilance and, even more, on a readiness to take trouble and devote hard work to a humane settling of issues well beyond our own perimeter. She came to an insight, also, into the helplessness that many human beings feel in the face of encroachments, into the timidity and self-preservative apathy of onlookers, into the fear of not being numbered among the right people and the dread of what the neighbours might say. She began to recognize how powerful was the force of inertia on the erosion of cherished freedoms and decencies. She is not yet the exclusively private person that she still hopes to be again. She has contended at every level with nuisances from the R.A.F. at Benson, and in the days of the Chalgrove affair these were many. Having expended many hours of her time on helping farmers against Whitehall, she has devoted hours of it to combating their demolitions of ancient trees and their encroachments on rights of way and rights of common; she has an ambition to make local government at the parish level the lively and democratic affair that in theory it should be but in practice rarely is. It was the belief that local government is at any rate one defence of the individual against injustice and servility and bureaucratic indifference that prompted her in 1968 to serve as Clerk to the

Newington Council. Many consequences have flowed from one shattering summer afternoon a decade ago. But passionately concerned as she is with local affairs, there are many times when she deeply resents them. The day is all too short for the things that she most wants to do, and she longs for an undivided mind to turn to the aesthetic creativity that gives her her deepest and most abiding fulfilment.

*

Life in Newington in the 'fifties and 'sixties offered strong contrasts to that in the neighbouring village of Berrick Salome at the turn of the century and to that in the Far Oakridge of my boyhood. In his evocative study of Berrick Salome Mr. Moreau has written that 'each member of the community knew everybody else and was a personality to the others. . . . They enjoyed enormously the little feasts and treats and shows; they loved their football; they loved their cricket. . . . They clustered together in the Church and Chapel and sang in their choirs.'[1] In Far Oakridge everybody was known to everybody else, and though there was much courage and humour, the prevailing mood was sombre, breaking out occasionally into violence. In wet summers and autumns the farmers, in enforced idleness, gazed with gloomy frustration at their rotting crops, rotting often until ears of corn sprouted. Everybody was poor.

Newington is marked by a down-to-earth ordinariness. People as often as not know only their immediate neighbours. One or more members of most families are employed in well-paid or relatively well-paid work with the British Motor Corporation or Pressed Steel Ltd at six-mile distant Cowley. In wet weather the farmers wait confidently for a dry spell, when out roll the combine harvesters, if need be in fours or sixes and even after dark; in a few hours the harvest is safely gathered in. But there are no feasts or treats, football or cricket; there is no chapel and the church is deserted except by two or three. There is well-being and much good sense. Since both work and recreation are sought usually away from the village, life is not eventful in any obvious sense. Compared to sombre, isolated Far Oakridge, where before the First World War, I was told, nobody was known to have visited London and only a few nearby Gloucester or Cheltenham, and the equally impoverished Berrick Salome where, however—to quote the verdict of the same author—people 'knew

[1] *The Departed Village* by R. E. Moreau, 1968, p. 165.

the now lost secret of being happy on little', Newington seems as contented as it is prosperous. Of course the better one comes to know a place the more aware does one become of rivalries and tensions and even ugliness beneath the seemingly untroubled surface. As we came to know Newington better and to become more closely identified with its affairs, the more intimately were we able to study, for example, the oldest and most constant feature of English rural life, namely the operations of landowner or tenant farmer in relation to resident villagers. To salvage green lanes, for instance, or commons or even rights of way from ubiquitous enclosure has proved an enterprise that demands not only unceasing vigilance but occasionally physical courage. But this particular story is many centuries old; neither the cast nor the plot has altered much since Norman times; the alliances have altered not at all.

CHAPTER TEN

GOVERNMENT BY TRUSTEES

AN INEVITABLE consequence of the Tate Affair was to cause me among others, both in Great Britain and abroad, to take a hard look at the trustee system under which the flames had taken hold so quickly and raged for more than two years. I myself had worked under the system for so long that I had come to accept it almost as an inevitable feature of the order of things. Certain doubts about it that had lodged somewhat casually in my mind were brought under scrutiny by a chance remark made shortly after the affair had ended. 'Of course you realize', Robin Darwin, Principal of the Royal College of Art, said to me, 'that what happened at the Tate could never have happened at all if you'd been under a Ministry instead of under Trustees.'

As I have had a longer experience of serving under Trustees than any living director of a British national gallery or museum it may not be foolhardy to offer a few brief reflections upon the system under which a number of these institutions are governed. It so happened that shortly after my retirement I was invited by *The Times* to contribute two long articles on the subject, but I preferred to wait until the passage of time had afforded a clearer perspective.

At the time of the affair the Tate, together with a number of other national cultural institutions, was governed by a diarchy, that is to say by a Board of Trustees appointed, for seven-year terms, by the Prime Minister, and by the Treasury, headed by the Chancellor of the Exchequer. In March–April 1965 the functions previously belonging to the Treasury were transferred to the Secretary of State for Education and Science. The powers of the Trustees are not referred to in the relevant Act of Parliament and are accordingly unaffected by this transfer, and my friends at the Tate tell me that these remain, in practice as well as theory, precisely what they were. Trustees are subject, like government departments, to the financial control of the Treasury, and they do not concern themselves with routine administration, staff promotions and the like, which are the

The four grandchildren:

Miranda

Sarah and Susannah

Hugo

'Jour d'Eté' being stolen from the Tate Gallery on 14 April 1956

responsibility of the director. Appointments to the staff are made by selection boards nominated by the Civil Service Commission on which Trustees and the director serve. The staff—at least the Tate staff—assumed that they were Civil Servants until some date in the early 'sixties, when it appeared that they were only quasi-Civil Servants, expected to conform to Civil Service practices but in fact employees not of the Crown but of the Trustees. This discovery about their status had an extremely disturbing effect upon my colleagues.

Like all systems of government the trustee system has advantages and drawbacks. Chief among its advantages is that it brings to the service of the Gallery—from this point I will refer specifically to the Tate, having no direct experience of the functioning of other national institutions—a long succession of public-spirited and cultivated men, some of them passionately preoccupied with painting and sculpture and all actively concerned for their welfare. Four of the ten Trustees are practising artists; the others—a number of them art collectors on a large or a modest scale—may be directors of banks, shipping lines, stock-broking firms, chains of shops and other commercial enterprises, lawyers and writers on the arts.

Whether it was the case with other similar institutions I do not know, but almost every Trustee within my experience soon became closely identified with the Tate and formed in some cases a lasting affection for it. Royal Academicians, whose first loyalty lay elsewhere, were less positive in their attachment, but of recent years they have rarely been appointed Trustees.

Under the trustee system an impressive volume of intelligence, diverse experience, knowledge of the arts and good will has been available to the Tate and at no cost to the taxpayer at all. Trustees are proud to serve the Gallery and are mostly assiduous in their attendance at their monthly meetings.

The chief disadvantage of the system, in my opinion, is the price paid of necessity for another of its advantages: the independence it confers upon the Board of Trustees. Under their rule the Gallery is free from political (as distinct from art-political) pressures and from bureaucratic interference. Where the formation of the collection is concerned this independence is invaluable indeed: a buffer against philistinism not to be lightly sacrificed. But this independence is virtually absolute. In theory the Trustees are responsible to the Prime Minister, who is in turn responsible to Parliament. The

o

Prime Minister, however, knows no more of their doings than he happens to read in the newspapers, and when these have come, on occasion, under discussion in Lords or Commons the government spokesman has invariably suggested that the matter at issue be left to the discretion of the distinguished gentlemen who comprise the Board of Trustees, who enjoy the Government's entire confidence, and so forth. The Trustees, in effect, unlike anyone else in the government machine, are dictators, responsible, in practice, to no one.

So far as the formation of the collection is concerned there is, to my mind, a good deal to be said for such 'irresponsibility', but so far as the staff is concerned it is otherwise, for they are subject to an authority, itself answerable to nobody, from which there is no legitimate appeal; an authority, moreover, not only not composed of professional administrators, but not necessarily including a single member with experience of administration.

The discovery that they were employees not, as they supposed, of the Crown, but of their Trustees, dismayed the staff not only of the Tate but of a number of similarly governed institutions.

A discussion about the government of the national art galleries and museums took place in the early 'sixties at a 'Directors' Conference', consisting of the heads of the national galleries and museums, which meets at irregular intervals. On this occasion a substantial and highly articulate majority voiced a similar disquiet. The solution favoured was the abolition of Boards of Trustees, their replacement by Advisory Councils, and the transfer of Trustees' powers—except in so far as they related to the formation of collections, the holding of exhibitions, conservation and the like—to a government department. Such a system, it was agreed, while retaining the most valuable feature of the trustee system, namely the services of public-spirited men of taste, would put an end to the drawbacks of it outlined above. In a handbook, designed for guidance of the Tate Trustees and prepared under their close supervision in 1955, the relation between the Trustees and staff is defined as 'comparable to that of a Minister in charge of a government department to his permanent officials'. No relation could in fact be less comparable. If a serious error is made by an official in a Ministry, the responsible Minister resigns, while in an art gallery or museum the Trustees, in similar circumstances, are apt to lay the blame, implicitly or even explicitly, on the staff. Trustees almost never resign, and it is relevant to note that whereas resignation by a minister or enforced retirement for an official may have—in the latter case is almost certain to have—grave consequences for their careers, for a Trustee resignation has none but peripheral consequences. They have been known to threaten to resign as a means of bringing pressure to bear on their fellow-Trustees or the staff, who are thereby placed in an awkward predicament, knowing as they well do that he who so threatens may take an action which would have an impressive effect at no cost at all to himself.

A significant feature of the discussion at the Directors' Conference I have referred to was the entire satisfaction with their system of government expressed by directors of institutions responsible to a Minister but with Advisory Councils.

With the conclusions of the Directors' Conference in question I was in wholehearted agreement. The trustee system, in my experience, is susceptible of functioning as perfectly as any, but subject to one condition, and that a crucial one. In a previous volume I quoted Kenneth Clark as saying that 'If there is something rarer than a good artist it is a good trustee'. If there is something rarer than a good trustee it is a good chairman—a very rare person indeed. It is my own experience that provided the chairman is a man of such a kind—I have earlier cited Sir Evan Charteris and Sir Jasper Ridley as just such men—the trustee system is ideal, but that if he is not a person of such a kind—and is it not perhaps too much to require that he should be?—it is a system that leaves much to be desired. The good chairman needs not only to be a public-spirited man of affairs, an enthusiast for the arts, intelligent, zealous and possessed of authority, for these are qualities—fortunately for the Tate—not uncommon among Trustees, but he needs in addition to be benevolently disposed towards the staff, courageous, candid, disinterested, and above all just—almost a superman in fact. Of the first cluster of attributes I mention authority last, for all the chairmen of the Tate—with the exception of one who reluctantly undertook the office during the war as a patriotic duty—have possessed it. It is a common attribute because, in addition to the authority that the occupancy of the chair bestows upon all but the least authoritative, his fellow-Trustees rely upon their chairman to be in close touch with the Treasury and with the staff—far more fully informed, in short, than they on the technical, financial, art-political background of any subject about which they are called upon to make decisions, and to have given close study to all the relevant papers. The influence of the chairman is apt to be decisive, not only as regards routine decisions, about whether to buy or not to buy, to accept or to decline a proffered loan or exhibition and the like, but over the entire character of the Board as a whole. I believe it to be no exaggeration to say that the character of a Board is liable to be more radically altered by a change of chairman than it would be by the replacement of the other nine trustees.

The efficacy of the trustee system of government is dependent, then, upon the chairman's being a man of preternatural endowments. Such men are notoriously rare and when they appear their services are inevitably in constant demand. It seems to me, therefore, that to perpetuate a system which depends upon so rare a combination of high qualities in a single person—and that person probably already overburdened with other responsibilities—is unwise. Were responsibility for the national galleries and museums to be transferred to a ministry or ministries, and Boards of Trustees to be replaced by Advisory Councils, responsibility for their administration would lie with professional administrators, and the right of appeal by staff would be ensured; likewise a real, instead of nominal, ministerial responsibility. On the other hand an Advisory Council would allow full scope for the exercise of its members' discernment and enterprise—which is, in fact, precisely what interests most Trustees. (How many times have I not heard Trustees—in particular artist-Trustees—disclaim all interest in any aspect of gallery management except in so far as it related to works of art!)

During my years as Director the constitution of the Tate (apart from its establishment by Act of Parliament in 1954 as an institution independent in law as well as in fact of the National Gallery) remained unchanged. The composition of Boards of Trustees, however, their attitudes towards the staff and the way in which they exercised their powers underwent changes which, though sporadic and gradual, culminated in their virtual transformation. When I first went to the Tate the 'tone' of the Board of Trustees was set by aristocratic men of taste, who behaved as though they were responsible amateurs who were in general guided by the advice of a professional, in the person of their Director. They maintained this attitude even when they were themselves highly perceptive collectors. I am thinking of such men as Sir Evan Charteris, Lord Crawford, Sir Jasper Ridley, Lord Sandwich, and Lord Howard de

Walden. Of course they did not invariably take the Director's advice, but they were consistently disposed to do so. I am not alone in regarding aristocrats as exceptionally qualified to serve as trustees. While Director of the National Gallery, Charles Holmes wrote to Robert Ross that 'had I your gift of tongues I would write an essay on "Lords and their Uses" which would melt even your icy Liberal heart. Of course I refer to the old and crusted brands . . . You quite underestimate the pleasure of working under men who are placed above the envy, intrigue and petty ambition of commoner men and the advantage to public business that comes from lack of friction.'[1]

As such men became less available, however, the tone was set by artist-Trustees and by knowledgeable men belonging to the same sort of world as the Director and his staff. During my last years the Trustees tended more and more to assert their individual tastes and even to bring forward works, without notice to me or to anyone else, immediately before Board meetings, and such works were on occasion bought without my opinion even being asked for. The mutual deference of the Trustees to one another made it embarrassing for them to oppose anything brought forward by one of their own number. Conversely works brought forward by me after close consultation with the senior staff were sometimes rejected. After a meeting when this had occurred, a member of the staff who now occupies a senior post at the Tate observed angrily that 'the painting or sculpture certain to be turned down by the Trustees is one which has the enthusiastic and unanimous support of the staff and is by an artist whom the Trustees themselves have decided should be represented'. This tendency on the part of the Trustees to regard themselves as the experts and the staff as mere administrators to carry out their wishes became sharply manifest only after the retirement of Lord Cottesloe as chairman in 1960. Lord Cottesloe is an aristocratic man of taste and a discriminating collector, who invariably showed the utmost regard for the opinions of the staff. I do not suggest that the procedure I described was habitual, but it was sufficiently frequent to disturb the staff and to indicate a differing relation between the Trustees and themselves. In earlier years it would have been inconceivable. Artist-trustees, who have become increasingly influential at the Tate of recent years, fall into a very special category. With regard to the kind of art that they themselves

[1] *Robert Ross*, ed. Margery Ross, 1952, p. 324.

practise their judgement is usually, as one would expect, extremely perceptive. With regard to all other kinds they are apt to respond either with a want of sympathy or else, in order to avoid any temptation to prejudice, with an excessive tolerance.

But the circumstance that revealed beyond question the seriously changed relation between Trustees and staff was the secret appointment by the Trustees of one of their own number as my successor. In the event they had to be reminded that the prerogative for such appointments belonged to the Prime Minister and the appointment was not confirmed. Indeed the very fact of the appointment's having been made was publicly denied, but there is abundant, including written, evidence to the contrary. As a Treasury official said at the time, had the attempt succeeded the entire relationship between Trustees in major institutions and the staff for whose welfare they were responsible would have been gravely unsettled. The Trustee in question, after the failure of his candidature as my successor, applied for the post of Keeper of the Gallery's collection of British painting and sculpture prior to 1900. In this he was successful. Two years later he was succeeded by Martin Butlin, a highly regarded specialist on the work of Blake, Turner and other British artists of the period and a member of the Gallery staff for nine years.

*

In spite of its serious shortcomings—provided that the powers of Trustees were confined to the development of collections, exhibitions and the like, and that administration were subject to a Minister to whom the Trustees were also responsible—I believe that the trustee system would be the most satisfactory means of managing the specialist activities of a museum. It is tempting, especially for a director, in office or retired, to favour a director's being vested with authority for ultimate decisions regarding purchases, the acceptance or refusal of gifts, the organization of exhibitions. The risk, quite simply, would be too great. It is possible to secure the dismissal of a director for misconduct, but for errors of judgement almost impossible. Moreover, in an institution maintained by the taxpayer a director responsible to nobody is no less anomalous than a Board of Trustees responsible to nobody. (In the United States and certain other countries where museums are privately maintained their governing bodies are free to arrogate or delegate powers as they wish.) The present danger, however, is not the over-powerful director but the over-powerful trustee.

It would be dangerous, then, if the scope of the Advisory Councils that have been suggested as an ideal alternative to Trustees were to be merely consultative and not deliberative. The selection of works of art is not something to be ultimately left in the hands of any one man over a period of years. The expertise of staff is indeed indispensable in matters of connoisseurship, of information about what examples of the work of any given artist are available at any given time, of the physical condition of a painting or a sculpture, and so on. But also the matured judgement of works of art that has been formed through many years of experience of them and of response to them, and of many kinds of them, is a judgement that should be seriously taken account of by any Board of Trustees. But neither should it enjoy ultimate authority. A Board of Trustees should, that is to say, genuinely deliberate about such matters; if it does, its decision is more likely to be sensible, and there is no inherent reason why a decision reached in this way should reflect any lowest common denominator of opinion. The Tate Trustees have not at any time been prone to decisions of this sort. But two things appear to me, in a word, to be essential; the one is answerability; the other is clearly defined circumscription of their authority within the boundaries that I have suggested.

I am, of course, not the only man to point to these problems in this decade, nor is Britain the only country in which they have emerged. I quoted a judgement of Mr. Bryan Robertson's in my last volume; I end this chapter with another verdict of his. 'Power . . . is manipulated in England too often for the implementation of amateur opinion rather than of professionally authoritative knowledge.'[1]

[1] *Private View*, Bryan Robertson, John Russell, Lord Snowdon, 1965, p. 164.

CHAPTER ELEVEN

LEAVING THE TATE: ST. ANDREWS

MY LAST months at the Tate were lived in an eerie limbo. My retirement at the end of September was announced in April 1964. At the end of July my old friend and close collaborator, Norman Reid, was appointed to succeed me. It would have been wrong—apart from continuing to bring forward works for the consideration of the Trustees and proposals about exhibitions— to attempt to exercise any influence over long-term policies. Over one issue it was a relief: this was the completion of the building, which was engaging the close attention of the Trustees. About the desirability of the completion of the unbuilt rear-quarter of it there was no doubt in anybody's mind, but about the projected substitution of a vast steel and glass box for the existing Victorian-classical façade I was relieved to have to offer no opinion. Such a construction would have added to the Gallery's accommodation and amenities but—however irrationally—I would have shrunk from having any part in the destruction of Smith's handsome and lovable façade. The best solution seemed—as it seems to me still—to replace the long-obsolete military hospital next door with a new building designed specifically to accommodate the modern collection.

After my last Board meeting on 17 September I felt like a shadow —a role to which I was unaccustomed; no less strangely, a shadow benignly regarded.

The director of an art gallery, particularly one concerned with modern art and most particularly the national collection of it, becomes accustomed to arousing hostility, to hearing reports of statements about him which, if he were a private citizen, would tempt him to bring action for slander. I have given an account in some detail of one area of my own experience that received an unusual amount of public attention, but most directors of art galleries whom I have known well have confessed to moments of distress and even of despair. I remember hearing Charles Holmes say that, though in general he had no belief in ghosts, he believed that the National Gallery, of which he was Director, was quite literally haunted by evil spirits, so acutely had he suffered there. These words, spoken many years before I had any notion of entering his profession, struck me as hyperbolic.

So it was that the ubiquitous expressions of goodwill by collectors, artists, members of the public, tributes in the press, farewell dinners, although delightful, heightened my sense, during the last months of my directorship, of existing in a shadow world. After the last Board meeting I attended on 17 September even the shadows grew paler. But that meeting was marked by a memorable event.

I told the Trustees of several conversations that had taken place between Henry Moore and myself concerning a matter of great importance to the Tate.

Several years before, in July 1960, when I was visiting him at Perry Green he had invited my opinion about a friend's suggestion that the house be preserved as a memorial after his death and all his unsold work remain there and the collection perhaps added to, saying that he himself had serious doubts about the feasibility of such a project: the difficulties seemed too formidable. I replied that the cost of the upkeep would be enormous and Perry Green was relatively inaccessible.

Henry received, and with evident relief, my negative response, with its implication that some already established institution would be preferable as providing a more accessible site and at no cost to his estate. As though I had referred explicitly to the Tate he said that after fourteen years as a Trustee he had formed a deep affection for the place and would prefer the collection of his work there to be augmented. The idea, then, that the principal collection of his work should be at the Tate was entirely his own. Directors of art galleries have at times to solicit benefactions: it was the more satisfying that this one was due entirely to the spontaneous impulse of a generous man.

During the intervening years this proposed bequest had been the subject of discussion between us. Henry had once told me that before making a journey by air he had drawn up a provisional will leaving everything he possessed to the Tate.

Two nights before my last Board meeting he had called with his family at my house in Chelsea before all four of us went to the Tate for a dinner in Miró's honour, and told me that he had decided definitely to make the much discussed bequest and authorized me to tell the Trustees of his intention. He had given me a rough list of individual works and of various categories of works which it was his intention to include. This list—which, of course, I showed to the Trustees—was in manuscript, and as he had no copy he asked that it should be returned to him for further consideration. In view of Kenneth Clark's intention (which I had already reported to the Board) of bequeathing a splendid group of drawings, Henry had said that he saw no point in adding to these, but I replied that I believed that the Trustees would welcome the inclusion of some maquettes. He intended, in the final list, to exclude casts of bronzes already in the possession of the Arts and British Councils in the hope that these would eventually find their way to the Tate.

The accommodation of a few of the largest bronzes offered serious problems: their size would make it impossible to show them in the present building; its rusticated façade as a background made an outdoor site impossible. These, perhaps, should remain in their deeply impressive landscape environment at Perry Green. But as the list was not a final one, to bring these problems to the attention of the Board would have been premature.

As Henry had often spoken to me of his dislike of the Duveen Sculpture Hall—in which, on account of its great height, the source of light was remote from the sculpture shown there so that its forms were apt to lack definition—I told him that I thought the Trustees, when a new building was erected, might consider setting aside space for a Moore collection. This possibility seemed to delight him, but I made it clear to the Trustees that it had been raised by me and there was no question of any condition regarding the manner of the collection's display being attached to the proposed bequest.

The Trustees expressed their utmost pleasure at this splendid bequest—a bequest which a little lightened my sadness at severing connection with an institution with which my interests, my affections, indeed my entire way of life had been for so long so intimately identified.

The bequest was treated as confidential for about two years—as was prudent, considering that its terms had not been precisely agreed—but news of it, 'leaked' to a Sunday newspaper, gave rise to a spate of controversy and speculation. At the Royal Academy Dinner in 1967 the Prime Minister, Mr. Harold Wilson, announced it in the most appreciative terms and stated that it was the intention of the Government to make a special grant of £200,000 for its accommodation.

Not long afterwards a letter signed by a number of highly
respected young artists was published in *The Times* protesting
against the singling out of a living artist for such conspicuous
honour. Its implicit denigration of a man widely acclaimed as the
foremost living sculptor, and one, moreover, who had shown consistent generosity to his younger contemporaries, was read with
astonishment and indignation. It later appeared that the signatories
were under the impression that the entire sum to be allocated for the
extension of the Tate, namely £2,200,000, was to be spent on
building a gallery to accommodate the Moore collection. When it
was made known that the sum to be so used was that named in the
Prime Minister's announcement, several of them expressed their
heartfelt regret to Moore.

I walked out of the Tate on 2 October for the last time as its
Director, oppressed by regret at leaving the only public position I
had ever wanted, my colleagues and the wide complex of responsibilities that my directorship brought with it. I had decided that my
departure from the Tate should end my involvement in the London
art world and, except for the Friends of the Tate, I resigned from
the various committees on which I served.

So I walked out into the street as into a void. It is a common
weakness of our nature that we are more conscious of the deprivation
of privilege than of the enjoyment of it. Far from taking pleasure in
a lifetime's health, we are scarcely conscious of it; yet illness can
immediately bring us to despair.

Suddenly, after a third of a century, to have no public function
is a strange sensation; I missed even activities peripheral to my
duties at the Tate which—when I had thought of them at all—I had
thought of as drudgery. Such sensations pass quickly, especially if
one is so constituted as to look to the future rather than the past. I
delighted in the prospect of being able to give to writing periods
longer than weekends. Paradoxically, I looked forward to looking
back.

There are many people—including several of my own friends—
who are masters of the art of living and are able to experience their
lives fully while they are living them. I am not one of them. To me
life, as I have lived it, has seemed too confused and fast-moving to
be experienced fully. Experiences, even the most deeply felt, have
at the time a dream-like character and seem entirely 'real' only in
recollection. It was principally for this reason that I had begun

Summer's Lease, the first volume of these memoirs. But to write a full-length book at weekends involves constant interruption of trains of thought, and I looked forward eagerly to longer periods of writing. *Summer's Lease*, on which I had been engaged since the middle 'fifties, was finished a few months after I had left the Tate and published just a year later. But, except in rare cases, the writing of books—certain popular categories apart—is, economically speaking, a luxury. After payments to agents, typists, the tax-collector, the residue is insignificant—especially for a slow writer such as myself on subjects of a limited field of interest. And so a few days after leaving the Tate I took up an appointment as art adviser to the publishing division of the British Printing Corporation in an office in Hertford Street, Mayfair. The conditions of work there offered a bizarre contrast to those at the Tate. In a smallish room on the first floor were four people besides myself, two of them typing continuously, the other two talking constantly on the two lines of telephone. I shared a table with Hugh Elwes, editor of *Discovering Art*, the weekly periodical we were producing.

Nominally an 'art adviser', I was in fact a proof corrector working in an inferno. In the meantime there was much discussion, initiated by John Chancellor, then head of the publishing division, about a modified English version of the Italian weekly *Maestri di Colore*.

On 22 October, examining a very rough mock-up, I noticed myself described as editor. Although I had joined the Corporation as an adviser merely, I was attracted by the prospect of learning a new profession and accepted the obliquely proffered invitation. My proposal that the new periodical should be called *The Masters* was accepted, and I was given authority to initiate new issues and to commission texts from British authors even when we used Italian colour plates, and to make changes in these if the authors doubted the authenticity of any of the paintings reproduced. Each issue of *The Masters* was devoted to a single painter; it consisted of a brief biographical introduction, a longer critical appreciation, seventeen colour plates and a smaller number in black and white, a guide to further reading and to the whereabouts of works by the painter in British public collections.

The response of the most authoritative scholars to invitations to contribute texts was immensely encouraging: Anthony Blunt wrote on Poussin, Kenneth Garlick on Lawrence, Geoffrey Keynes on Blake, Michael Levey on Bronzino, Benedict Nicolson on Wright of Derby, Herbert Read on Vermeer and Bosch, Graham Reynolds on Constable, Michael Jaffe on Rubens, and Kenneth Clark had agreed to write on Henry Moore, to name but a few. *The Masters* was received with enthusiasm, especially by art students and others of the younger generation.

Owing to circumstances remote from editorial control it was decided to end the series in September 1967 with the hundredth number. There were times when I felt that the editing of *The Masters* was a logical continuation of my efforts at the Tate to make the most serious artists widely known.

*

On the morning of 15 October 1964 I received a very long letter written in a small hand. I judged it to be the sort of letter (of which directors and ex-directors of art galleries are frequently victims) in which an account of a worthless work of art is accompanied by an expression of the owner's desire to sell it. I accordingly deferred reading it until after breakfast. I was entirely mistaken about its contents: it was an invitation from a group of students at the University of St. Andrews to accept nomination as their candidate for the rectorship.

I marvelled at the unexpectedness of the invitation, but after consultation with Bob Boothby, a former rector and friend from Oxford days, I decided to accept it. I was the more attracted by the invitation because Scotland, in the course of my rare visits, had been a country in which I felt very much at home, and two of the four most intimate friendships of my life had been with Scots, Tom Rowat and Athole Hay.

Richard, our son-in-law, was dangerously ill—so dangerously that Lucy sometimes slept at the Edward VII Hospital; our household was disrupted as Elizabeth assumed responsibility for the grandchildren, and I was deeply involved in an unfamiliar enterprise. Accordingly, I gave no thought to the election at St. Andrews—even though one of my supporters, Margaret Baron, visited me in London to give me news of the campaign. Interest being intense, she urged me to visit the University, as all the other candidates had. Such a visit, she said, would be of particular value in that St. Andrews people were always inclined to suspect others of reluctance to go there on account of the awkwardness of the journey. I told her that I could not take any part in the campaign, but that in a country celebrated for its moors and streams it must be made clear that I did not kill animals, birds or fish, and that in the country of John Knox I was a Roman Catholic. Whatever curiosity Margaret Baron's visit might have stirred was dissipated by a telephone call from Lucy that Richard's condition had become critical.

Exactly a week later, on 14 November, another of my supporters, Spencer Hagard, telephoned to tell me that I had been elected. I was, I believe, the first person primarily associated with the visual arts to become rector of a Scottish university. Ruskin was elected in 1871 but disqualified as holding office at another university, that of Slade Professor of Fine Arts at Oxford.

That St. Andrews, unlike the English universities, has a rector, is due to two causes, one secular, the other religious. Before the foundation of St. Andrews in 1410 many Scottish students had studied in England, but war between England and Scotland, and the recognition, during the Great Schism of 1378–1418, of Benedict XIII—the Avignon Pope—by Scotland, combined to sever academic intercourse between the two countries. The turbulent condition of Paris—which had begun to attract Scottish students —early in the fifteenth century made the establishment of a Scottish university a virtual necessity. The system of government derived in part from continental rather than English models, from those of the Low Countries but also in part from those of Orleans and Angers, whose institutions in turn derived from those of Bologna, although in a less democratic form.

Bologna had attracted students through the eminence of its teachers of law. The students—many of them of mature years and of good standing in their own countries, affluently beneficed and non-resident clerics (cathedral dignitaries, for example)—were mostly foreigners and principally German. In a city-state in which they enjoyed no civil rights they needed to co-operate, therefore, in students' guilds or 'universities' for their own protection and welfare. Moreover, as Rashdall commented long ago, 'prolonged exile was a serious penalty, to which a body of young men of good position in their own cities, many of them old enough to be entering upon political life, would naturally submit with reluctance. The student-universities represent an attempt on the part of such men to create for themselves an artificial citizenship in place of the natural citizenship which they had temporarily renounced in the pursuit of learning or advancement.' It was a logical corollary of this that Bolognese students, having a natural citizenship, were excluded from these student-guilds or 'universities', just as professors, being citizens of Bologna, were likewise excluded from office in them.

The four 'universities' of legal studies in Bologna were in origin, therefore, private societies for the welfare of their members, to whose constitutions the students had bound themselves by oath and whose sanctions, therefore, were spiritual as well as temporal. These statutes, revisable only after long process, were administered by an executive officer, the rector, and a student council. The rector was not elected by the students directly, but indirectly—by ex-rectors, the newly elected councillors and an equal number of special delegates. It was in other words a form of self-government rather like the societies of merchants who combined in national companies when working in a foreign city, within but constitu-tionally independent of, though upheld by, the city of Bologna. It was not an arrangement that arose from an ideal of student-partici-pation in any contemporary sense. However, given their mature years and standing, and their muscles well developed by their deal-ings with the city—whose commercial prosperity postulated that students should not exercise their undoubted medieval right of migrating elsewhere if dissatisfied—the jurist universities of students were able also, at Bologna, by tough boycotting of unpopular teachers and of students who attended their classes, to dominate the doctors' guilds as well. Not that the doctors had not themselves, through a too close identification with the city, fostered an antagon-ism of interest. But the domination did not last long. By the end of the thirteenth century, to propitiate the students, the city was paying the salaries of the doctors, who hitherto had been paid by the students themselves. Effective concern for the excellence of the university as a teaching institution was, therefore, in other hands and students and their rectors gradually lost all but a fraction of their former control. But though they had once selected their own professors, at no time had they claimed or exercised academic control of curricula or examinations.

When the Scottish universities of the fifteenth century were founded—by the respective local bishops—there was a hope of establishing them as schools of theology and law. It is this hope that is probably responsible for their partial imitation of the student-university of Bologna. But the hope was too ambitious for a country so poor and so little populous as Scotland; the Scottish students

were arts students and extremely young. From the beginning, therefore, student government was a mere form. Indeed, the academic
constitutions most closely followed were those of the universities
that had been frequented by Scots about this time, that is to say
(the older medieval universities of Paris and Oxford being torn by
too many dissensions) those of the new universities in Germany and
the Low Countries.

The office of rector was inherited, therefore, indirectly from
mediaeval Bologna. In Bologna the rector, who was required to be
a 'secular clerk, unmarried, wearing the clerical habit', took pre-
cedence over all archbishops and bishops (except the bishop of
Bologna) and over cardinals. The expenses of his office were met
from the fines he exacted from the members of the university. The
expenses must have been crushing. At Bologna's sister university
of Padua the installation of the rector was celebrated by a tilting-
match for which the rector was required to provide 200 spears and
200 pairs of gloves for the combatants. At Bologna he was forbidden
to 'dance or make to dance with trumpets' for a month after his
election. A particularly expensive custom grew up of stripping the
newly elected rector of his clothes, tearing them up and requiring
him to redeem the shreds for exorbitant sums. A statute of 1552
forbade the 'too horrid and petulant mirth' which marked these
occasions, which it did not, however, abolish. It is not surprising
that students became anxious to avoid election, and in order to
prevent him from absconding before the end of his year of office
the rector was not allowed to leave the city without the permission
of his council or without giving surety for his return.

It is only a semantic accident that in Bologna an association of
students was termed a 'university' and an association of doctors a
'college', whereas at Paris and in Oxford it was the other way round.
Nor does it matter; for in the Scottish universities, as in their German
models, college and university were virtually identical. The consequence was, however, that in the Scottish universities teaching was
restricted to a permanent body of regents, as it was not in the
medieval universities, with a curious difference for St. Andrews in
that a system of rotation obtained there, so that each regent taught
a group of students throughout all their four-year course.

It is indicative of a low standard of education—the system was
abolished in the eighteenth century—and this standard and the
youth of students account for the fact that from the very early days

The author at his Installation festivities as Rector of the
University of St. Andrews, 1964

Beauforest House, 1969

the election of the rector, who was in effect a working vice-chancellor, was restricted to graduates. It was restricted to them and to men in orders as early as 1475. In 1625 the franchise was restored to all members of the university but only heads of colleges were eligible for election. In 1642 the franchise was denied to students except for those in divinity and in the senior arts years, and the 'viri rectorales' were heads of colleges and a professor or two. This arrangement obtained for nearly two centuries and for much of the time was complicated by a curious circumstance, or device, whereby four 'viri rectorales' ruled in rotation.

In the nineteenth century, however, fresh winds began to blow, and 'the one hundred and eighty or so country youths who formed the student body were soon at odds with the handful of conservative old men who attempted to govern them'. The only leverage they had was the rectorial election. It was not much, seeing that both suffrage and choice were so severely circumscribed. They countered by the argument that to elect any of the officially eligible candidates was inconsistent with the oath to elect a man 'majoris dignitatis ac nominis'. In 1825 Sir Walter Scott was elected. The election was voided, but there were negotiations in consequence of which all matriculated students were to enjoy the right to vote. But since their choice was still unfree, their discontent was not allayed. Glasgow had taken the initiative in opening the rectorship to outsiders and throughout the 1830s had elected leading politicians. To the students this was a new dawn; to the senate it was a deterrent against change.

But as the years went by, juniors became seniors and the old order began to crumble. The process was no doubt expedited by a few incidents, as when one rector, a principal of a college angry that his own college had only one official rectorial candidate, refused to surrender his gown of office at the end of his term and had to be coerced by the university commissioners. In 1858 half the vote was for a 'vir rectoralis' and half for Sir Ralph Anstruther, a much respected landowner of East Fife. The retiring rector gave his casting vote for Sir Ralph. This could not so easily be voided and the Lord Advocate advised that he be installed.

But in this same year was enacted the Universities Bill, which opened the office of rector to anybody fit for it who did not hold a teaching post in a university, with an amendment to the original Bill that disfranchised university staff. Contrary to the fears of many, nineteenth-century elections were not purely political in character, though until 1892 every election was contested by two candidates, of whom one was usually sponsored by the Conservative Association and one by the Liberals. The latter were much more imaginative and more successful; the former preferred to nominate party figures and had many reverses until they won with Balfour in 1886. Disraeli had lost to J. A. Froude in 1868. Two liberal victories were voided: Ruskin as holding an Oxford chair; James Russell Lowell, American ambassador at the time, as being an alien—a precedent disregarded in the election of Nansen in 1925 and of Marconi in 1934.

There appears to have been little consensus, however, about what it was that a rector was supposed to do. In 1862 Sir William Stirling-Maxwell, the Conservative Member for Perthshire, took his office very seriously. 'Your rectors', he declared in his rectorial address, 'have certain duties to perform here and they ought to be chosen chiefly with a view to the efficient performance of these duties.' Yet the very next rector—a Liberal victory this time—was John Stuart Mill, who defeated the Lord Lieutenant of Perthshire, Lord Kinnaird, and in his three-hour address in 1865 Mill called his office the 'honorary presidency' of the university, leaving it obscure how such a presidency differed from that of the Chancellor. It would seem that for most of the time the effective head of the university was the senior college principal, and in 1889 a new office was inaugurated, the principalship of the university, the size and scope of the University Court being also extended. St. Andrews itself was growing in numbers. But the existence of a Principal was not construed as entailing that the rectorship was purely ceremonial. In 1892 the Marquis of Bute became rector, a man with a passionate personal interest in St. Andrews, and engaged in a long struggle—he was elected for a second term three years later—over policies with regard to Dundee with one of the finest Principals—Donaldson—St. Andrews has ever had. The Principal won, but honourably.

But after Bute the rectors were quiet men as far as St. Andrews was concerned. Andrew Carnegie, a munificent benefactor, had two terms and was followed by a succession of great public figures. Between the wars, as a historian has commented, it seemed at first as if the rectorship were to become a St. Andrews version of a Nobel prize for literature and then of a Nobel prize for peace. It was a period in which it enjoyed great prestige but the old dissatisfactions grew. Should a rector be a 'working rector' or not? He was apt to appear once during his term of office, for his installation and his rectorial address, and then to disappear for ever. Smuts was installed a month before the end of his term, in October 1934; Marconi was elected in 1934 but died in the spring of 1937 before he had put in an appearance at all. In these circumstances a St. Andrews graduate who had already served the University, Lord MacGregor Mitchell, won an emphatic victory in 1937 over Hugh Walpole. He died a year later and was succeeded by another St. Andrews graduate, Sir David Munro, who for the same reason won comfortably over Admiral Sir Roger Keyes. The war intervening, Sir David ruled for eight years, the longest term in history. The election of so close a neighbour as Lord Crawford in 1952 is an indication, I think, that this wish was still operative, as also was that of Lord Boothby in 1958, who also made a point of concerning himself wholeheartedly with university affairs. In 1964, after my own election, the students gave me clearly to understand that a working rector was what they preferred.

In fact, in the last two decades, the function of a working rector in the Scottish universities has approached more closely that of the medieval university proctor—and in Oxford and Cambridge the proctors were sometimes called rectors; to a large extent, though not entirely, he has to do with representing and working for the interests of the students as a distinct group. It may well be that in the still fresher winds blowing through universities students will prefer to represent and work directly for their own interests themselves rather than elect an older man to do it for them or even with them. Indeed in 1968 some of the Edinburgh students nominated one of their own number for the rectorship. Inchoately, and for entirely different reasons, it is an interesting reversion to the Bologna of over 700 years ago.

In the circumstances of 1964 the best course seemed to me to keep in close touch with the students (I promised them that I would meet their Council before every meeting of the University Court that I was able to attend) and to do what I could to foster interest in the visual arts, to which little attention had been paid.

Following a warmly welcoming letter from my supporters I made, on 21 November 1964, my first visit to St. Andrews. Twelve of them wearing their scarlet gowns were waiting for me at seven in the morning at Leuchars Junction. They took me first to Balcarres (where I was to stay), the house of my old friends David and Mary

Crawford, the only people I knew in Fife, and then to a gay break-fast at the Peat Inn, a place out in the country several miles from St. Andrews. Over that hospitable table, in front of a blazing fire, began the ever-widening complex of my friendships with students. On that memorable occasion my hosts talked mainly about the university and its future, with an earnestness that, far from preclud-ing, served to stimulate wit. One was able to discuss serious issues without cautious preliminaries; the habit of serious conversation was evidently an integral part of St. Andrews.

The students made it clear to me that they relied upon their rector to safeguard their interests, and that my own term as rector would cover a highly critical three years, as St. Andrews and Dundee, which since 1897 had formed a single University, were to go their separate ways in 1966 or 1967. The impending separation, which it was acknowledged would gravely impoverish both, was fatalistically accepted. It seemed to me ironical that 'the split' was to take effect shortly after the new Tay Bridge would bring the two institutions, hitherto relatively remote by road, within less than half an hour's drive of each other.

Breakfast over, we visited the Students' Union, where I was received with a few discreet hisses and a vast drumming of feet upon the floor, which I at first took for a hostile demonstration, but was assured that it was, on the contrary, a token of welcome. After talk-ing with many students I walked through the streets of the little town of St. Andrews, for which—like many another—I felt an instant love, which grew with every successive visit. With Walter Scott I wondered 'why it should agitate my heart'.

In the Middle Ages St. Andrews, with its vast Gothic cathedral, its still earlier priory and its castle—all now in ruins—standing close together on a bleak and windswept promontory facing the sea, must have been one of the most spectacular sights in Europe. How this remote and inhospitable place should have become the focus of so much of Scottish history is mysterious. In spite of the pervasive aura of the Middle Ages pre-Reformation records are meagre: there are, I believe, not even any engravings which show the city as it was before John Knox 'preached it into ruins'. Its early history, as Stevenson wrote, 'broods over St. Andrews like an easterly "haar", grey and cold and blinding, a curtain of mist'.

That evening I enjoyed my first experience of the political sophis-tication and good sense of the students: I was entertained to dinner to meet the proposers of the other rectorial candidates, so that any divisions generated by a fiercely contested election should be promptly healed.

On another evening Lord Crawford took me to call on the Principal of the University, Sir Malcolm Knox. During our visit the Principal's attention was directed almost exclusively towards Lord Crawford, but as we were leaving he said that he presumed that I would not wish for the usual religious service in connection with my installation. I asked him whether he supposed me to be an atheist or knew me to be a Roman Catholic. I told him that I would be most happy were the usual service to be held. Subsequent negotiations disclosed, however, a degree of bigotry in some senior sections of the university that I was unaware still existed anywhere in the world, so that ecumenism was entirely unilateral. The date was 1964, and how remote it seems from the now prevailing climate of increasing goodwill and co-operation between the churches. But even then a wind of change was blowing. Before my three years had expired, at a Catholic Hierarchy Low Week reception, a bishop said to me, 'I want you to meet my friend the Moderator of the Presbyterian Church', and introduced me forthwith. On my last visit as rector to the university an honorary degree was conferred upon Dr. Grey, Archbishop of St. Andrews (now Cardinal).

One problem greatly preoccupied me: who was to serve as my deputy, or, as he is called in Scotland, my assessor. A rector, non-resident and ignorant of Scottish universities, can obviously render effective service only if he has the close co-operation of an assessor with intimate knowledge of the University. There was one outstanding possibility, a man who had graduated from St. Andrews with a double first class degree, who lived in the neighbourhood, was liked and admired by the students, had been the highly valued assessor to my two immediate predecessors, namely Sir John Carmichael. But he had been an unsuccessful candidate for the rectorship and was personally unknown to me. After discussing the matter with the Students' Representative Council and with their emphatic approval I invited him to become assessor again.

After a brief hesitation he accepted, to my intense pleasure. As his London office was also in Mayfair we were able to meet whenever the need arose. Before long we became close friends. Thanks to his understanding helpfulness and that of David Crawford I was kept well informed and prudently advised. On 24 November in Dundee I presided for the first time over the University Court. I am an indifferent chairman even in propitious circumstances, and being ignorant of the backgrounds of the issues under discussion and of the personalities of my colleagues round the table I must on this occasion have been peculiarly ineffective—a circumstance that the prevailing courtesy prevented from being conspicuous. On subsequent occasions, even though I studied the agenda minutely with John Carmichael and was closely informed about student attitudes, I never acquired the grasp of procedure, the sense of timing, the knack of encouraging the shy, of curbing without humiliating the loquacious—or most of the other talents a chairman needs.

Most human beings, I suppose, watching or recalling some public ceremony, wonder what it feels like to be a participant. I am no exception, but I had never, in my most extravagant dreams, imagined myself as the occasion for the splendid ceremonies prepared by the students in connection with my installation in St. Andrews and Dundee during 18 and 19 February 1965.

Early on the first morning, a flag flying from every flagpole in the town, Elizabeth and I went to the West Port (an ancient gateway), where I was formally welcomed to the University and the Burgh, inspected kilted cadets to the sound—at once so mournful and so exhilarating—of bagpipes, and was presented with the scarlet gown of a student (or bejant, as he is called at St. Andrews) which I immediately assumed (having, for twenty-four hours, student status). We then climbed into the Kate Kennedy coach, which was drawn by 'Blues' around the city, accompanied by a crowd of students in their scarlet gowns. (Kate Kennedy was the supposed niece of Bishop Kennedy, founder, in 1450, of St. Salvator's, one of the University's constituent colleges. In 1460 Kennedy put a bell into his new tower of St. Salvator's, naming it Katharina; she is still commemorated in an annual procession, though now as the attractive and respectable niece of the bishop.)

At each of the thirteen stops, at residences and the like, I was wittily welcomed and presented with a gift. At Dean's Court it was a copy of Machiavelli's *Prince*, as an aid, no doubt, in countering the supposed guile of the academic Establishment; somewhere else a shield to protect me from its assaults, and a shepherd's crook to enable me to guide my flock. The 'Blues' drew the coach so fast that we were able to make an extra stop for their refreshment. (Bob Boothby told me afterwards that on a similar unscheduled stop he had accepted a goldfish-bowl filled with whisky, and that in consequence the stop had been protracted by the need for a brief sleep, but that by taking a short-cut and by an extraordinary burst of speed by the 'Blues' he had kept punctually to his schedule.)

In the evening one of the great St. Andrews traditions was re-enacted, when a long procession of students carrying blazing torches marched along North Street and right out to sea along the pier in the blustery dark, then back along the Scores (the seafront road) and on to the West Sands where the Rectorial Bonfire was lit, and the students, one by one, threw their torches into it as they sang. For a few hours St. Andrews became again what it had been years ago, 'the Singing University'. As the procession passed along the Scores it stopped in front of the Principal's house, where we were having dinner. The students expected to be welcomed by the rector in whose honour the procession was held. The door remained closed; the Principal did not disclose to us that the procession had arrived.

Later that night we went to Dundee so as to be ready at Tay Ferries Terminal for our welcome early the following morning. This was as warm as that at St. Andrews. Again we boarded the Rectorial coach for a drag by 'Blues', this time through the busy streets of an industrial city, preceded by pipers and followed by a great crowd of scarlet-gowned students, to City Chambers, where we were welcomed by Lord Provost McManus. We then walked in academic procession, preceded by the two University Macebearers, to the parish church of St. Mary for the Service of Dedication. In the afternoon came the Installation Ceremony itself. This was held, for the first time in the University's five hundred years and more of its history, in Dundee, as Caird Hall accommodated larger numbers than any place in St. Andrews itself. It was the climax of the two-day celebration and for me an ordeal in several respects.

I had had the privilege of nominating three honorands for Doctorates of Law. Two of these were Professor Ernst Gombrich and Cecil Woodham-Smith. As a third I wished to honour David Jones (who was not well enough to make the journey) or Oskar Kokoschka (who was abroad). The University generously allowed me the third later on, when an LL.D. was conferred on Henry Moore, whom, as already overwhelmed with honours, I had not chosen among my original three, none of whom, however deeply and widely admired, had been recipients of honours commensurate

with their achievements. In addition to her outstanding gifts as a
historian, I had a special reason for wishing to honour Mrs.
Woodham-Smith.

One of the most humiliating and tragic facts about the history of
these islands is the failure of peoples otherwise politically gifted to
evolve a form of government which the constituent parts could
happily accept, or, more bluntly, Britain's ill-treatment of Ireland.
Cecil Woodham-Smith's *Great Hunger*, written on this side of the
Irish Channel, was for me a splendid token of amendment.

Caird Hall was densely packed by some thousands of students in
uproarious spirits. The Principal seemed to be nervous at having to
preside, owing to the inability of the Chancellor, the Duke of
Hamilton, to do so on account of illness; his relations with the
students were not cordial and it was evident that the atmosphere was
tense. The graceful, long, unfolding arcs of pink and blue toilet
paper, some of it falling—by chance or design—near Sir Malcolm
and Lady Knox, provoked him to an angry outburst and a threat
that unless noise and demonstrations ceased he would cancel the
entire function.

The students responded to the threat with a low prolonged roar of
rage. Sir John Carmichael whispered 'I'm afraid they are going to
run amok'. However, though the installation of rectors in other
Scottish universities has often been attended by acts of violence, the
throwing of eggs and tomatoes, bags of flour and even of potatoes,
at their rectors, at St. Andrews this has not been the case, and the
attitude of the students towards their rector is positively protective.
They did not run amok, and as Professor Gombrich, Mrs. Woodham-
Smith and I had Doctorates of Law conferred upon us and our merits
were being extolled by the Dean of the Faculty of Law the uproar
petered out.

I then took the Rectorial Oath, put on my purple robe of office and
proceeded to my first and most exacting duty: to deliver my
Rectorial Address. To have the attention of some three thousand
expectant students and critical academics for three-quarters of an
hour, to follow predecessors as eloquent as Kipling and Barrie, Lord
Balfour and Lord Boothby, or as learned and fluent as John Stuart
Mill, General Smuts or Lord Snow—and this with a voice so hoarse
that I doubted whether I would be heard at all—was a very alarming
ordeal. The prolonged cheering when I got up to speak and the
ebullience of the audience all but resigned me to delivering my

Address unheard. To my delighted surprise I was listened to in unbroken quiet. My theme, *Independence 65*, was a plea for the spirit of critical objectivity.

The installation was followed by a Rectorial Dinner at the conclusion of which, to my amazement, messages were read out from the Queen, the Prime Minister (Mr. Harold Wilson), the Leader of the Opposition (Sir Alec Douglas-Home), my predecessors Lords Kilmuir, Crawford, Boothby and Snow and the other rectorial candidates. (A cable from President Johnson was delayed until a day or two later.) The dinner was followed by the Rectorial Ball, at which an American woman student said to me, 'I've suffered on your behalf: I was putting up a Rothenstein poster during the election and a supporter of another candidate pulled down the ladder and I broke my collar-bone. But not before we'd changed all the Ps (for parking) into Rs'.

Next day I was again given gifts, one of which I particularly treasure: an elaborate cigarette-smoking machine constructed in the Engineering Department to enable me to smoke vicariously and avoid lung-cancer.

The installation and its attendant ceremonies had two results for me, one obvious, the other wholly unexpected: an enhanced devotion to St. Andrews and in particular to the students—and an admiration for politicians. I was all but annihilated by public activities in which I was invariably received with the most generous enthusiasm, whereas politicians, who in the course of comparable activities are often treated with indifference and hostility and are subject to perpetual criticism, appear to flourish. Not long afterwards I discussed this matter with a Member of Parliament. 'It is not talked about', he said, 'because we politicians like our eloquence and administrative ability and so on to be praised, but the simple fact is that three-quarters of political success depends on physical stamina.'

My three years' rectorship of St. Andrews was a source of almost unalloyed pleasure, although it was frustrating to be the recipient of such wide-ranging friendliness and hospitality yet be able to do so very little in return.

I was instrumental in securing an elegant degree scroll designed by Reynolds Stone and set up by the Curwen Press; I fostered the aim, promptly realized, of the appointment of a professor of fine art and the idea, widely supported but as yet unrealized, of the

establishment of an art centre; I gave fairly effective support to the
remedying of several causes for student discontent. These were very
modest achievements indeed, and they exacted no cost at all.

The rector is nobody's rival and in any case a transitory figure.
The relations, nevertheless, between a rector, now largely, though
not entirely, non-working, yet the successor of men who were, for
centuries, the active heads of the University, elected by the students,
and the principal, a permanent official, responsible for the day-to-day
running of the University, are somewhat anomalous. There are, I
suspect, occasions when principals have doubts about the desirability
of a system that brings the holder of a historic office into an uneasy
partnership with the university's effective head. Sir Malcolm Knox,
who was the Principal during my first two years of office, made no
secret of his disapproval of the students' election of a Roman Catholic
and I gathered from certain of my predecessors that he disapproved of
them no less, although on other grounds. But I deeply respected the
dignity and good sense which the students invariably showed in our
discussions, formal and informal alike.

Almost invariably I was greeted in the early mornings of my arrival
by scarlet-gowned figures at Leuchars Junction. Before almost every
meeting of the University Court a meeting was held of the Students'
Representative Councils of both St. Andrews and Dundee, at which
matters particularly affecting the student body were discussed, with
on occasion mildly dramatic results.

My meetings with the students were not predominantly official.
We met constantly. Nothing could have been more enjoyable than
their hospitality, their candid and cheerful talk. It is perhaps
invidious to name a few of the many who have become constant
friends but I will do so all the same: David Caldwell, Spencer
Hagard and Michèle Aquarone, now married, Alonso Roberts, Peter
Shelton, Iain Orr, Jennie Forbes, Margaret Baron. . . .

On my later visits, so as to be more readily available to the students,
I used to stay at St. Salvator's College, but I was enchanted by East
Fife and made frequent visits to my friends in the country, especially
the Crawfords at Balcarres.

One fact that should be recorded emerged from one of our
midnight conversations. The genuineness had been impugned of a
letter several times published (once in a book of my own) from several
of the impressionists, Degas, Monet, Pissarro and Renoir among
others, to Sir Coutts Lindsay in which tributes are paid to Turner.

'They cannot forget', it concludes, 'that they have been preceded
... by a great master of the English school, the illustrious Turner.'
As Sir Coutts Lindsay was a near relative of David Crawford's I
asked him whether the letter was in fact genuine. 'It has disappeared',
he replied, 'but my father saw it.'

With David and Mary Crawford and with Cecile Carmichael I
made many expeditions to houses in the neighbourhood. Didn't
someone describe Fife as 'a beggar's mantle fringed with gold?'
The description fits it: the central and western parts are bleak, but
the coastline and its immediate hinterland, though rocky and austere,
many of its trees gnarled and bent by the fierce east wind, and often
fogbound, is one of those regions which take an immediate and
enduring hold upon the affections: the chain of fishing villages,
Crail, Anstruther, Pittenweem, Elie, where the painted fishing-boats
offer the same contrast with the grey stone buildings along the shore
as the scarlet gowns of the St. Andrews students with the town's
grey ruins and austere but elegant Regency streets.

One icy afternoon in January 1967 David Crawford drove me over
to tea with Admiral Sir William James. We found him waiting for us
on the pavement outside his house in Elie. He was eighty-six and a
gale was blowing in from the sea. 'I had to keep a space clear', he
called out, 'as I know you're no good at reversing, David.' The
Admiral is a grandson of Millais and the subject of his notorious
painting 'Bubbles', and he spoke frankly about the Millais family,
dwelling upon her children's dislike of Effie Millais and her lack of
sympathy with her children except one son, Everett. I cannot
recall many of his age so fully in possession of all their faculties, so
full of zest for life. There were no doubt enmities, rivalries, skeletons
in cupboards, but to an outsider the Fifers seem to be closely united
by ties of extraordinary goodwill. In no house I visited did I ever hear
a word of denigration of a neighbour.

Early that April I accepted an invitation from Fordham University, New York, to serve as visiting professor of the History of
Art for the autumn term. Since it therefore became impossible for me
to perform my duties as rector up to the expiry of my term of office
in November, I went to St. Andrews at the end of June for the con-
ferment of degrees in order to say goodbye to my friends.

As I sat through a second graduation ceremony the next morning,
that of Saturday 30 June, I decided that to remain for a further day,
with its pleasurable obligation of attendance at services at the Catholic

Chaplaincy and the University Chapel, and meeting so many students and members of the Faculty together, would involve fare-wells both more formal and perhaps more emotional than I was prepared for. My last official duty finished, I got into the Car-michaels' car and they, understanding my feelings, distracted me with a visit to Falkland Palace. By this time I had come to regard John and Cecile Carmichael as among my most valued friends; I delighted in their forthrightness, their wisdom and their rare kind-ness. (The previous summer I had been taken ill in St. Andrews, and he had arranged for his car to meet me at King's Cross and drive me straight to Newington—nearly fifty miles.)

That evening I went to Kellie, a superb castle with a distant prospect of the sea, built in the sixteenth century and intact. Most habitable castles have been modernized, but not Kellie: it is still without a main staircase; one climbs to the upper floors by narrow stone steps inside turrets at its corners. The chief interior feature is the seventeenth-century plasterwork, as elegant as it is bold. Hew and Mary Lorimer are ideal proprietors of a spectacular dwelling, which, like the Crawfords, they appear to manage with minimal outside help. There I spent two idyllic days, neither reading a word nor receiving a letter nor answering the telephone, but sitting in the formal garden under a hot sun, my gaze drawn constantly to the castle, so unbelievable for all its massiveness that it would not have surprised me if it had vanished like a mirage. Those two idyllic days of affectionate, intelligent company of the Lorimers assuaged the melancholy of parting from St. Andrews. My interest in Hew's sculpture was enhanced by the fact of his master's being our close friend Eric Gill. The cast of one piece, an eight-foot-high carving of Our Lady of the Isles, which stands on the Island of South Uist, is especially impressive in its austere dignity. On the Sunday evening Monica Lorimer drove me to Leuchars, stopping the car for a silent moment at Strathkinness to allow me a last glimpse, down a shallow depression, of the distant towers of St. Andrews bathed in a lilac light.

I had a strange sensation that I have never had on leaving any other place that I should never see it again.

Students at both St. Andrews and the new University of Dundee invited me to accept nomination for a second term. I told them that the administration might well think a rector a fool for three years, but if he stayed longer and became more involved in the affairs of

the university and more fully informed they might think him a knave
as well, which would diminish such influence as he could exert on
behalf of the students. This I felt so strongly that I was not even
tempted; so large a part of a rector's usefulness is due to his being
an outsider; after three years he would cease to be one.

To have been rector of St. Andrews was an unforgettable experience. I wish I could adequately express my gratitude to the
students for electing me, and for their trust and manifold kindness;
to my old friends David and Mary Crawford, and to my new friends
John and Cecile Carmichael, whose unique knowledge was always at
my disposal and whose houses were always open to me, and to Hew
and Mary Lorimer, who gave me their friendship, all of whom also
gave me an insight into the magical 'Kingdom of Fife'.

CHAPTER TWELVE

THE DAIMON OF PROGRESS

OUR CENTURY has been marked, in every sphere, by swift and accelerating change. It was therefore inevitable that painting and sculpture, and the little world in which they are made, evaluated, bought and sold, should also have undergone radical change.

The crucial development has been the progressive enfeeblement and the eventual dissipation of the once widely inspiring western European tradition. It was a tradition based upon the imagery of the natural world, whether hieratic like Giotto's, heroic like Michelangelo's, visionary like Blake's, 'realistic' like Courbet's, caricatural like Daumier's, or idealistic like Ingres'—to mention but a few of the infinite variety of ways in which it could be treated. This tradition was like a river with many tributaries and only now when it has all but disappeared does it begin, in retrospect—in spite of the infinite diversity of the artists who have worked within it—to have a kind of unity. How secure this tradition seemed, when I was a boy!

Roger Fry, then considered in many quarters a dangerously subversive critic, came to Bedales when I was at school there to give a lecture. Apart from his denigration of a popular Victorian painting of a Roman centurion, I remember only one point that he made, namely that Cézanne, far from being the anarchist that he was widely held to be, differed from his predecessors only in probing visible reality more deeply. (Picasso recently quoted Cézanne, as saying about nature, 'one never pays enough attention'.) It was precisely because tradition seemed to be so secure that conventional artists, collectors and critics (that is to say the vast majority), when works by Van Gogh, Gauguin and Cézanne were forced upon their attention, were able to treat them with such unrestrained vituperation. These masters were in fact endowing this tradition, so soon to disintegrate and disappear, with a final surge of blazing energy.

There prevailed, then, a general notion that there existed a

tradition based upon the close representation of nature (as exemplified in the work of the impressionists, for instance, or, at home, of
the leading members of the New English Art Club), or of the free
interpretation of nature (as exemplified in that of the revolutionary
masters just named and their followers). Academicians thought of
themselves as the true guardians of this tradition and of these
masters as anarchists. The fact that from around 1910 this tradition
was being radically challenged by such painters as Kandinsky was
scarcely known in Britain and when the work of artists such as the
three masters already named, as well as Seurat, Rouault and
Vlaminck, which only a few years later would have been thought of
as an integral part of the European tradition, was shown in Fry's
Post-Impressionist Exhibition of 1910, it was contemptuously
received not only by conservatives but even by a number of pro-
gressives, blind to the fact that such painting restored something of
primitive vitality and simplicity to a tradition showing manifest
signs of decadence.

Foreign painters whose work was basically traditional, such as
Bonnard, Vuillard, Utrillo, Modigliani, the young Picasso, as well as
Cézanne, Van Gogh and Gauguin, gradually became accepted, but
that of the revolutionaries, Kandinsky, Duchamp, the cubist
Picasso and Braque, remained little known—little known in London
and in the provinces almost unknown. But in the provinces almost
nothing was known about any of the artists I have mentioned.
There were a few exceptions: there was an enlightened tradition of
collecting in Glasgow and at the Whitworth Gallery, Manchester,
which included in its admirable collection of water-colours the work
of revolutionary figures such as Klee at a surprisingly early date.

London in the 'thirties was, of course, much more sophisticated,
and through the magnificent benefactions of Lane and Courtauld
and the writings of Fry and others the work of the great continental
masters from Manet and Cézanne to Bonnard, Vuillard, Matisse and
the young Picasso was already widely admired.

The historic significance of the work done by the best British war
artists (in both wars) has, it seems to me, escaped notice. Ours is an
age when the visual arts are becoming—and in innumerable instances have already become—esoteric, private communications or
even soliloquies. The work of the British war artists is the last
successful example of the serious treatment, on a grand scale, of
public themes, with dignity and conviction. Their achievement has

not received due recognition, partly because art of such an explicitly public character is outside modern sympathies, and partly because many of the best examples are lost, on the walls of the Imperial War Museum, among a multitude of works which are of value only as records.

The Second World War had a transforming effect on the entire art world. Not only was the influence of the old Establishment eroded until it ceased to exist, but a new public and new critical attitudes came into being—attitudes which before long were the exact opposite of those which had previously prevailed.

During the war the fact that relatively few paintings and drawings were on exhibition and the rarity of exhibitions enhanced their value in the public's eyes, and the fact that almost all of them were by the most serious living British artists focused public attention on modern art as never before. These circumstances fostered a responsive, open-minded attitude. Britain's isolation had the effect of enhancing the interest of artists in their predecessors, but it was not long before the work of most of them became part of the ebb and flow of an emerging international art. Traditional figurative art was still practised, often with conspicuous success, by survivors from earlier epochs such as Kokoschka, Augustus John and a number of others, but the new international style became increasingly abstract.

The decades between the end of the war and the present day saw the break-up not only of the—continuously evolving—figurative tradition but eventually of the whole concept of tradition. Tradition was replaced by a variety of movements which, whatever the distinction of the work of many of their adherents, quickly lost their cohesion and authority and were eclipsed. There are various reasons for this break-up of the Western figurative tradition and the brevity of the movements, some successive and others contemporaneous, that have followed. The most obvious is the changing character of society. In many spheres of human activity continuous change has become endemic: in social habits and conditions, attitudes towards religion and politics, to name a few among many. There is another and also immensely influential reason. As the knowledge of the pioneers of modern art, the impressionists and Cézanne, Gauguin, Van Gogh and Seurat, grew with the ever-increasing attendances at art galleries and the dissemination of colour reproductions of their work, one question became more and more insistently asked. Why were these masters unrecognized during their lifetimes, abused when they were not ignored, and mostly unable to sell their work—abused and ignored by the most influential art gallery directors, collectors and critics?

The answer—unlike the answer to many comparable questions—was simple. There had prevailed a conviction that a kind of sacred norm existed, a tradition not of the comprehensive kind alluded to, but a conventional academic tradition, deriving remotely from the Renaissance, with a concession here and there to romanticism, realism and other vital movements that had modified it when practised by the masters. But the exponents and supporters of this popular academism regarded any radical departures from it—most particularly departures that might have endowed tradition, in the larger sense, with new life—as manifestations of anarchy. The work of the modern masters was denigrated simply because it was a radical departure from this sacred norm: in a word because it was *new*.

The natural reaction—though so extreme as to be irrational—to the abhorrence of the new was the assumption that anything new was likely to be better than what preceded it. Innovation was admired as irrationally as it had earlier been condemned or ignored. Almost as irrationally, at least, for it is indeed the case that the large majority of the finest painters and sculptors have been innovators. But the conclusion often drawn from this indisputable fact is that art inevitably progresses through innovation, and it is not a valid conclusion. Unlike science, art does not necessarily progress. Science is a collective pursuit; scientists take the fullest advantage of their predecessors' achievements: they begin where their predecessors have left off. With artists matters are entirely different. Of course they draw inspiration from the vision of other artists, but the sheer magnitude of the achievement of a certain master can bring an epoch to a close: Michelangelo, Raphael and Rembrandt, for instance, revered though they were, did not have disciples whose stature exceeded theirs; it is even doubtful whether their example was of much immediate practical value. The great innovators realize new values, but usually at the cost of abandoning old ones.

On account of the disastrous errors of those who were supposed to be best qualified to judge the innovating masters I have named, those qualified to judge of the new today mostly hold their peace—at least in public. They have lost their nerve. They examine, nervously, a painting of a uniform black or a uniform blue or one resulting from a

R

naked girl rolling on wet pigment: suppose after all the artist turned out to be a Cézanne. . .!

That Picasso is a greater artist than Michelangelo is not explicitly asserted, yet the general assumption that prevails is that innovation is desirable in itself and likely to be an improvement on what has gone before. Innovation, in short, is equated with quality, whereas in the history of art times of progress, of decline, or of stagnation succeed one another or intermingle.

*

Throughout my early and middle life I was accustomed to hearing artists—successful portrait painters and a few extremely careful bachelors such as Steer excepted—speak of the difficulties of survival. Indeed even fashionable portrait painters were not immune. McEvoy, for instance, unable for a while to pay his rates, shuttered up all the windows of his London home to give the impression that it was closed, while he worked there undisturbed. Wyndham Lewis, Spencer, Ginner, David Jones, Roy de Maistre, Bomberg, Henry Moore, Barbara Hepworth and Ben Nicholson and scores of others voiced to me or in my hearing their anxieties about their neglect by dealers, collectors and critics, and their ill-usage by the still influential Establishment dominated by the Royal Academy.

After the Second World War the climate was entirely different. Abuse provoked by the Picasso-Matisse exhibition at the Victoria and Albert Museum and the abuse by Munnings of the same two masters after he became President of the Royal Academy were widely regarded, not, as they would have been before the war, as condemnations of eccentricity by responsible authorities but as manifestations of hooliganism.

From the 'forties to the 'sixties the concept of tradition withered away. I did not make systematic visits to colleges of art, but when I was invited from time to time by staff or students I noticed no drawing from the life or still-life. When there were models posing the students were either improvising freely on the theme of the nude, or more often painting abstracts entirely unrelated to their ostensible subject, on which their backs were often turned.

Not only did 'tradition', in the comprehensive sense in which I have used it here, evaporate, but all movements, however conspicuously successful, enjoyed ever briefer spans of life. A single example will serve to make this point. The New York school of action painters which emerged as a mature movement in the late 'forties and continued to flourish in the 'fifties aroused enthusiasm among young painters throughout the Western world, and in the United States pride in the first American art movement to make a forcible impact abroad. When I visited New York in the 'sixties, though Pollock, de Kooning, Gottlieb, Rothko and several of their colleagues were held in high repute, action painting, as a movement, was as remote, for the younger painters I met, as social realism or even as cubism. It was an episode in the long history of art, an episode that gave New York unprecedented prestige as a creative centre, but already half-forgotten.

The contempt of the academic Establishment for originality and innovation, then, had a large share in the conditions at present prevailing in the visual arts. But there is another factor that has been crucial in effecting the break with the past which has been pervasive and enduring. This factor is the dominance of abstraction, a dominance extending well beyond non-figurative art.

When I first saw paintings by Mondrian and Kandinsky, paintings and sculpture in Mall Studios by Nicholson and Hepworth and sculpture by Brancusi when I visited his studio in Paris, I thought of them as avant-garde rather than radically revolutionary. Widely different though these artists were, their work had in common (although by no means invariably in the case of Kandinsky) an almost classical sense of proportion and a classical serenity of spirit. But in retrospect these and other works of a similar character appear to me to be decisive manifestations of the total break with the European tradition based upon the phenomenal world, however freely interpreted in the interest of idealism, satire, caricature, fantasy, 'moments of vision', symbolism or any other motive. Abstract art has been defined and described many thousand times, but Herbert Read's lucid and succinct description is as good as any. 'The abstract artist', he wrote, 'can affirm the subjective nature of his activity, and abandoning all attempts to reproduce even the phenomenal character of an object, or indeed any forms given by the direct experience of the eye, he can proceed to project on his canvas an arrangement of lines and colours which are entirely subjective in origin, and which, if they obey any laws at all, obey the laws of their own origination.'[1]

Abstract art represented an attempt, by excluding all national,

[1] *Art Now* (1933), p. 100.

local, old or modern imagery and associations, to achieve, through its formal qualities alone, 'something', according to Ben Nicholson, 'with a universal application'. It was neither an ignoble nor an irrational ideal: to evolve a language of form that would always speak directly to people of all times and all places; a language which would confine itself to themes that could not be better expressed in other media, in that, for instance, of the photographer. Abstraction is a concept very much in accord with the division of labour. Abstract art is the art of the 'specialist' in the production of form and colour.

I believe that the phenomenal world offers a criterion for a figurative work of art, however visionary, however caricatural, however idealistic, however fantastic. Its existence provides an indication of how to evaluate a Rowlandson or a Daumier, a Raphael or a Palmer, a Fuseli or a John Martin. The more impassioned advocates of abstraction have frequently written as though the consistent aim of figurative artists was 'imitation'. Realism is a relatively modern phenomenon, but even realists have not 'imitated' nature but interpreted her within a highly evolved 'aesthetic convention. Direct 'imitation' of nature in the absence of such a convention is an impossibility, as (in addition to the convincing arguments of aestheticians)[1] is shown by the most gifted 'primitives', artists unschooled in this highly evolved aesthetic convention, even by a 'primitive' of genius, such as the Douanier Rousseau who 'imitated' nature as closely as he could.

Re-reading *Art Now* I came upon a passage which expresses, precisely, what seems to me to be the basic difference between its author's and my own convictions regarding the relation of the phenomenal world to the artist. 'Landscapes and portraits have, so to speak, their own personalities', it runs, 'and it is easy for the representational painter to mask his own lack of personality in the impersonality of things.' But is there a single example of some moving subject: a storm at sea, the interior of a forest, a sunset or a sunrise, a venerable face, an exquisite naked figure, in which any such theme is portrayed in a manner that moves us by a painter who has to mask his lack of personality in its impersonality? I believe, on the contrary, that the phenomenal world is not a pretext for an artist 'to mask his own lack of personality', but that it is, on the contrary, a vast complex of life-giving essences, of forms and colours.

'Imitation' (besides being impossible) is a pejorative word, but

[1] See E. H. Gombrich, *Art and Illusion* (1960).

certainly painters as different as Rembrandt and Courbet, Constable and the impressionists sought to represent the reality of their subjects, and even a painter as remote from being an 'imitator' as Picasso told me that he had never painted a picture that had not its point of departure in something in nature. The influence of abstraction has been to sever the link between the artist and the phenomenal world, and I believe that the severance is disastrous in its disintegrating effects.

This implies no denigration of the finest abstract artists, but I regard them as a class apart. The abstract painters and sculptors I have named, and a number of others have splendid achievements to their credit, but achievements of a highly specialized, autonomous order.

The work of all figurative artists, even the most visionary, the least 'realistic', is directly related to the phenomenal world, which provides its essential nourishment. It provides it also with a criterion of judgement, rough and ready though it is, unavailable for that of abstract artists, each example of which—to quote Herbert Read again—'is a Law unto itself'.[1] The collapse of the tradition, more precisely the complex of traditions, of art related, intimately or remotely, to the phenomenal world, and the dominance of an art each example of which 'is a law unto itself', has ushered in a time of critical anarchy. It has often been observed that each generation in an evolving tradition has shown its originality in terms of opposition to the immediate past. But for the young artist of today there is no tradition to oppose, no powerful Establishment to defy. The Establishment, in terms of a group of influential multiple office holders, exists today as always, but instead of being repressive, as it formerly was, it is in general eager to identify itself, without reserve, with whatever innovation is currently fashionable. The Royal Academy itself is no exception: it courts, assiduously, the currently fashionable, though sometimes with amusingly ambivalent results.

*

In several important respects the position of academies has changed: membership confers little distinction and modest material benefits. In earlier times to be a Royal Academician was likely to ensure, if not a fortune, at least a livelihood. There has been during the present century a tendency, accelerated since the war, for the reputations and the material success of artists to be made by the

[1] *Art Now*, p. 100.

commercial galleries, most particularly by those that actively foster the interests of individual artists.

The chief exhibition gallery of modern art before the war was not the Whitechapel Gallery, Burlington House—or even the Tate. It was the Leicester Galleries, housed in modest premises on the south-east corner of Leicester Square. Here were held, owing to the perceptiveness of Oliver Brown and his partner Cecil Phillips, the first exhibitions in England of Cézanne, Renoir, Pissarro, Van Gogh, Matisse, Picasso, Klee. At Brown's memorial service in 1967 Kenneth Clark said in his address that 'anyone who bought two good examples from each of these exhibitions would be a millionaire today. Nobody did.' There must be many who owed their first sight of the work of these and many other masters to the Leicester Galleries and I should like here to acknowledge my own indebtedness to its pioneering activities. Its rooms were as familiar to me as those of my parents' house for almost as long as I can remember. Of course there were certain artists whom they exclusively represented, Sickert, Max Beerbohm and many others of high distinction. But they did not 'promote' them—at times almost the contrary. I used to be amused—and occasionally frustrated—when I was focusing my attention on a picture in order to decide whether to bring it before the Tate Trustees; Brown would hail me cheerfully and, standing between the picture and me, would dilate with enthusiasm about it or even some other picture. The Leicester Galleries, after two moves, still flourish, but the chief focus of attention today is not the gallery that holds a long succession of one-man or 'mixed' exhibitions as the Leicester Galleries did, but those which intensively promote members of a carefully selected 'team'. Of these the most spectacularly successful is the Marlborough, which was established by H. R. Fischer and Frank Lloyd in 1947 and whose 'team' includes Henry Moore, Francis Bacon, Ceri Richards, Kokoschka, Ben Nicholson, Victor Pasmore, John Piper, Sidney Nolan and several other of the foremost painters and sculptors of the day. The interests of all of them are assiduously fostered. Mr. Fischer keeps in almost constant touch with his artists. The prices of almost all works of art have risen but, although I know little about the details, I believe that the Marlborough pay their artists a regular income as well as ensuring that they receive substantial prices for their work. 'Before the Marlborough took me on,' a painter said to me, 'when my former dealer owed me £25 I used to call to collect it, and after a couple of hours' argument I'd come away with £10.' The best dealers have become so influential that they confer on 'their' artists a status comparable with that formerly conferred by membership of the Royal Academy. So influential are they that even artists of high talent find it difficult to survive without their collaboration. Fortunately dealers with a perceptive eye for talent and good-will towards artists are not uncommon, certainly in London and New York.

*

It is difficult to make valid generalizations about people engaged in the most monotonous vocations; how much more difficult when artists—whose calling depends upon, or accentuates, highly individual personality—are in question. Nevertheless, during the decades in which I have had direct experience of them, it is possible to discern certain pronounced changes of attitude.

Before the Second World War artists were apt to regard themselves as members of a superior caste, superior, in their sensibilities, their perceptions, but above all, in the loftiness of their aims, to the generality of their fellow-men—qualities which they also readily conceded to poets, novelists and workers in other creative fields. Membership of this élite was regarded as incurring heavy responsibilities towards their fellow-artists and art in general. This was the case whether with artists such as Charles Ricketts and Charles Shannon, who led aloof and fastidious lives, very far indeed from the madding crowd, or such as Augustus John, who although he rejected a number of the generally accepted moral values nevertheless resigned his membership of the Royal Academy in 1938 when that body refused to exhibit Wyndham Lewis' portrait of T. S. Eliot in their Summer Exhibition. From my childhood until about the late 'thirties I remember frequent discussion among artists regarding matters of ethics; whether, for instance, it was not 'wrong' that so and so should not be elected to membership of such and such a body. Admittedly my father was exceptionally preoccupied with the ethical aspect of art politics. I remember seeing the correspondence between him and the president of an unimportant society of lithographers about its refusal to elect Lucien Pissarro to membership. To this my father contributed more letters than most artists today would write appealing against their own death-sentence. Of course artists 'protest' today, against the war in Vietnam, the establishment of an airport at Stansted and the like, but, in general, collectively. In the earlier days I am attempting to recall most artists were, if not exactly their brother's keepers, at least closely— though of course not always benevolently—concerned with one another's doings.

After the Second World War, with the decline of institutional religion and the immense popularity of the originally despised masters of modern art, Cézanne, Van Gogh, Gauguin and certain of their successors, art became, as T. E. Hulme called it, 'spilt religion' and leading artists themselves came to be regarded as almost mystical figures, and the reigning body of aesthetics was one reminiscent of Croce, its influential exponent in the English-speaking world being Herbert Read. According to this aesthetic, subject is irrelevant, representational art is not art proper, for representation is a means to an end, the arousing of emotion, and art proper has nothing to do with ends, being itself a pure expression of emotion. The doctrine that art proper is the self-expression of spirit is illuminated by the negative definitions of art of Croce and his English disciples. 'It is not physical fact, for this is to allocate it to the category of concept and of reason; it is not a means to pleasure and entertainment or the production of any intended effects by techniques, for this is to allocate it to the category of the economic and the magical, of desire and utility; it is not moral, for this is to allocate it to the category of ethical activity, of will and principles of good and evil; it is not knowledge, being preconceptual, but (since it does not presuppose knowledge) better than knowledge.'[1]

Neither the generality of artists, nor even of critics, is familiar with the writings of Croce and his derivatives, but the aesthetics of philosophers, particularly during the 'thirties, 'forties and 'fifties, exercised, largely through the writings of Herbert Read, a pervasive influence upon both. Artists came to regard themselves not as a modest élite with wide-ranging sensibilities and responsibilities but rather as unique individuals capable of producing a primary self-expression of spirit through pure emotion. And they became articulate as never before. 'Of all the bad features of the art world today', Francis Bacon observed to me, 'the worst is the "statement by the

---

[1] This succinct summary is taken from Father Vincent Turner's contribution 'The Desolation of Aesthetics' to the symposium *The Arts, Artists and Thinkers*, edited by John M. Todd (1958).

Artist" by way of preface to the catalogues of an exhibition of his work.' An anthology of such 'statements' would already make bizarre reading; to future generations much of it would border on fantasy. Whether it is due to the continuous physical struggle with refractory material or some other cause, the pronouncements of sculptors were noticeably more relevant to their own individual aims in their own work and less susceptible to panoramic philosophizing than those of painters.

But already, by the 'sixties, the artist as the personality expressing a unique vision, the unique possessor of lyrical intuition, seems to his younger contemporaries a slightly pretentious figure. The very idea of a living artist being regarded as a 'master' has become repugnant. (For them Picasso is simply an Old Master who happens to be alive.) Their attitude was clearly reflected in a letter to *The Times* following the announcement of Henry Moore's intended bequest of a collection of his sculpture to the Tate. No British artist is regarded with greater admiration or affection than Moore. The letter did, indeed, rest on a misconception, but it was also a pro-test against the apotheosis of a living man. It is a current assumption that younger generations recoil from the mediocre and insignificant among their elders. In the history of art the contrary has been more usually the case. The recoil of the American action painters against the social realism (in which some of them had even participated) which preceded their own movement was, indeed, in essence against a kind of art called into being by legislation which, however socially benevolent, compelled many artists to portray subjects refractory to their natural interests, and which produced a huge volume of work that (with some splendid exceptions) seemed provincial and irrelevant to the 'mainstream' of the arts. But the recoil of younger generations is more frequently not from faceless exhibitors in academies and salons, but from the most significant of their elders.

*

Demythologization of the living artist is accompanied by the first beginning of a possible demotion of the unique original work of art as the only proper object of purchase by the lover of art. This demotion is itself but a function of an alteration in the economic structure of society. The works of the western world were created for small aristocratic or mercantile classes or for a church not disposed to sell them. Today wealth is more widely distributed. A public interest in the arts, scarcely conceivable for liveliness and distribution even half a century ago, is stimulated by the activities of art galleries, by colour reproduction, television, radio and other agencies. But the larger part of the major and a large proportion of secondary painting and sculpture have already passed into or are destined for public possession; inflation has made modern works of art vastly expensive and they are difficult to buy, even for many of those who can afford them, owing to the concentration of the art trade in a few small areas in a few great cities.

The art trade plays a highly important part in the art world. The major international dealers have the power of creating artists' reputations as academies had in the eighteenth and early nineteenth centuries, although reputations cannot be long maintained without talent to justify them, but it is doubtful whether the art trade is now as well adapted as it formerly was to meet the needs of the public, more particularly in Britain. In the United States, on account of the high prestige of art collecting, a tax-structure that favours collectors making gifts to public institutions, and abundant wealth, private buying of painting and sculpture still flourishes. In Britain conditions are entirely different: dealers who have discussed them with me have estimated the number of collectors on any considerable scale at no more than twenty or thirty. These and public galleries cannot create a very substantial demand; indeed the dealers in the more expensive objects sell—they tell me—a high proportion of them to foreign buyers. Yet year by year—as increasing gallery attendances and the sales of colour reproductions show—the interest of the British public in the arts grows continuously. What does this public require? Not expensive original paintings and sculpture—so much is perfectly clear: they cannot afford to buy them. Nor 'popular' works, that is to say shoddy, derivative works: visits to art galleries, reproductions of works by the masters, have made it too sophisticated.

The logic of our situation is obvious—and for the painter and sculptor ominous: namely that the widespread enthusiasm for the arts can be met only by the supply of multiple units of some kind. Not reproductions, but large numbers of originals such as artists' prints or casts. Print-making flourishes on a very high level and there is no reason why enormous editions of casts should not be of high quality. But the production of originals in the requisite vast numbers necessitates the use of new technologies which inevitably affect the character of the product, and leave the painter and sculptor in the position of a practitioner of a 'handicraft'. The designers of the new multiple—and readily replaceable—units will be artists; there is no reason why they should not be very good artists indeed. But they cannot be painters and sculptors in the sense that they have been from Giotto to Picasso, from Pisano to Moore. It may be objected that there will always be scope for the fine painter and the fine sculptor. But the prospects for these arts, were they to survive primarily as 'handicrafts', would be bleak. Great artists usually appear when there are many others similarly engaged: Masaccio, Michelangelo, Rembrandt, Goya; they are none of them isolated phenomena, but the apexes of pyramids very broadly based. There is a sense in which even the dreariest hack is contributing his mite to their achievements.

*

Revolutions appear, in the long perspective of history, less radical than they seemed to contemporaries—to whom, on occasion, they marked the end of the world. In writing of the present situation I am, of course, aware of the temptation to exaggerate its radical character; no less of the tendency of elders, evident through the ages, to criticize—on grounds not justified by posterity—the work of their younger contemporaries. But I can only bear witness to what I see, and I am in any case reflecting not upon the talent or originality of my own younger contemporaries, among whom there is much of both. On my visits to art schools I have been impressed not only by the talent and originality of many students but by the craftsmanship they bring to the making of their constructions. It is the situation in which they have to exercise their vocation that arouses misgiving.

It seems to me that the disintegration of the Western tradition— again I use the term in its most comprehensive sense—has also occasioned the disintegration, more or less rapid, of the movements that have accompanied and succeeded its demise. The widespread abandonment—often by artists of outstanding talent—of the external world as a source of their themes has transformed art from a public into a private language—a language intelligible to very few or else a soliloquy. Occasional utterances by artists whose work is the most remote from any reference to the phenomenal world suggest that at a certain level of consciousness they recoil from the fact that, whatever its qualities, their art cannot convey other than aesthetic values. 'The function of the artist', wrote Robert Motherwell, 'is to make actual the spiritual that is there to be possessed.' According to Mark Rothko, 'subject is crucial, and only that subject matter is crucial which is tragic and timeless'. The opinions of these two gifted painters and intelligent men deserve the utmost respect, but I cannot see how the work of the one can convey spiritual truth or that of the other the tragic. They were no casual comments; they were printed in the catalogue of the exhibition, The New American Painting, brought together by the Museum of Modern Art, New York, and held at the Tate early in 1959.[1]

Human beings' preoccupation with themselves, their fellows, their environments and their ideas surely precludes an enduring interest in art forms which by their nature frustrate the representing of any of these and, therefore, of any comment upon them. The film, the still photograph, can both represent and comment, but the paintbrush can accomplish something beyond the reach of both. A Rembrandt and even a Whistler have made images, for example, of the dignity and pathos of old age that are unforgettable, an integral part of the human heritage in a sense impossible for a film-maker or a still-photographer. I am now speculating about the future, near or far, but for the present, painting and sculpture even of a remotely traditional character are boring to the sophisticated public.

Pop art has been regarded, with some plausibility, as a harbinger of a renewal of interest in the phenomenal world. But the interest is strictly qualified. The subjects of pop are indeed taken from everyday life, which is treated, however, as though it did not really exist, as though, in fact, pop painters shared—as artists—the recoil of their non-figurative fellows from the phenomenal world. Pop art does, of course, make some appeal to the predominant preoccupation of human beings with themselves and their environment, which accounts largely for the widespread interest that it has evoked. But

[1] The work of its seventeen painters, Pollock's 'drip' technique apart, drew much of its inspiration from Europe. 'The pure psychic automatism . . . in the absence of all control by reason and aesthetic and moral preoccupations', for instance, had been recommended years earlier by André Breton, but it was far more evident in the work of the Americans than it ever had been in the deliberately calculated fantasies of the European surrealists. But it was not so much the originality of the ideas expressed as the audacity, the wholeheartedness and the scale of it, that made an impression so deep. The time was also ripe: an exhibition of similar American work at the Tate five years earlier had made no stir at all and little impact on artists.

it is as though the artists are asserting, even in their closest imitations of objects of daily use (hamburgers and the like), that 'we don't for a moment take this subject *seriously*'. The world of pop does not convince us of its reality as do the worlds created by other artists farthest from 'realism'—Blake, Daumier, Klee, Henry Moore or a surrealist. The work of such as these assumes the existence of the world of normal vision; that of pop artists assumes—in spite of their everyday subjects—that it has no real validity. Vintage pop painters, too, in their successful attempts to disguise, by their imitation of newsprint, the fact that their lines are brushstrokes, and by their colours, invariably of uniform hues, that appear to be applied not by hand but through perforated screens, implicitly deny that their paintings are, in fact, paintings at all. 'I want my painting to look as though it had been programmed', said Roy Lichtenstein; 'I want to hide the record of my hand.'

In spite, therefore, of their 'popular' themes (often closely based on strip cartoons, soup-tins, 'hot-dogs' and so on) their consistent implication is that the world as we experience it—solid, ethereal, beautiful, ugly, tempestuous, innocent, cynical, humorous—has little relevance for the artist.

Pop art represents a rejection of the comprehensive Western tradition no less than the abstraction against which it purports to react. A rejection, in fact, more radical than, for example, action painting. The latter painters were deeply involved with the physical act of painting, and to that extent their methods, if not their aims, were related to those of their predecessors.

*

It seems to me, then, that a succession of revolutionary movements of extraordinary diversity has now lost coherence. The revolution is at an end. Every element inherited not only from the Western tradition but from the sense of fantasy of Klee and the surrealists, from the classical sense of order of such men as Brancusi, Mondrian and Nicholson, from the formalized humanism of such men as Moore—all has ended in a nihilism which torrential outpourings of laudatory criticism cannot conceal. And there is no phase, either, of the Western tradition—again I use the term in its most comprehensive sense—or of any of the movements that derive from or recoil from it which will serve as a basis for new beginnings. A single instance will indicate how little power to inspire remains to it. In

1937 a small group of gifted and extremely perceptive painters, of which Victor Pasmore and William Coldstream were the leaders, returned to 'straight painting', based on the often forgotten truism that the visible world really exists, on the rejection—as one of their associates described it—of 'the fatal doctrine that painting is all art', on the belief that the aesthetic element was a by-product of the direct relation of the artist with appearances. The participants, eventually known as the Euston Road Group, took as their point of departure the visual attitudes which underlay French painting from David to Cézanne. Nothing could have been more rational than this programme or at its best pursued with more intelligence and sensibility. I am thinking in particular of some of Victor Pasmore's Thames-side landscapes. But the fact that the programme proved impossible to sustain—in 1947 Victor Pasmore became an abstract painter as austere as Mondrian or Nicholson and the others all went their separate ways—tells us, however deeply we may regret it, that the realistic tradition, even in its noblest aspect and revived with understanding and skill is, for the time being, played out.

*

I am not by disposition a prophet, but I would find it difficult to believe that, with the volume of talent and the high sense of craftsmanship and the unprecedently wide enthusiasm for the visual arts, the future will prove as black as it now appears. I would even hazard an indication of a possible basis for new departures. It seems to me that the artist will eventually have to come to terms with visual reality, but that to do so he will have to view it from a new and idiosyncratic angle. Picasso, of course, does just this, but Picasso is now an Old Master, a god who, though worshipped, exerts little influence on his younger contemporaries. Bacon, though not universally worshipped, is widely listened to. 'One wants to be as factual as possible', he said, 'and at the same time to unlock certain areas of sensation other than the simple illustration of the object.' These words of Bacon's seem to me to offer an indication of a possible way to the formation of an art that will draw sustenance from the visible world and a more comprehending response from an avid public.

Posterity, as it eventually does, will distinguish between sheep and goats, but for us, especially where, say, the art of the under-forties is concerned, the difficulties of assessment are uniquely formidable. The work of Moore and Bacon and others of senior generations is related, however tenuously at times, both to nature and to the art of the past. But much of the art of their juniors is not only entirely unrelated to the art of the past or to nature but so disparate in character and medium that one kind is incomparable—at least today—with another. Intuition may tell us, often emphatically does tell us, of a difference in stature between two artists whose work is of a similar order. But how is one to compare kinetic with pop? Or, more difficult still, how to compare any of these with serendipity, the art deriving from taking advantage of pure accident, or with the product of the co-operation of the artist with the computer? Even when the 'Fine Arts' of painting and sculpture fell into clearly recognizable categories, aestheticians, in their preoccupation with art as an 'expression of emotion', rarely referred to individual works or to their specific effects upon the spectator. Had they given these their close attention their generalities about 'lyrical intuition' and their panoramic philosophizing might have been less remote from actuality. As things are, these little-read yet highly influential thinkers have contributed, by their relegation of any art except that conceived as the product of the pure aesthetic element to an inferior sphere, to the present situation. It is a situation in which one critic has observed that 'a great flood of objects are presented to us in the art galleries which wouldn't have been regarded as works of art at all a hundred years ago. But we respond to them as works of art; they function as works of art in every way that can reasonably be required of them.' 'What happens', he asked, 'when everyone agrees to treat the forged banknote as if it were genuine?' Of course the banknotes are not all forged. Posterity will recognize some genuine currency and some pieces of high denomination—but criteria for their detection have been eroded. We have our individual intuitions—the basis on which judgments must be formed—but they are increasingly difficult to bring to bear in the prevailing flux. This flux is, I have argued, the product of a variety of forces, of which not the least influential is a widely diffused conviction that art proper is exclusively the expression of 'pure subjectivity', as Maritain described it, that the aesthetic impulse, though of course essential, is necessarily conditional on the elimination of extra-aesthetic, extra-personal, objectives. But art is like happiness, an end most effectively pursued when its pursuer is at least partially preoccupied with extraneous aims. However confidently they express themselves, I know that today many artists are oppressed by their rejection, under pressure from the prevailing aesthetic, of external subject, of social function and other extra-aesthetic aims (those now denigrated as 'imitation', 'illustration' and the like), which commits all but those few rare spirits—the pure abstractionists—to a perpetual search for themes in a vacuum insulated from life, which begets in turn a perpetual striving to be unlike everybody else.

The situation is not so unpropitious as I have suggested. There is a minority of independent spirits who ignore alike the claims of an all but extinct academic tradition and those of 'pure subjectivity'. Art, as the proverb has it, is long, and there are other circumstances, chief among them an abundance of talent and skill, which make it unnecessary to be despondent about the future. One thing, however, is certain: if we could foresee it we should be astonished.

CHAPTER THIRTEEN

BEAUFOREST HOUSE AND THE OLD RECTORY, NEWINGTON

NEWINGTON began to weave its spell over our imagination—at any rate Elizabeth's imagination—during the mid-winter of 1946–47. We had bought a house at Shillingford and every day Elizabeth drove over from Garsington, where we then lived, to paint and decorate it. Her way took her through Newington, and her imagination, and emotions, were captured—especially on the return journey—by the leaving behind of an environment for the retired and for commuters, sensible and convenient, and the plunging into what felt like deep country. From the top of Primrose Hill, a half-mile or less from Newington one would look out over the Thame valley to the twin humps of the Sinodun Hills, mysterious, ancient, inscrutable. As one followed the signpost indication, one's eye rested on a mass of trees, with the steeple of a church thrusting out from among them and, just visible, the uncompromising square Georgian mass of Newington House. Approaching more closely, one passed the gateway to Newington House, its piers surmounted by the heraldic griffins of the Cecil Bisshopps (as we came to learn later), proud, theatrical, contemptuous. Beyond the church on the other side from Newington House was the Old Rectory. But this we never saw; it was hidden behind a wall and among the trees, but we knew that somewhere by the grounds of these two houses flowed the river. We were aware of a presence that was casting a spell among the woods and by a river.

It was not long after this that we had our first glimpse of the Old Rectory. On a summer's day—8 August 1948—we went to Newington House to lunch with some friends, Lady Bradford and her mother, Mrs. Lawson, who at that time owned it. We told them we did not intend to put down our roots in the sensible, cosy, easy-to-run Queen Anne house at Shillingford; we spoke of our weekly journeys in search of houses. 'I think', said Alison Bradford, 'that

I know exactly what you want.' She disappeared and returned with a ladder. We climbed it and peered over her wall. We saw a rather derelict but beautiful house set in an utter wilderness. But we knew at once that our longings would be satisfied if we could live there and that nowhere else should we ever feel at home.

At the time there was still an incumbent living in the Old Rectory but his departure was already planned. Immediately, therefore, we began overtures for its purchase, should it prove to be within our means. The Rural Dean told us that it was too historic a house for sale to be considered. To this view we found it difficult to reconcile ourselves, and in the months that followed our obsession grew to such a degree that every moment of leisure was spent in what was, strictly speaking, trespass. The fences had fallen and decayed, and the large wooden gates were always open—in fact it proved impossible to shut them—and we used to wander admiringly among the nettle, the briar, the thickets of sycamore and ash and elm, of blackthorn and snowberry, the piles of bindweed and tall tussocks of couch grass. So impenetrable were some areas, undisturbed for decades, that snakes were numerous (one was killed entering the house), and there were minor accidents. Vincent sprained an ankle falling over what turned out to be an invisible box hedge of two feet high, and Lucy was ill with nettle rash. The largish grey stone house was built overlooking the narrow, winding Thame on a man-made plateau some fifteen feet above river level. The grounds are wedge-shaped, sheltered towards the east by a row of tall oaks and elms; bounded on the west by the river Thame; its base the churchyard wall and the wall over which we had peered with Alison. The house was itself easy to enter; windows were never fastened. We would roam over it, too, with enchantment, and return to Shillingford to fetch a water butt to set under a particularly large hole in the roof or a ladder to remedy a badly overflowing gutter.

The condition of house and garden saddened us, but our longing was by now too passionate to permit us to regard it as anything more than easily surmountable and quite ephemeral. We persisted in our negotiations. Owing to its lamentable appearance of dereliction, the house elicited only alarm and despondency when in the end the Church Commissioners put it on the market. In consequence, in March of 1951 our offer for it was accepted.

The dream was realized at last. Immediately for almost every afternoon and a large part of many days Elizabeth—accompanied by two Alsatians and a litter of eight puppies—was in the grounds planning the repair or erection of fences, attempting the first few yards of clearance, directing the first tentative operations of reconstruction and repair. At the time we had a regular part-time gardener, Larry King of Warborough, whose good humour and fortitude carried us over many problems and whose comments would express, with strong pungency, the cynicism and independence of the south Oxfordshire countryman. He accompanied us from Shillingford to Newington without flinching. But our friends were appalled. 'Surely', they said, 'you are not going to live back of beyond in that wilderness?' By June the grounds were fenced and the most essential stonework and brickwork was done. The last furniture removal took place on 18 June, and we were free not only to work but also to sleep in the one place that for so long had obsessed us. Sometimes I have thought, shoulder-deep in nettles, that even if all my energies at the Tate had been entirely misdirected I should at least have contributed a little to rescuing from desolation one beautiful corner of England.

In all the redemptive labours over the years that followed I took a very subordinate part. The house and the garden offered full scope to Elizabeth's constructive vision and her practical resource. Both of us were aware that yet again we would have achieved little had it not been for Vincent's high confidence and the flair for garden design and the manifold ingenuity that he promptly developed. The first obstacles were overcome; a beginning was made on clearance of the jungles; by 18 June the house had a few rooms ready to camp in. But there was no plumbing of any kind yet reinstalled, and the skilful plumber who had been removing basins, sinks, bathtubs, W.C.s, disappeared. The water supply, in any case, came straight from the river; there was an old filter bed but it was useless and had been by-passed. When after some weeks a bath was installed the bath water was brown. From the river water was pumped electrically, but the pump was rarely trouble-free for long (the dirty water fouled the valves) so that for perhaps two years, until mains water reached us in 1953, Elizabeth spent a portion of every day, sometimes as much as two hours, repairing breakdowns in the pump house. Our drinking water we used to carry over in a bucket from the stableyard tap at Newington House next door.

Not only did we never experience an instant of regret—even with her American upbringing in hygiene Elizabeth was happy to pump water from a river in which, upstream, cows were standing knee-deep cooling themselves in the shade of the willows—but even the first weeks of camp life had a sense of homecoming that exhilarated us and has never left us. For many months Elizabeth was exhausted: to labours by day she added vigils by night. There were too many experiences not to miss: river mists, low over the meadows, reflecting moonlight or pink dawn; weird cries of aquatic birds in the dark; the ecstatic din of the dawn chorus. Many hours of the night she spent in an enraptured listening and watching.

Over the years, little by little, Beauforest—we renamed the Old Rectory after the name of the last Augustinian Abbot of nearby Dorchester at its Dissolution in 1536—was rescued from its earlier decades of neglect and became a place of deeply satisfying beauty, both orderly and magical. The house is now substantially as we want it. Early visions of what the garden design should be have had to be radically modified from the experience of a difficult soil and of westerly gales; they have suffered, too—as whose have not?—from the tribulations of life beyond our garden gates. There are times when Vincent is dejected at the gap between conception and execution. But in addition to countless shrubs and other perennial plants—and 120 varieties of the old roses—some 200 trees have been planted within our gates, and since much thought has always gone to choices that fit into or complement the flora of the district, we often momentarily forget that the landscape that now surrounds us is not self-sown by nature but constructed by ourselves.

Much of the early work was like archaeology: a clearance of brushwood to disclose a pre-existent beauty of proportion and mass. It was like archaeology in the more usual sense also, for in many places in which we have dug for horticultural reasons we have also turned up old building stone and carved masonry. Even in our dish-washing we look out on the simple Norman doorway of St. Giles' Church just over our garden fence. It has been impossible for us, even had we wanted to, to be unaware of the past.

Newington—originally called Niwantun—is in fact not strictly the name of a village but of a parish and a manor. It was an estate made over, at the behest of King Cnut, by Emma (his wife, previously the wife of Aethelred and by him mother of Edward the Confessor) to the Benedictines of Christ Church Cathedral, Canterbury. Manorially it was the administrative centre of an estate that comprised four hamlets: Holcombe, a few yards away from the bottom of our garden; Brookhampton, next door to Stadhampton, a mile and a half away to the north; Britwell Prior, four and a half miles to the south-east; Berrick Prior, two miles to the south. The Abbot of Christ Church was also Archbishop of Canterbury and Primate of England, so that not long after Anselm and Lanfranc Newington was manorially the affair of the Prior and ecclesiastically of the Archbishop. It was, that is to say, a 'peculiar'—exempt from the jurisdiction of the local bishop (of Lincoln, up to the Reformation, of Oxford afterwards). It was Canterbury's only Oxfordshire estate, though the Priory possessed two in Buckinghamshire, at Risborough and Holton. Risborough is Monk's Risborough, and from time to time in the fourteenth century Newington, too, appears as Monk's Newington, Newenton Monachorum.

There is much material concerning Newington's medieval history in the Dean and Chapter Library at Canterbury, but it awaits a competent medievalist. How the Canterbury Black Monks administered their estates is familiar, however, from R. A. L. Smith's *Canterbury Cathedral Priory* (1943) and from the first volume of Professor David Knowles's *The Religious Orders in England* (1949). There is no doubt that Benedictine farming was always good, at any rate up to the late fifteenth century—they had hardly taken over their Newington estate before (quite unlike its immediate neighbours) it was showing an increase of 30%; but its high peak as far as Canterbury is concerned coincided with the Priorate, from 1285 to 1331, of a very remarkable monk, Henry of Eastry, in whose time the Newington estates were regularly inspected twice a year by a monk-warden 'usually armed with a bow and arrows' and his lay-clerk. The farming was mixed, as has always been the case in this part of Oxfordshire, but arable probably predominated. By the end of the fourteenth century, however, all the manors of Christ Church had been let out on lease, though the monks seem to have been still assiduous in their assessments of husbandry when leases fell in and in the repair of their properties. (In 1487 there was a lease of some of it, for fifteen years, to an ancestor of our own part-time gardener Larry King, who was substantial and public-spirited enough to bequeath, in 1505, a cow for the repair of the village road. The will was witnessed by a Thomas Moores, a descendant of whom also worked many years for us.) It is difficult to believe that in the sixteenth century the monks were unaware which way the wind was blowing. It is fairly certain that the Canterbury Benedictines deliberately let their rents run down: the net income of Newington recorded in 1535—even allowing for a 20 % under-valuation—is a small revenue from an estate of more than 2750 acres, being in fact less than the almost contemporary salaries of the new Regius Professorships at Oxford and Cambridge.

The troubles hit the Cathedral Priory in September 1538 when the shrine of Thomas Becket was pillaged and waggon-loads of precious metalwork and jewels rolled away to assuage the Crown's insatiable thirst for money, the small works of art being auctioned locally. As is the English genius, the grossest injustice was perpetrated with scrupulous attention to legality. But for the history of English art there is no need for the myriad qualifications that attend the relevant social history; England was in a few years robbed of much of her finest architecture and of almost all her artistic masterpieces of whatever kind. It was the shattering of a visual culture as well as of a way of life, and it took two centuries for English painting fully to recover from it.

Canterbury Cathedral Priory surrendered to the Crown, as a Priory, and was suppressed in 1540; a collegiate chapter was constituted instead. It became, in other words, a new secular cathedral and in the same year was re-endowed with most of the possessions of the old Priory, although not, it appears, with Newington.

The study of its history has immeasurably deepened our affection for the place in which we are privileged to live. Not many yards away from our house there stretches eastwards an enormous field from a ridge of which we can run our eyes over the whole extent of the ancient ecclesiastical manor. The experience is a deeply moving one. From various parts of Newington one can see a variety of phenomena particular to an industrial civilization, from a power station to cables and pylons. But from the ridge of the field from which we contemplate the old manor of Canterbury everything that we see, as far as the Chilterns, is as it was centuries ago.

Monastic manors taken by the King were sooner or later sold for cash and many were disposed of at once on existing leaseholds; some changed hands two or three times in the succeeding decades, often splitting up in the process. Thirty years later, one John Oglethorpe, the natural son of 'George Oglethorpe of Newington', was lord of the manor and armigerous. It is hardly a coincidence that this John was nephew of the rector of Newington through the Dissolution period, namely Owen Oglethorpe, the President of Magdalen College,

Oxford, appointed to the living by Cranmer in 1538. (He later crowned Queen Elizabeth.) The Oglethorpes were said to be a Yorkshire family who had settled in Oxfordshire at the beginning of the sixteenth century. John Oglethorpe's son, also called Owen, was High Sheriff of Oxfordshire in 1583 and again in 1594.

As in most parts of the country the transition to lay ownership was smooth, the new owner and lord of the manor being the same man, or the same sort of man, as the pre-Dissolution leaseholder. The Canterbury monk-wardens had of course employed a permanent staff through which to manage their estates, the principal officer for every group of them being a lay steward, who also held manorial courts, and in each of the manors serjeants or bailiffs. It was these men who in the first instance for the most part took leases on the Canterbury estates throughout the last 150 years of the Priory's history and whose children, subsequently, bought their leaseholds, and found themselves doing as lords of the manor what for decades they had been doing through leasehold or by delegation.

Another Benedictine establishment suppressed by Henry VIII was Gloucester Hall in Oxford, part of whose remaining buildings, 150 years afterwards, were occupied by the nascent Worcester College. When I was an undergraduate of Worcester my rooms during my second year were medieval and their past was that of the Black Monks. We have not discovered any local relics of Beauforest's medieval past, nor was there, as far as one can see, any close relation between Newington and Gloucester Hall, which for a century housed Canterbury Monks, or—except as a source of ready cash on occasion—with the later Canterbury Hall.

*

Although it is only in recent months that a full awareness of the ecclesiastical past of Newington rectory has overcome our resistance to acknowledge it, from an early date we knew that from the Reformation onwards it had seen a succession of highly placed and probably absentee rectors. As we wandered in the churchyard and pulled out the weeds that hid the tombstones and scraped away the moss from their surfaces to read the names we would ponder on the contrast between the distinguished ecclesiastics who had held the living and the thirty (at least) unmarked mounds identifiable as graves only because they are in a graveyard, and a few graves still with their wooden crosses extant or with simple boards erected over them from which the painted names have long ago been erased by weather and time. The earlier tombstones have death's heads carved on them; the later carry complacent cherub faces. We came to learn, however, that the rating of the Newington rectory in the money or salary market was probably high by at least the middle of the thirteenth century.

In 1257 the rector was a Ralph de Cropper, and he was the beneficiary of a papal provision. We do not know who was petitioner for this provision or why the petition was made. But a papal provision implies that by 1257 the Newington rectory was worth making application for. Such applications were complex and costly, and needed strong support. It implies, therefore, a rich endowment in glebe and tithes.

But although the list of rectors continues more or less unbroken, there are no personalities that so far we can attach to these names until the middle of the fifteenth century. From 1456 onwards, and quite abruptly, the rectors are all Oxford men, principally from Merton College, All Souls and Magdalen. Some are certainly priests; some are not. All are Fellows of their Colleges; some are lawyers; some are clearly in the royal service in one capacity or another. All are pluralists: some holding the living with cathedral dignities, some holding it with other livings with or without dispensation. One of them, John Marshall (a Merton man), became Bishop of Llandaff in 1478.

Of the curates who actually did the work at Newington as substitutes for the rectors, or of the vicars who possibly preceded them, there is no record whatever, any more than there is of the landless labourers to whom they were the ecclesiastical counterparts. That their duties were of crucial importance, civilly or socially as well as spiritually, is plain when one reflects that the fundamental unit of living, as real and more unifying than the manor, was the parish.

Newington has always been deeply rural, so that it would be extraordinary if the medieval parsonage were unlike its eighteenth and nineteenth century successor in its ample provision for pigsties, stables, barns and outhouses of every kind. Like many another, it would have looked like a farmyard. 'Here the parson lived and worked; walking from the stable to the altar, and from there to look after his pigs and his cattle; sharing with his people in the task which occupied so much of their waking hours and of their thoughts, that of making the earth bring forth her increase.'

Of the medieval or sixteenth-century embellishments of the parish church there is no inventory known to us. The parish had, however, by then lived through more than 500 years of Catholic life, so that it is reasonable to expect the usual and functionally necessary chalices and ciboria, a monstrance, candlesticks and candelabra, a processional cross, a crucifix, chasubles and copes embroidered and in several colours, priest's linen and altar linen, missals and other liturgical books, a chest or two and coffer. There would inevitably have been a carved madonna and a few saints. Manorially, as has been said, the process of the Dissolution of the Monasteries was smooth, and injustice was done with scrupulous attention to legality. In other respects and in respects that touched ordinary people its aftermath was more like the destruction done at St. Thomas' shrine in Canterbury. When the Edwardian commissioners rode round Oxfordshire, they were more indulgent to some churches than to others. To St. Giles, Newington, they were harsh. From the accumulation of the equipment and gifts of several centuries there remained, after their passage in 1553, the items recorded in an inventory of the things that might be safely kept to the use of 'our sovereign lord the king', namely '3 bells in the steple, a chalice withoute a patente'. For the neighbouring church of Warborough a couple of miles away there is an inventory both of what it contained in 1552 and of what was left behind in 1553; though in Warborough the treatment was slightly milder, the story is again one of pillage. The church plate and sometimes lead and bells were carted away for melting down to pay for the war against Scotland; the rest was auctioned in the churchyard. The procedure was identical with that of some years earlier. It is hardly surprising that there had been risings, or that in the 1550s the protests were put down with the brutality that has always characterized the English ruling class when its interests were threatened, or that several west Oxfordshire priests were hanged from their steeples.

*

The story of the post-reformation rectory is much better documented and will be found in an Appendix (page 255). But this documentation relates only to pluralist and largely absentee incumbents; about the village or the parish there is virtually nothing. There is little in the parish chest, and little in the Bodleian. As Elizabeth and I have wandered round the churchyard, we have been acutely aware of the transitoriness of everything about us in this respect also. Of a place that has been inhabited for at least a thousand years very little remains from the past. Relatively few records, as I have observed; little building, and even of what appears on early nineteenth-century maps much has disappeared almost without trace. Owing to death or migration there is hardly anybody living in Newington whose memory goes back even half a century; there are no more than a few snatches of memory of what life was like in the 'twenties; there are no traditions and no legends other than one of a tunnel under the river. Even the local pub has disappeared (it is now a private house), but the daughter of the recent landlord has recalled for us her father's description of how shepherds driving their flocks along the road would stop for a drink. Another village woman who used to work for us would describe how the people had to rely entirely for their water supply on the river: how they used to draw it in buckets from a dipping platform, or little jetty, built for them by the local Rural District Council, out over the little ford, Holcombe Ford, at the bottom of our garden, carrying their water home on shoulder yokes. She described, too, how cattle were driven to this same ford, which was indeed used interchangeably by man and beast. Some years later, when Elizabeth became Clerk to the Parish Council and enjoyed access to parish records, she found that almost every parish meeting from 1894 to the 1950s, apart from those convened to discuss charities, had been taken up with the problems of getting the Rural District Council to install a pump so that the villagers would not have to walk across so large an area of mud—and often flood water— to reach their dipping platform upstream from the animal watering pool. But for a place that had had associations with people as various as the mother of Edward the Confessor and Henry James pathetically little, we felt, had remained.

But to some of this puzzle the churchyard holds the clue. Almost none of the rectors are buried in it; they were much too grand and much too busy to develop an association beyond the receipts from glebe and tithes: most of them, we suspect, were, like Henry James, fleeting visitors. In the days when records are normally abundant the rector looked to his patron and the curate to the squire, and neither looked very much to the common people of England. Many of the latter are buried in the churchyard, but just as in life they were labourers without land so in death they are parishioners without names. I have already recorded that at the dissolution of Canterbury Cathedral Priory the great bulk of the estate passed into the hands of the Oglethorpe family—a member of it, the President of Magdalen, was rector at the relevant time—from whom it passed into those of three landowners. The local social and economic pattern of land-owner, tenant-farmer and village labourer was established early.

This we appreciated comparatively recently, and it began an understanding of several features that had intrigued us from our first years at Beauforest. We had been exercised by the fact that, as a village, Newington appeared to have no centre other than the public house and never to have had one. It was also curious that the only part of the 'village' in which there were and had been cottages had strung itself out along a line of road that ran into a wide green lane that we discovered on our early walks, little used and in parts ob-structed, which itself pointed inexorably eastwards to Chalgrove and Brightwell Park, just over the parish boundary.

It turns out that it is not surprising that Newington has no centre and never had one. For Newington, as we came to see, was never a village in any sense; it was the administrative centre of a manor and a parish that comprised four hamlets scattered over an area which until quite recent times was notorious for the roughness of its roads. The social and economic life of three of them were part and parcel of the three villages to which they were contiguous. The fourth was Holcombe—the hamlet at the bottom of our garden—and the estate having for two hundred years been in the hands of the lord of the manor of Brightwell Baldwin to the east, its life looked eastwards.

The road thither was the green lane along which we used to ramble and which, with her customary flair for field archaeology, Elizabeth had already diagnosed as probably an important key to the district's history. A visit to the map room of Bodley and the genial assistance of its librarian revealed that all the cartographical sources disclosed the same prominence of this ancient lane as the nerve of an east-west axis of communication. It sums up, in fact, Holcombe's social and economic history over many centuries.

The evidence of the churchyard about the poverty of the place has also turned out to be quite accurate. Holcombe was where it was entirely on account of water, and, as I have already narrated, we were, in our early years at Beauforest, no less dependent on the river than our Anglo-Saxon ancestors. But it has been decrepit and full of poverty for many centuries. In 1665 it held only six taxable houses, two of them being farmhouses, the rest cottages; in 1755 there were ten 'tied' cottages; in 1838 nineteen occupiers. The gardens appertaining to the cottages are in some instances of a meagreness to which we can recall no parallel.

We used to wonder about these old cottages and why they appeared so stricken with poverty. That pauperisation was among the effects of the early nineteenth century parliamentary enclosure commissions is a commonplace of many economic historians, but when eventually Elizabeth examined the enclosure awards of the neighbourhood she found Newington in much worse plight. In every neighbouring hamlet the awards show plots of land allocated to cottagers in compensation for their loss of rights in the open field and of privileges on commons and waste. But there was no parliamentary award for Newington; the commissioners were not invited to make one. The land had already been long enclosed, and no compensation whatever had been made to the cottagers for ancient rights and privileges. That their poverty was heightened by these losses is a fairly clear inference. Elizabeth found it tragic that in the very first effective meeting of the newly constituted parish council of 1894 the principal business was an urgent request for allotments of land; nothing was ever done.

A woman, now over eighty, who used to work for us, one of the rare characters who was born in the neighbourhood and lived in it all her life, used to tell us how her family had to pay threepence a week for school fees and was reluctant to spare her, though the Newington school-house was only a few yards from their cottage; whenever she went to school she took with her the family mending. Yet her father was a farmer-butcher and carrier who owned his own house, immeasurably better off, therefore, than his neighbours.

Another mysteriously missing village perquisite that used to puzzle us was right of common: there was a faint tradition that somewhere or other, in addition to Holcombe Ford, the village had once had some five acres of common. It was an unplausible tradition, seeing that there appeared no obvious site for it. Eventually, however, tithe maps and a tithe commutation award, of 1839, confirmed the tradition and disclosed where it was, namely, the ancient wide green lane discussed earlier; like many another English road, it was cropped as pasture and (when the weather was not too wet) traversable by pedestrian, horse, horses and gig. Now that we are in the twentieth century the villagers run a risk of losing this as well.

Without security from land-ownership in the feudal sense and with no competition, as there is now, from nearby industry, the lot of the cottagers of Newington had been for a century or two a near-subsistence struggle for survival that hinged entirely on the tenant-farmer. The historian of Berrick at the turn of the century has written that 'it is impossible to exaggerate the gulf between the farmers, who were the sole source of regular paid work, and that majority of the community who had to "keep in with them" in order to survive'. It is a situation whose transformation is still recent history, so that, although farmers no longer hold efficacious sway over their fellow-men, we find that some of them behave atavistically to this day, or as if nostalgic for the days of their predecessors' prime. We find, too, in the offices of local government, the same unholy equivalents of the last four centuries.

Yet just as an octogenarian of Berrick, reporting on the hardship under which his life had been lived, concluded with the comment that somehow things had been 'more civilized then', so local people who have from time to time worked for us have shown all the indigenous style of living that characterizes south Oxfordshire and have delighted us with the dry, earthy, cynical humour that greets the tragedies no less than the comedies of life. But to its loss, as has been observed, Newington has never been a village but a manor and a parish of hamlets. There is no centre to it. Indeed both the Old Rectory, at any rate since 1774, and Newington House, since 1664, have turned their back on it. Both look away from the road to the river and to the Berkshire hills. In consequence, the beauty of Beauforest is a secret one, and from the earliest days the discovery of it was like being made the favoured recipient and beneficiary of a secret. As gradually and painfully the squalor in which we had found Beauforest was overcome and its particular genius began to emerge with the confident progress of the labours devoted to it, this extra-ordinary beauty held us under such enchantment that at times it was difficult even to work. We were visited with a species of guilt-complex. 'Why', we asked one another, 'should we have the privilege of living here?' We reminded ourselves that many others had lived here over many other centuries; that for some time the house and the grounds had stood derelict; but we have never wholly exorcized our sense of mystified privilege. Nor have I ever overcome the pangs of homesickness that, abroad or in distant parts of England, I experience with ever-increasing acuteness. Beside the Sea of

Galilee and the Neva, the Bosphorus and the Pacific I have been haunted by the vision of Newington, trance-bright, in pre-raphaelite detail, whatever the season of the year, and at the centre of the magnetic field the austere Georgian house and Elizabeth among her roses, pruning or gathering with the look in her eyes 'as though', Stanley Spencer used to say, 'she were going to cry'—the look that expresses love and loyalty, candour and benevolence, the look impossible for eyes behind which even a shadow of slyness or self-interest lurks. But although my inward eye is drawn to this centre I roam in imagination through the whole enchanted place. England is still, is only just ceasing to be, through the disorderly proliferation of bungalow and caravan, a country of beautiful villages, but Newington has a special beauty, enhanced for those who know it by being hidden. Newington's face is turned towards the river. To northwards there is no bridge across it for a mile, to southwards, apart from a ford at Drayton, none until Dorchester. Nobody who does not cross the river ever sees Newington's face: the wooded banks rising above the wide horseshoe curve of the Thame; the bright green grass between; Newington House, the church and Beauforest House from the top of their steep bank serenely overlooking the flat river meadows to the west.

APPENDIX

THE POST-REFORMATION RECTORY OF NEWINGTON

IN 1540 the rector of Newington was a very senior Oxford man, Owen Oglethorpe, who had been a Fellow of Magdalen College since 1526 and President of the College since 1535. He had been appointed to the rectorship in 1538, holding it with two prebends, a canonry and five assorted College livings, the combined emoluments of which might well have yielded an income somewhat in excess of the salary of an Oxford Head of House in the 1960s. Diplomatic in temperament and emotionally attached to Catholicism, Owen Oglethorpe found himself in trouble between radicals and conservatives in the College and resigned the Presidency in September 1552. The death of King Edward VI brought a change in his fortunes and the deanery of Windsor was added to his preferments. He was also, in 1553, rector of Haseley, only a few miles from Newington. He became Bishop of Carlisle in 1557, and two years later the unhappy man—a quiet conservative living through troubled times—was in trouble again. There was no Archbishop of Canterbury to crown Queen Elizabeth (the see was vacant); the Archbishop of York refused; the Bishop of Durham said he was too old. Oglethorpe was suffragan of Durham and the next in line. He crowned the Queen in January 1559. He is said to have regretted doing it, and a few months later joined other bishops in voting in Parliament against yet further measures of the Crown to lay hands on ecclesiastical money; subsequently they refused the Oath of Supremacy and were deprived of their sees. He died at the end of the year.

That rectories within reach of Oxford and Cambridge should contribute, or continue to contribute, to the salaries of university pluralists was to be expected. From the early Reformation to the nineteenth century the practice of pluralism was supposed to be regulated by the Statute of 21 Henry VIII ch. 13, *Spiritual Persons abridged from having Pluralities of Livings*. Masters of Arts or

Bachelors of Divinity of either University shared with chaplains to the nobility temporal and spiritual (dukes and archbishops were allowed six chaplains each) the privilege of holding without dispensation livings with cure of souls that were not more than thirty miles apart. A rationalizing argument ran—it was one used by Francis Bacon—that for learning in theology and eloquence in preaching pluralism was the price that had to be paid, and possibly there were rectors in Oxfordshire and some at Newington who came out at the weekends to preach to the parishioners in their care. But usually they were served by curates. In his diary for 14 January 1776 Parson Woodforde, at that time in residence at New College, wrote that 'the Post which should have come in last night, did not come till 10 this morning on account of the snow. Scarce ever was known so deep a snow as at present. Many carriages obliged to be dug out near Oxon. No Curates could go to their Churches today,—Not one from our College went today on account of ye snow.' By and large, however, the conclusion of ecclesiastical historians appears to be that the county suffered in this respect through proximity to the University.

The Newington living, then, was used to supplement the emoluments of Oxford worthies; from the mid-sixteenth century (excluding Oglethorpe) its rectors included seven Heads of Colleges and a couple of professors. It may well be that there were other attractions. A pleasant house in the country would be for many a welcome refuge in the not infrequent incidences of plague. Trinity College, for example, had such a refuge in the parsonage house at Garsington, specifically rebuilt for this purpose under the terms of the founder's will. Corpus Christi had a house in Witney. All Souls, which owned the parsonage at Stanton Harcourt, retained four rooms in it against the circumstance of 'pestilence or other contagious disorder' in the city. Magdalen and Oriel at different times sought safety in Wallingford and Ewelme. Thame was another such refuge on the east side of Oxford. There were many of them. The Newington parsonage was or had become pleasant enough. In its present state it is an aggregate of buildings that are, in the main, of three different dates. The oldest, of which a substantial part remains and of which more remained until about 1935, when a wing was demolished, is Tudor. There was replacement of or additions to older medieval buildings and what looks like a reasonably attractive sixteenth-century country house began to emerge. Returns some decades later show the rectory to have been of substantial size. The 'big house' had been built in the 1640s, and in the 'hearth' tax returns of 1665 this house ('Mary Dunch widdow') was rated at twelve hearths, and the rectory ('Doctor Brabone') at ten.

The Oglethorpes were the lords of Newington for at least a century. An antiquarians' survey of 1717 recorded that 'Newington House belongs to Sir Cecil Bishop. Here are two Mannours. Sir Cecil has 1, Berrick Prior, Newington and Brookhampton; 2, Holcomb belongs to Mr. Stone.'

These were two of the families—and their tenant-farmers still more—concerned with the revenues of the rector of Newington. A third, and perhaps the richest, was Catholic. In the early seventeenth and in the eighteenth centuries the owners of Britwell Prior, whose first post-Dissolution owner had again been the Oglethorpes of Newington, were the Simeons, and after them, by inheritance, the Welds. Both families were Catholic. The tithe system was in operation over all these lands, along with rectorial glebe. It clearly yielded a steady income. There is no doubt that the system made the rectory of Newington an institution locally much resented. The resentment persisted after commutations. After the disjunction of Britwell Prior from the Newington parish, for instance, in 1867, although its tithes had been commuted for £129 and there were eight acres of glebe, only £25 was allocated to the new rector who did the work. The rest went to the rector of Newington. As late as 1892 it proved impossible to alter this inequitable arrangement. 'The thing', said Bishop Stubbs, 'has to be borne.'

As has been said, the living went to Oxford men. Within the general pattern there are minor variations discernible. The rectorship being under the jurisdiction and in the patronage of the Archbishop of Canterbury, and All Souls College having the same Archbishop as its Visitor and patron, it is not surprising that the largest single block of Oxford scholars consisted of Fellows, and indeed Wardens, of All Souls. Of the four Wardens who were rectors of Newington at least three were, in quite different ways, remarkable men. The first, Seth Holland, was perhaps the most remarkable of them all in that he was a man with religious convictions and also with the courage of them. Holland had become a Fellow in 1535 and Warden twenty years later. Cardinal Pole, Archbishop of Canterbury, whose chaplain he was, appointed him to Newington in 1557 and also to the deanery of Worcester in

T

place of the last abbot of Evesham. Elizabeth succeeded to the throne; Pole was dead. Steadfast to his convictions, Holland was removed from the wardenship in 1558 and deprived of his rectorship and his deanery in the October of the following year. He went to the Marshalsea prison and there died at the beginning of March. He was buried in St. George's, Southwark, 'out of the Kings Bench Prison—being brought to the Church by about three score gentelmen of the Inns of Court and Oxford, for he was a grett lernydman'. Three of his colleagues, too, shortly left the College; one of them, Jasper Heywood, *poeta et philosophus haud incelebris*, became a Jesuit.

Holland was followed almost immediately and for a decade by a local man of a very different character from Drayton St. Leonard, the next parish on the further bank of the river Thame, Clement Perrott, Fellow of Lincoln College in 1535, who had been a canon of Lincoln for a quarter of a century from 1535 and rector of the immensely rich Middleton Stoney in 1544. He survived quite unscathed through every convulsion of his times and became rector of Newington in 1561. There was a large number of girls in the Perrott clan, of whom one married into the Newington Oglethorpes —she became wife of High Sheriff Oglethorpe.

It is as certain as makes no difference that Perrott actually lived at the rectory; his family was just over the river. But there was another reason why a cleric in major orders might well like a country house in the sixteenth century. Robert Hovenden, the dynamic and immensely able and courageous Warden of All Souls from 1571 to his death in 1614, became rector of Newington in 1572. Five years later he married. His situation was not altogether easy. Clerical marriages were legal, but Queen Elizabeth disliked them, and several obstacles were put in the way. These overcome, there remained for an Oxford Head of House the difficulty that wives or 'other women' were not allowed to reside in cathedral or college precincts. Hovenden married his Katherine in Newington church (the marriage is entered in the register) and it looks as if for much of the time he kept her in the rectory, administering All Souls—he was a first-rate administrator—from his rooms above its gateway in Oxford High Street.

The rectors employed curates to assist them or to work as substitutes. It was a normal custom. There is a scattering of references by name to such curates in the Newington records. The churchwardens presentments of 1605, for instance, are endorsed by a Henry Hurst. They concerned sexual misdemeanours, as they did a century later when in 1721 a William Hull endorsed documents concerned with the public penance of Elizabeth Hayborne 'in a white sheet', for fornication or adultery. There is a Mr. Evans. In 1681 the church-wardens presented Mr. Robert Thorne 'our curate, for not reading Prayers in our Chappell every Sunday in the morning and evening. There is no surplice to administer the Sacrament, or Register Book.' These things are run of the mill. Perhaps the most interesting entry of all is the legend, superimposed over the Commonwealth years, 'Ed. Archer, pastor by ursurpation, Dr. Sheldon being the lawful Rector'.

Dr. Sheldon is, of course, Gilbert Sheldon, who had become a Fellow of All Souls in 1622 and Warden in 1635. He was appointed to Newington by Archbishop Laud in 1639. Sheldon was a man of wide-ranging abilities who knew everybody: much of the Restoration Settlement was his work, and his ideas about church-state relations were, therefore, pervasive for many crucial decades. He resigned his Newington rectory on becoming Dean of the Chapel Royal and then Bishop of London in October 1660. Three years later he was Archbishop of Canterbury.

Of all the remarkable achievements of this versatile man perhaps I may be forgiven for thinking that his greatest was his befriending of a young scientist (principally, at the time, I think, an anatomist), who had in the first instance been more or less intruded into All Souls by the parliamentarians, named Christopher Wren, whom he interested in his project of building a public theatre for university functions, hitherto held in St. Mary the Virgin's. For this Sheldon floated a public appeal in 1664, himself subscribing £1000. The appeal failed, and he bore the entire cost himself, £12,200 according to one source, £25,000 according to Wren. The Sheldonian theatre was opened five years later.

I have already suggested that the patronage of Newington rectory was exercised primarily in the interest of supplementing the emoluments of Oxford scholars throughout a period when, in any event, fixed incomes were steadily decreasing in value. It is clear that the first step to it was to become domestic chaplain to the Archbishop of Canterbury or a chaplain-in-ordinary to the King. Over a period of 180 years there were at Newington six episcopal chaplains and three royal ones—to Charles I, William III, Anne.

Sheldon's successor, John Dolben, who had married the former's niece in 1657, was also a rich man—rich enough at any rate, in his thirties to make a large contribution after the Restoration to completing the north side of the Tom Quad at Christ Church, his own college, his arms as Archbishop of York being carved on the roof of Wren's gateway under Tom Tower, in commemoration of this. He was appointed to Newington by the King in 1660, immediately on the Restoration, for he was an ardent royalist who had been wounded both at Marston Moor and at the siege of York. He became a canon of Christ Church at the same time. Two years later his uncle, Gilbert Sheldon, now Bishop of London, made him Archdeacon of London; in the same year he became Dean of Westminster and won much credit for resigning all his parochial benefices. He was Bishop of Rochester in 1666 and Archbishop of York in 1683. He was a popular and 'conversable' man whose eloquence in the pulpit achieved a mention in Dryden. As a biographer wrily commented, 'perhaps the fact of Dolben having married Sheldon's niece was no hindrance to his promotion; but he deserved it by his merits'.

The rector from 1691–1708, George Royse, a Provost of Oriel, is entered in the registers as 'pleb', i.e. not gentry or above, and his successor at Newington was a linen draper's son from Wakefield, John Potter. But Potter had gone to a remarkable local grammar school, where Richard Bentley was an older contemporary, and become a classical and patristic scholar of at least competence and perhaps distinction. Like another of his Newington predecessors he was an ardent controversialist. By 1694, at the age of twenty, he was a Fellow of Lincoln College, by 1704 chaplain to the Archbishop of Canterbury and rector of Newington from 1708 to 1737. He had become Regius Professor of Divinity at Oxford the previous year— through, it was said, the interest of the Duke of Marlborough; like many ambitious eighteenth-century characters Potter was High Church and Whig. In due course, in 1715, and again through the Marlborough interest, Potter became Bishop of Oxford. But the income was only some £300 a year, so that he retained Newington. He became Archbishop of Canterbury himself in 1737, another exception to many generalizations about the eighteenth century, for clearly it was not always necessary to belong to the right family. There were, of course, many bishops of noble family and extraction, and these also included men of ability. There were indeed, according to Greville, two kinds of bishoprics, 'bishoprics of business for men of abilities and learning (e.g. Canterbury, York, London, Ely —the latter on account of its proximity to Cambridge) and bishoprics of ease for men of family and fashion (e.g. Durham, Winchester, Salisbury, Worcester).'

It is reported that Potter's eldest son grievously 'offended his father by marrying a domestic servant, and was disinherited, though amply provided for in church endowments'. In fact, he was provided, *inter alia*, with a stall at Canterbury and with the benefices of Lydd and Wrotham, both very rich and the latter notoriously so. A clergyman applied to the Archbishop for a licence to hold in plurality two livings forty miles apart. 'But', said the Archbishop, 'they are out of the distance.' 'If Your Grace will look at the map of Kent, you will find they are nearer than Wrotham and Lydd.'

From the character of many observations made from time to time about the eighteenth century one might infer that their authors believed that pluralism, favouritism in patronage, laxity in the discharge of ecclesiastical duties, were peculiar to the century. Of course they were not. But it was a century governed by property and patronage, in which preferment depended, above all, on the arts of discretion. It is the logic of an Erastian church and it is not surprising that the rare independent bishop found himself for years in charge of Llandaff or that in all the history of Newington there appears to have been only one rector prepared to speak his mind and take the consequences. Of Sheldon it was observed by Bishop Burnet (sometimes an acidulous critic) that he seemed 'not to have a deep sense of religion, if any at all' and that he spoke of it 'most commonly as of an engine of government and a matter of policy'. But when William Warburton, the friend of Pope and the emendator and improver of Shakespeare (as prebendary of Durham he had refused to wear copes, since they ruffled his full-bottomed wig) was consecrated Bishop of Gloucester in 1760, the preacher, himself subsequently a bishop, spoke more plainly still. 'Though the apostles, for wise reasons, were chosen from among men of low birth and parentage, yet times and circumstances are so changed that persons of noble extraction by coming into the Church may add strength and ornament to it; especially as long as we can boast of *some* who are honourable in themselves as well as in their families.'

For the rest of the eighteenth century the Newington rectory exhibited the strongest possible contrasts. From 1737 to 1771 it was held by a father and son, John and Philip Billingsley. John's father and grandfather had both of them been nonconformists of vigorous convictions vigorously expressed, and he had himself been a dissenting minister working in Dover. There he had wooed and won the sister of a Dover acquaintance, Philip Yorke (who became Lord Chancellor Hardwicke), and had conformed to the Church of England. As far as one can see, neither father nor son had any other emoluments; both died at Newington and are buried in the chancel, and both most probably lived there. How they lived I do not know. Probably much as did Parson Woodforde, but with a touch of nonconformist conscience and a touch of whiggery. Despite their antecedents, there is no memory at Newington of 'enthusiasm' or of anything like it.

The Billingsleys were succeeded by another quiet character, George Stinton, a Devonian who had been a Fellow of Exeter College from 1750 to 1767. He was rector from 1771 to 1781 with a prebend at Peterborough, and we can discover no further involvements of his other than with the Royal Society and the Society of Antiquaries, of both of which he was a Fellow. It was in his rectorship—the date, 1774, is carved over the dining-room window of the present Beauforest House—that what is now the central portion of this house was built or rebuilt. There are in fact various features (such as a concealed dragon beam) to suggest that an older Tudor structure was partly adapted and partly rebuilt in a Georgian idiom.

But the end of the century offered a contrast that belongs to near-fantasy. Stinton was succeeded by the Hon. James Cornwallis, the nephew of Frederick Cornwallis, then Archbishop of Canterbury, and the younger brother of Charles, Lord Cornwallis, who was conducting some of our campaigns against American insurgents in the New World. He has been described even by a pious Anglican historian as 'an aristocratic nonentity'. By way of Eton and Christ Church he had become a Fellow of Merton in 1769 and a Member of the Temple. But in that year Uncle Frederick, who had just become Primate, advised a career in the church rather than in the law. The advice was taken and preferments followed fast: a rich Kentish rectory at once, a second (Wrotham) in 1770, a third in 1773; a prebend of Westminster and the deanery of Salisbury in 1775. All these benefices were held simultaneously. He resigned his Kentish holdings on becoming Bishop of Lichfield in 1781, but was instead appointed rector of Newington. (It was in October of this year that his brother Charles surrendered to George Washington at Yorktown in Virginia.) In 1791 he wanted the deanery of St. Paul's, which Pitt refused but instead conceded that of Windsor. He resigned Newington on becoming Dean of Durham in 1794. In 1823, he succeeded to the earldom at the age of eighty-two (his brother's marquisate lapsing) having been bishop for forty-three years and apparently done nothing at all except live 'in great state at Eccleshall'.

*

After Cornwallis Newington saw another eighteenth-century character whose history is in some respects similarly outrageous but to whom Beauforest House owes much. From 1794 to 1802 (and it is possible that he lived at the rectory for longer) the rector was Charles Moss, whose father, also Charles Moss, was an extremely rich man and a bishop. The father had become Bishop of St. David's in 1766 with the consequence that the son became Archdeacon of Carmarthen the following January, at the age of three, and Archdeacon of St. David's the following December. Translated in 1774 to Bath and Wells the father had made his son Sub-Dean of Wells at the age of eleven. Some years later followed three prebendal stalls. The father died in 1802 and bequeathed the son £120,000. In consequence of this he appears to have retired from affairs—he enjoyed indifferent health—but accepted the bishopric of Oxford in 1807. He died four years later, unremarked but trusted and respected.

With a part of his wealth Moss built the present (north) front and the most recent portion of Beauforest House, embracing its present drawing-room and study, with corresponding rooms above, and a hall between. On it, I suspect, he extended only a fraction of his fortune; there are many features in which perfection of finish is seriously lacking. His wine cellar, however, is well-made and ample, and ecclesiastical gossip has it that he was most reluctant to exchange it for any episcopal residence.

When John Betjeman first saw this façade he at once declared he was sure it was by James Wyatt. The attribution is entirely correct. The north front of Beauforest House is manifestly by the same hand as the south front of the Great House at Great Milton, just over four miles away—in some respects the two fronts are identical— which is said to have been built in 1805, near the time at which the north façade of the Newington rectory was added to the central building of 1774; and the Great Milton addition is attributed by a contemporary to 'the late Mr. Wyatt'.

Phineas Pett, of Christ Church, and a man very busy in the diocese, was the last pluralist rector of Newington. After his death in 1830 the picture changes, and since Pett no rector has held another ecclesiastical office or another appointment of any kind. Pluralism was severely curtailed by law in 1838 and abolished in 1850. The hamlet of Britwell Prior, as has been observed, was detached from Newington and incorporated into the Oxford diocese in 1867. In fact there had been long periods during which no services at all had been held in the Britwell Prior church, perhaps because the lords of the manor were Catholics and set a bad example, perhaps because the Newington curates were underpaid or indolent or simply absent. (£30 to £40 a year was the usual eighteenth-century scale.) An eighteenth-century rector of Britwell Salome had complained that, though receiving no income for it, he had been ministering to the Britwell Prior parishioners who came to his church 'merely out of charity and honour to the government'. In 1738 another rector of Britwell Salome somewhat tartly commented that 'on ye 1st Sunday in every month ye service ought by custom of ye place to be performed and a Sermon preach'd att the Chappel belonging to Newington by ye Curate thereof. This Chappel tho out of my Parish is not above a furlong distant from my Church.'

Septimus Cotes, who was rector of Newington for half a century from 1845 to 1893 had been appointed by the Archbishop of Canterbury, but during his time the status of 'peculiar' was abolished and by the middle of the century its jurisdiction was firmly in the hands of the local bishop, the energetic, zealous, extremely able Samuel Wilberforce (the son of the evangelical abolitionist of slavery), Bishop of Oxford from 1845 to 1869.

There is no doubt that in Newington as through all the country there was a very different state of affairs prevailing in the Church of England in 1860 from what had prevailed thirty years earlier. In Oxfordshire the sale of advowsons or of the next presentation to a living had continued throughout the first half of the century, though no longer announced in the local press as once they had been. (In *Jackson's Oxford Journal* for 17 April 1784 there had appeared an advertisement for the sale by auction 'at Garaway's Coffee House, 'Change Alley, London, of the next Presentation and Perpetual Advowson of the Vicarage of Thame, Towersey, Sydenham and Tetsworth, situate nearly circular and within two miles of each other; the present value about One Hundred and Thirty Pounds: the present incumbent upwards of Sixty.') The Archbishop of Canterbury had defended the practice as late as 1836 on the ground that it enabled wealthy and respectable persons to secure livings and bring their talents into the church. But it was not long before Wilberforce was throwing his immense energies into the running of his diocese and exercising some choice of his own clergy through a college at Cuddesdon. There was also a considerable change in public opinion, and the causes of the change were multiple: a long-lingering fear of whatever it was that might have contributed to the French Revolution and Empire; evangelical gospel and Puseyite tractarianism; but above all nonconformist conscience and nonconformist rivalry—these, as a recent nineteenth-century historian has recorded, rather than the Whig commission of 1835, were the reasons why the Church of England ministry was a better one in 1860 than it had been thirty years earlier. In many respects the torpor of the eighteenth century and its detestation of 'enthusiasm' had been boredom and distaste after the endless (and profitless) theological controversy of the century before. But though theologically and politically driven off the field, the moral fervours won in the end and transformed this comfortable latitudinarianism.

Not that the transformation was not itself comfortable. As far as the country clergyman was concerned, the mid-century ideal was one of reverence in worship, some competence at preaching, some knowledge of theology and more of the Bible, some acquaintance with and solicitude for his people, but above all, the setting, by example, of a good moral tone. By now the clergy were nearer the level of the gentry, and indeed in many villages took over the older functions of the squire. The example was that of the gentleman and was the more effectively set if the squarson had a status that was likely to be looked up to. The example itself was the Anglican one of a full family life decently and commodiously lived.

Of Septimus Cotes who ruled as rector of Newington for the latter half of the nineteenth century little is known beyond his example of family life. He and his three wives are all buried in the churchyard. He had a coach-house and kept a gig; he drew up in 1870 an extremely informative map of the road system within the Newington parish. As far as can be ascertained, he was a top-hatted

figure very like old Mr. Ellison whom Flora Thompson has described
once and for all, and like Mr. Ellison Mr. Cotes preached much, I
imagine, on the rightness in God's sight of the social order as it
then existed.

But after the Second World War a day came when church attendance had so far declined that the three ancient parish churches of
Newington, Chalgrove and Berrick Salome were grouped together
into one cure of souls in the charge of the vicar of Chalgrove. When
the last incumbent moved away, the rectory house was for a time
deserted. In due course it passed into our hands.

INDEX